IMAGES
of America

ROEBLING

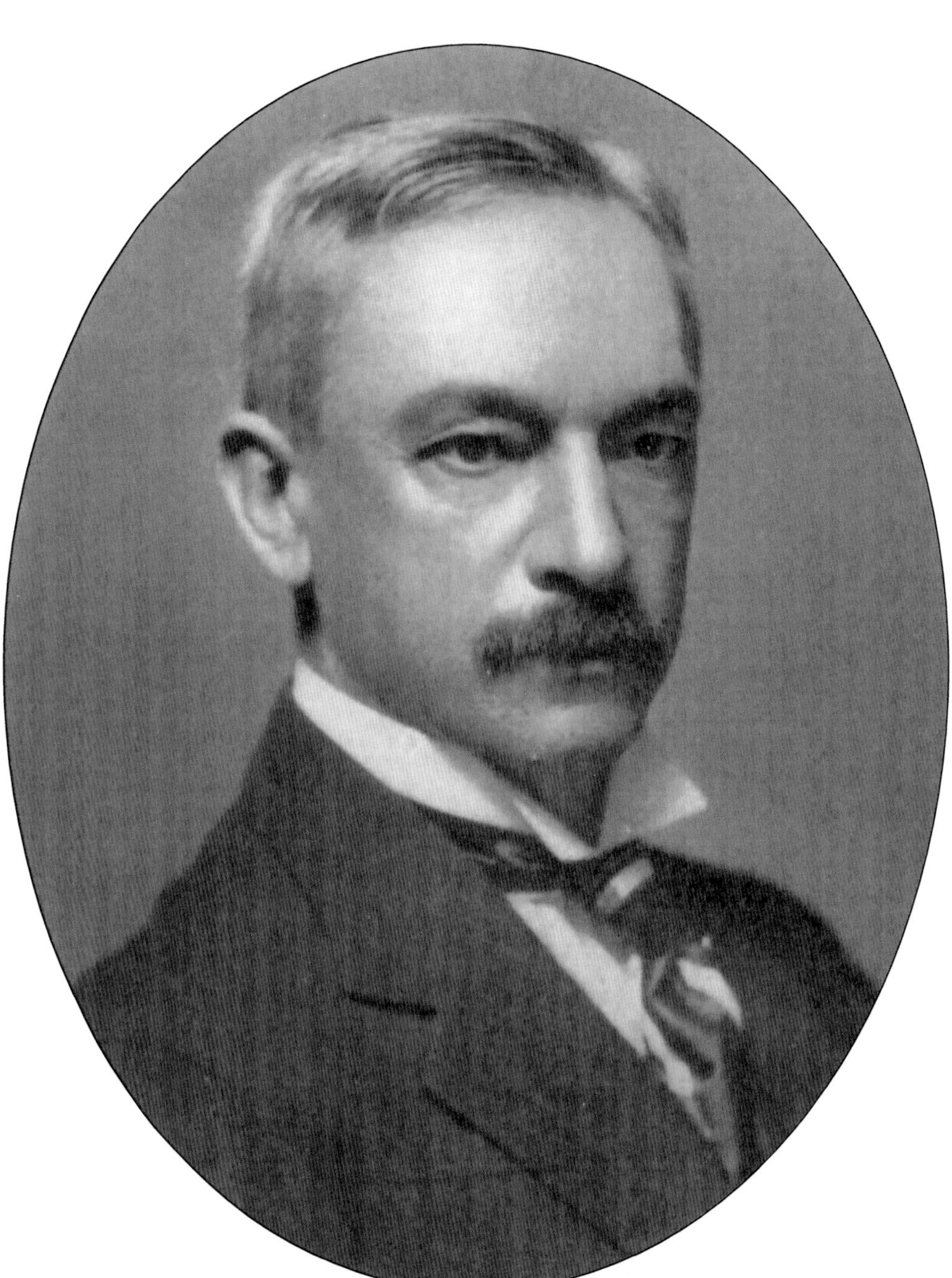

Charles G. Roebling (1849–1918), the third son of John A. Roebling, is considered to be the father of the village of Roebling. President of the John A. Roebling's Sons Company from 1877 until his death in 1918, Charles oversaw the company's expansion outside of Trenton, New Jersey. Charles designed and built the mill and the accompanying industrial town that became known as Roebling, New Jersey. All of the new mills and machinery constructed and used by the company were designed by Charles. The village of Roebling stands today as the founder's visible monument as a master builder and mechanical engineer. (Courtesy Special Collections and University Archives, Rutgers University Libraries.)

IMAGES
of America

ROEBLING

Friends of Roebling

Rose M. Menton, Daniel C. Roth, Michelle V. Scott, Joseph Varga,
Joseph B. Varga, Loretta M. Varga, and Paul M. Varga

ARCADIA
PUBLISHING

ISBN 978-0-7385-0510-7

Published by Arcadia Publishing
Charleston, South Carolina

Printed in the United States of America

Library of Congress Catalog Card Number: 2001086559

For all general information contact Arcadia Publishing at:
Telephone 843-853-2070
Fax 843-853-0044
E-mail sales@arcadiapublishing.com
For customer service and orders:
Toll-Free 1-888-313-2665

Visit us on the Internet at www.arcadiapublishing.com

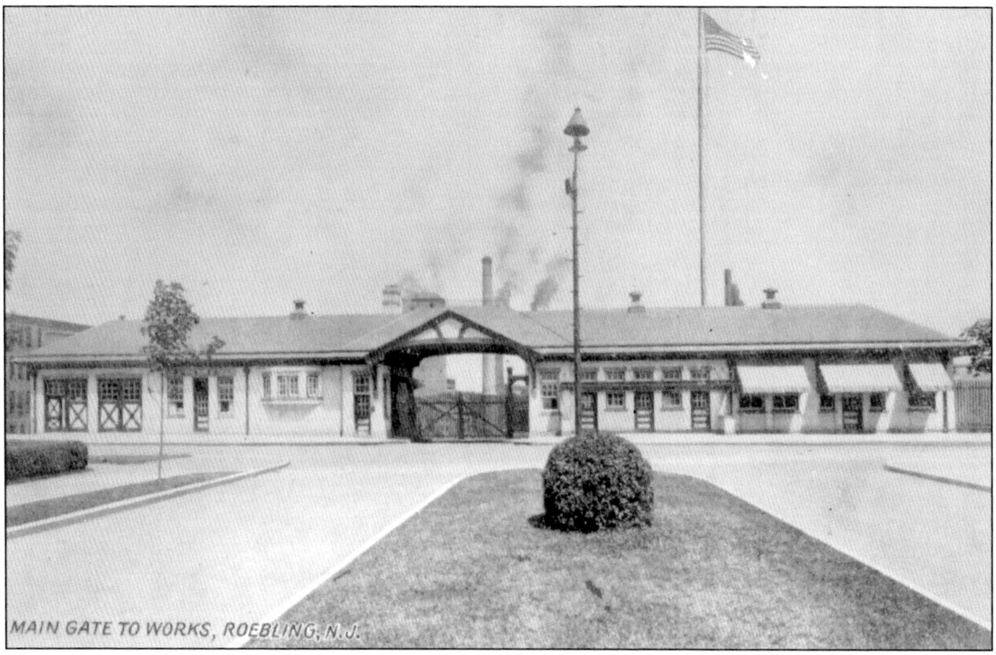

This was Main Gate No. 1 of the John A. Roebling's Sons Company, where thousands of workers would enter and leave each day. On the right side of the entranceway was the employment office and on the left, the village police station and magistrate office. Magistrate Tom Callery would listen to any complaints that occurred in the village and render a decision that would be appropriate to the complaint. The building had a prison consisting of three cells for the temporary detention of malefactors. (Courtesy Louis Borbi.)

Contents

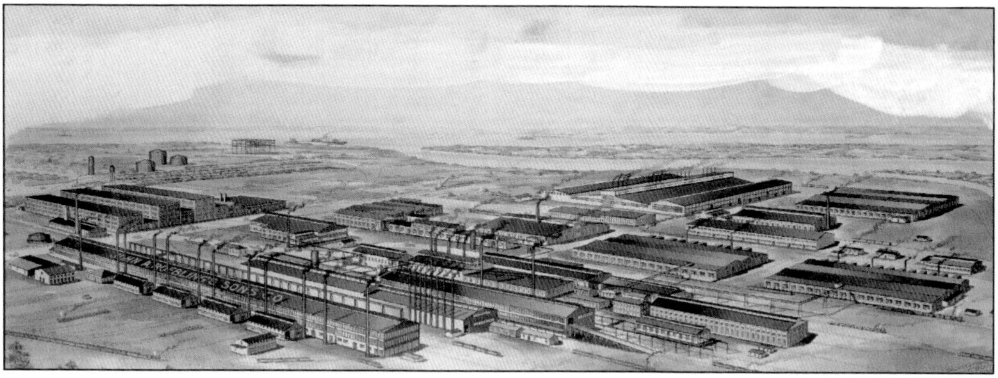

This 1923 engraving shows the Kinkora Works, the original name for the John A. Roebling's Sons steel mill, located in Roebling, New Jersey. (Courtesy Judy L. Winkler.)

Acknowledgments

There are many people who offered their assistance, knowledge, and time to us. We want to thank Gus and William Alexander, Shirley Alexander-Williams, Joseph Bordas, Maryann Bordas Bunnick, Dorothy Tonne Buzash, Steven Buzash, Pastor and Mrs. Iosef Chereches, Janet and Albert DeChristie, Rev. Jackie Lou Dennis Everett, Carl G. Friday, Janet Paykos Griffith, Bill Gyenge, Elizabeth Hovart, Hungarian Reformed Church, Irene Kaczoroski, Marion and Alex McDowall, William McGrath, Ted Mitre, Mary Arnold Montalto, Wendy Nardi of the Trenton Public Library, Bob Nelson, Donna Orfe, Shirley and Tom Pierson, Catherine Burkus Reca, Marie Reynolds (author of *Images of America: Browns Mills*), Bill Richardson, Carol M. Sheaffer, M.D., and her mother, the late Margaret Earlin Sheaffer, Yolanda Simko, Edward Skipworth of the Rutgers University Libraries, Ray Thompson, Peter Turco (for listening and putting up with us), Judy L. Winkler of the Invention Factory Science Center, Richard C. Woodbridge, Esq., Joseph Yeager, Mary Yetko, Mary and Peter Yurcisin, and Joseph D. Zahorsky.

We want to give credit to the following sources we consulted and used in this book: *A Story of the Public Schools of Burlington County, NJ*; McCulloch, David, *The Great Bridge*, Simon & Schuster, 1972; Roebling, Washington A., "In Memoriam—Charles G. Roebling," 1918; Don Rottenburg, "The Roeblings—Bridging the Generations," *Town & Country*, May 1983; Clifford W. Zink and Dorothy White Hartman, *Spanning the Industrial Age*, Trenton Roebling Community Development Corporation, 1992; *Iron Age* magazine and the many Roebling Company publications, including *Blue Center*, *Roebling* magazine, and *The Roebling Story*.

We also thank our families—Michael, Megan, and Matthew Scott, Corinne K. Varga, and Durinda and Amanda Roth.

A special thank-you and our deep appreciation goes to Louis Borbi, who allowed us to take full advantage of his vast collection of photographs, memorabilia, notes, and interviews with mill employees and villagers. Louis' collection goes back over 30 years, and without his curiosity, interest, and tenacity, much of Roebling's history would have been lost.

INTRODUCTION

In order for one to appreciate the village of Roebling, we must begin with the patriarch John A. Roebling, who was born in Mulhausen, Prussia, in 1806. He attended the Royal Polytechnic Institute in Berlin, where he and many others studied engineering and construction disciplines.

In 1831, Roebling, his brother, and others sailed to America. First, they settled in Pittsburgh and then traveled north to establish a farming colony, which in time was called Saxonburg. While working as a surveyor for the Commonwealth of Pennsylvania, Roebling found that the hemp rope used for pulling and lowering cars of the portage railway system was not efficient. He got the idea to make wire rope to replace the hemp rope. His first wire rope "mill" was behind his home in Saxonburg.

Roebling's wire ropes allowed him to design and construct many engineering projects. As business increased, he needed a new location for expansion. This led to the purchase of 25 acres of land in Trenton, New Jersey.

One of the high points of Roebling's career was the design of the East River Bridge, known to the world as the Brooklyn Bridge. While in its preliminary stages, Roebling suffered an injury to his leg, which resulted in his death from lockjaw. The building of the bridge fell upon the shoulders of Roebling's eldest son, Washington A. Roebling. During construction, Washington was stricken with caisson disease, also called the bends. The disease caused Washington to supervise the project from his apartment overlooking the site in Brooklyn Heights. Washington used a telescope to observe construction and communicated directions to the workers at the site through his wife, Emily Warren Roebling. After many obstacles, the bridge was dedicated on May 24, 1883.

Brothers Ferdinand and Charles Roebling were in New Jersey supervising the Trenton plant, which grew and flourished. In order to facilitate expansion, it was determined that an open-hearth furnace had to be built. There was no room around the existing plant, and land in Trenton was very expensive. Charles made a systematic search between Trenton and Burlington, finally selecting a site 10 miles south of Trenton at Kinkora, a rail station on the old Camden and Amboy Railroad. It was considered the proper site because it was close to Trenton. It had proper railroad facilities and had access to river transportation. On June 25, 1904, Charles signed a contract to purchase the land from Jacob F. Hoffner for $17,000.

After the land was purchased, Charles had to build the mill. Trenton was the closest city to find available workers. However, to ask hundreds of men to commute daily would be expensive and inconvenient. Charles knew that workers had to be hired to build the mill and, eventually, work at the mill. So, he planned and created what is considered one of the first company towns in the United States.

The building started in 1904 with the completion of the Roebling Inn. Now the workers had a place to room and board. The village housing was then built for mill workers, supervisors, and managers. Charles's village required a general store, bakery, drugstore, and school. He designed the water and sewer system for the village. He made sure there was room for fire and police protection, including a jail and medical services. The company owned and maintained the housing. They mowed the front lawn, did the repair work, painted the interior, and gave homemakers a selection of wallpaper to choose from. The company maintained the company housing until 1947, when the homes were put up for sale.

Charles planned the layout of the mill very carefully. Buildings needed for the manufacturing of the wire rope were conceived and constructed. Roads—paved and rail—made their way to the mill.

A variety of activities were available to the villagers. People could listen to the Marshall Band in Roebling Park. In the early days, villagers would watch silent films in the second-floor meeting room of the drugstore and, later, watch the sound movies in the Roebling Auditorium. Sport teams—the Blue Centers and the Bulldogs—played football. Roebling boasted championship teams in football, baseball, and girls' softball. Roebling became well known for its boxers. Some who had success were Gus Alexander, Joe Horvath, Carl Schaum, Harry Varava, and Danny Cooney, the "pride of Roebling."

There was ice-skating, roller-skating, and tennis on Ninth Avenue, as well as a six-hole golf course on Eighth Avenue. Live entertainment could be enjoyed in the Roebling Auditorium and in the Hungarian Home. The recreation centers on Sixth Avenue and Main Street and on Railroad Avenue provided billiards and bowling. The Scout Hut provided activities for Roebling's younger villagers.

Roebling became home to people of different ethnic backgrounds, including Hungarians, Romanians, Slovaks, and Swedes. The churches provided for the spiritual needs of its members. Sometimes, when a worker died, the church would help with the basic needs as well.

During World War II, the company and the village went all out to serve the country. The U.S. Navy used the submarine and torpedo nets produced by the mill. The nets would be used to protect naval blockades from the enemy and its firepower. War bonds were purchased and patriotic rallies were held. Over 400 of Roebling's young men served in the armed forces. Many of Roebling's women took their place in the mill.

In December 1952, the John A. Roebling's Sons Company announced the sale of the entire company. The mill that produced the wire rope for San Francisco's Golden Gate Bridge and other bridges, wire mesh nets used extensively in World War II, and elevator cables would have a new owner. This was a company where a member of the Roebling family was always at the helm and a company that did everything possible to provide for its workers and their families. It was the end of an era.

—Friends of Roebling in association with Roebling Garden Club
Rose M. Menton, Daniel C. Roth, Michelle V. Scott, Joseph Varga,
Joseph B. Varga, Loretta M. Varga, and Paul M. Varga

One

The Roebling Family

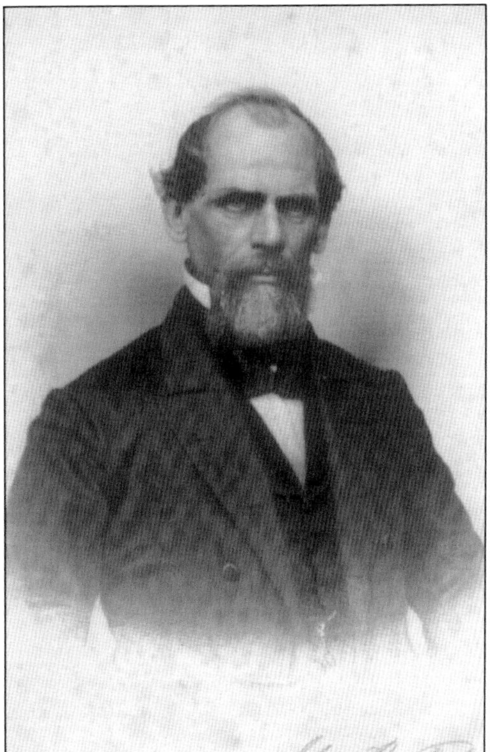

John A. Roebling (1806–1869) was a surveyor, a civil engineer, and a bridge builder. Roebling's first wire rope plant in Saxonburg, Pennsylvania, led to his success in the production of wire rope in America. Roebling was father of nine children, including Washington A. Roebling, Ferdinand W. Roebling, and Charles G. Roebling. John A. Roebling will always be known as the designer of the Brooklyn Bridge. (Courtesy Special Collections and University Archives, Rutgers University Libraries.)

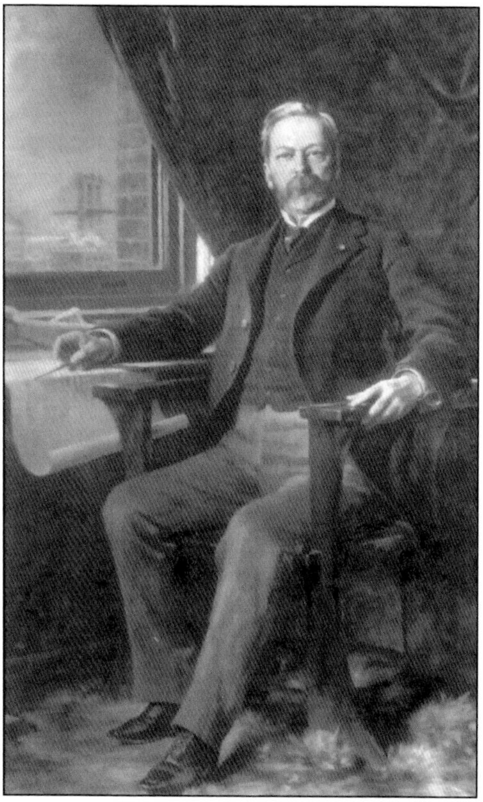

Washington A. Roebling (1837–1926), first-born son of John and Johanna Herting Roebling, graduated from Rensselaer Polytechnic Institute in 1857 with a civil engineering degree. He served in the Civil War with distinction. He would later complete the East River Bridge (Brooklyn Bridge) as chief engineer, due to his father's death. At age 84, Washington assumed the role as president of the company until his death at age 89. (Courtesy Special Collections and University Archives, Rutgers University Libraries.)

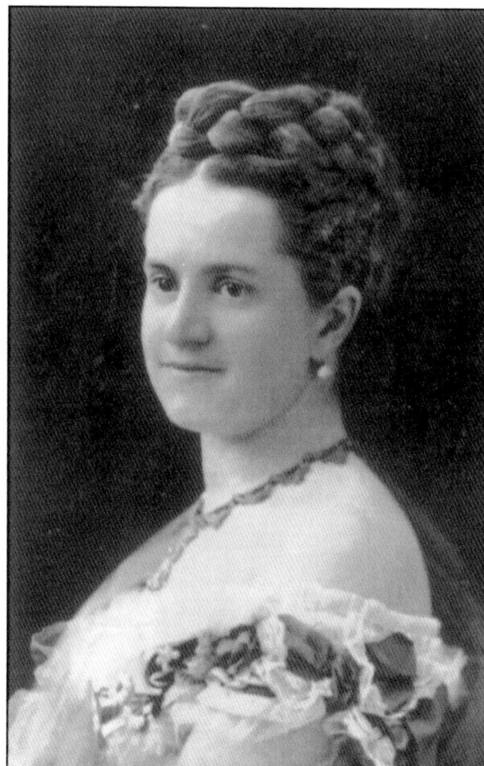

Emily Warren Roebling (1843–1903) was the wife of Washington A. Roebling and daughter-in-law of John A. Roebling. After John A. Roebling's death in 1869, the task of completing the building of the Brooklyn Bridge was given to Washington. In time, Washington became bedridden with caisson disease and relied on Emily to help him finish the enormous project. There are plaques commemorating this achievement on the towers of the Brooklyn Bridge. (Courtesy Special Collections and University Archives, Rutgers University Libraries.)

This photograph shows John A. Roebling II, Washington A. Roebling, and Siegfried Roebling. The Airedale, named Billy Sunday, was the only dog allowed to ride on the Trenton Trolley. (Courtesy Special Collections and University Archives, Rutgers University Libraries.)

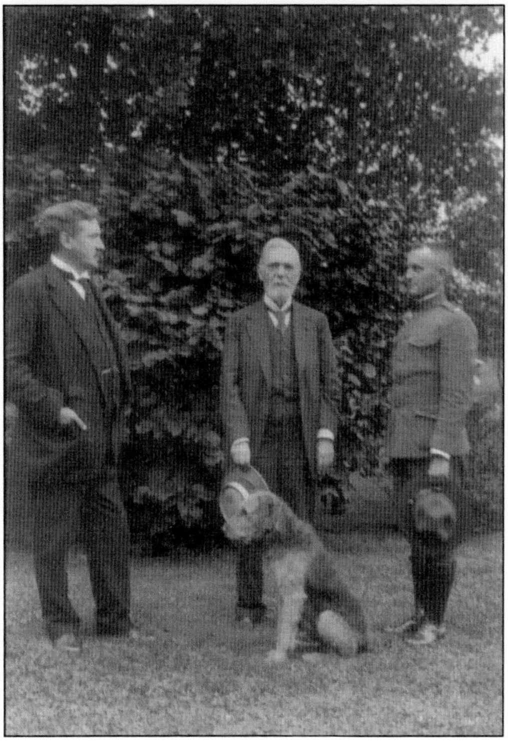

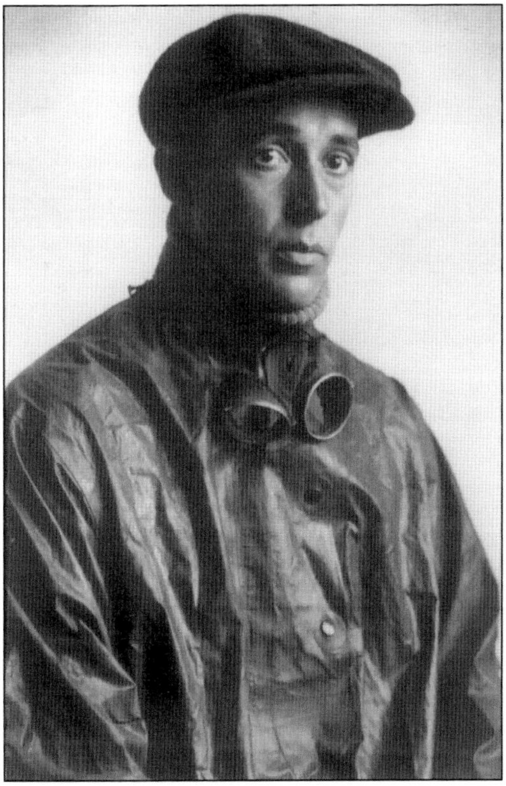

Washington A. Roebling II (1881–1912) was the only son of Charles G. Roebling to reach adulthood. He is pictured in auto-racing attire. He died in the sinking of the *Titanic* in 1912. (Courtesy Special Collections and University Archives, Rutgers University Libraries.)

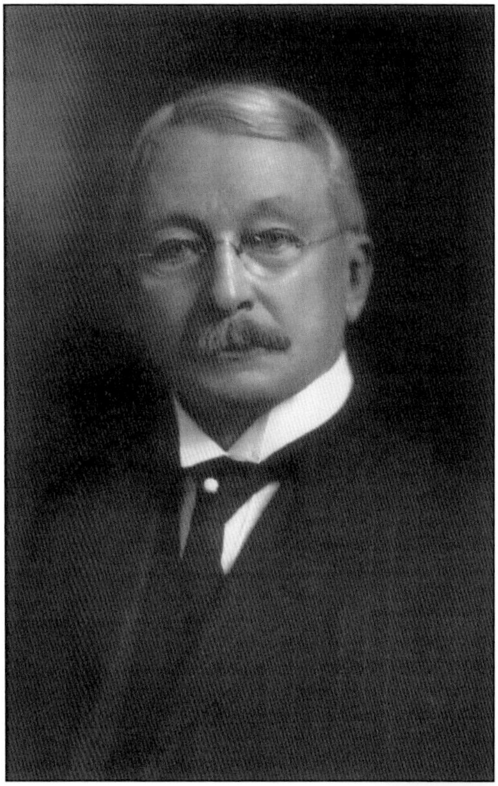

Ferdinand W. Roebling (1842–1917) had interests centered upon the sales and financial aspects of the business. Ferdinand explored new markets, suggested new or changed products, and built the whole business structure. (Courtesy Special Collections and University Archives, Rutgers University Libraries.)

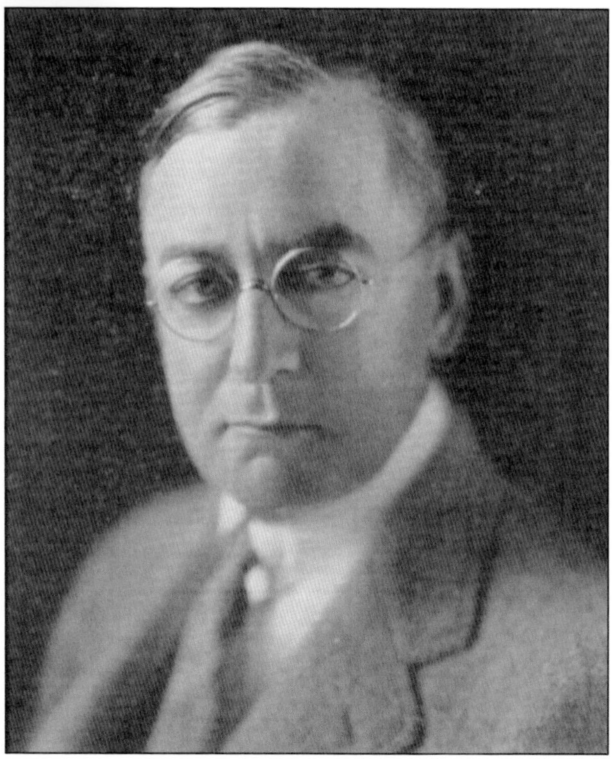

Ferdinand W. Roebling Jr. (1878–1936) was elected president of the John A. Roebling's Sons Company in 1926, following the death of his uncle Washington A. Roebling. It was during his presidential term that the company erected the George Washington Suspension Bridge across the Hudson River in New York City in 1931. Generous with his wealth, he was a constant supporter of various hospitals and churches throughout New Jersey. (Courtesy Carl G. Friday.)

Karl G. Roebling (1873–1921), the eldest son of Ferdinand, was the brother of Ferdinand Jr. Karl was originally named Charles Gustavus Roebling after his uncle, but he legally changed his name to avoid confusion. Karl joined the company after attending Princeton University. He worked in the various departments in the mill to learn the business firsthand. Karl headed the company for three years until his sudden death in 1921. (Courtesy Carl G. Friday.)

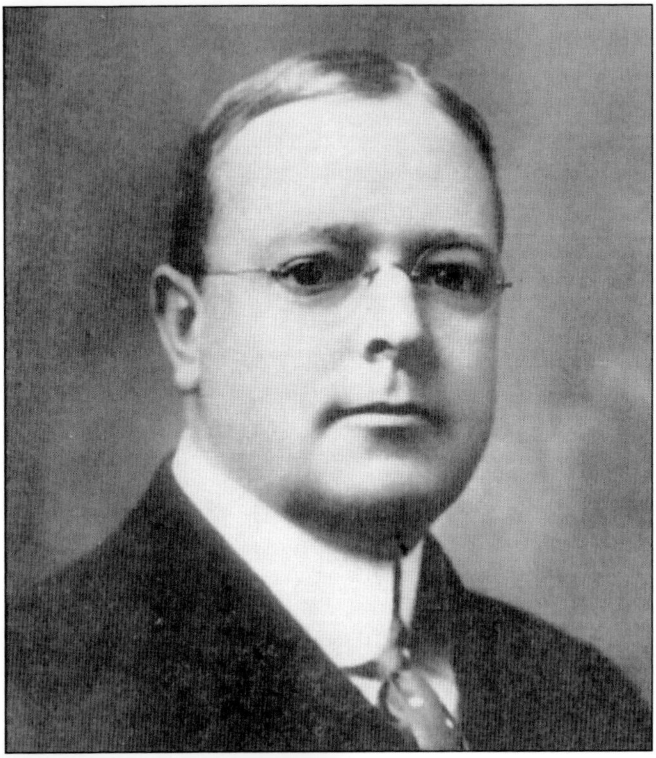

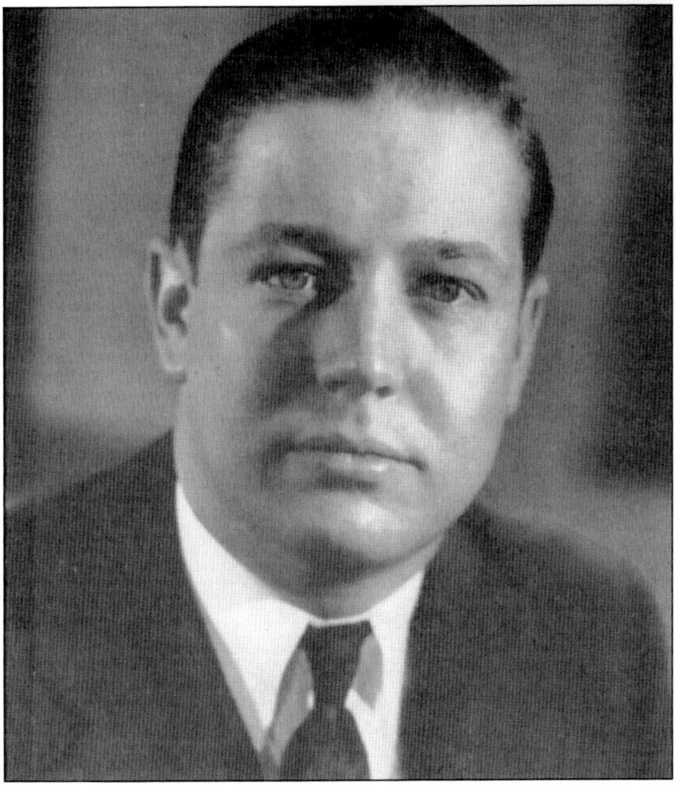

Charles Roebling Tyson (1914–1999) was the son of Helen Roebling and Carroll S. Tyson and grandson of Charles G. Roebling, for whom he was named. At the age of 30, he assumed the presidency of the John A. Roebling's Sons Company in 1944. Charles Tyson was the last president of the company before it was sold to Colorado Fuel and Iron. (Courtesy Louis Borbi.)

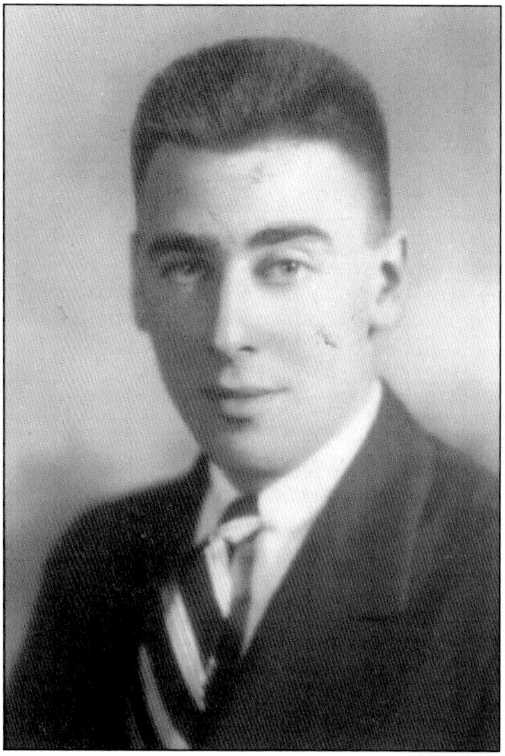

Ferdinand W. Roebling III (b. 1911), son of Ferdinand William Jr. and grandson of Ferdinand William I, was a vice president and assistant director of engineering *c.* 1944. (Courtesy Special Collections and University Archives, Rutgers University Libraries.)

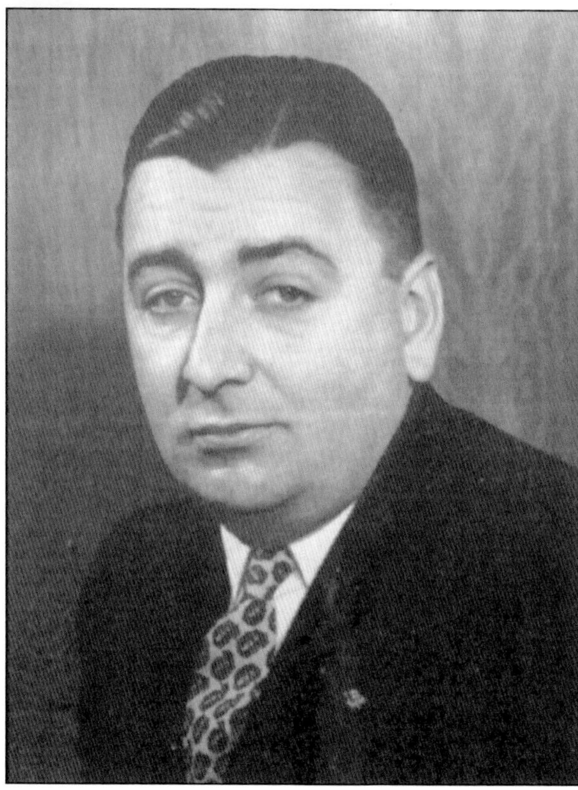

The Roebling tradition of active management of the John A. Roebling's Sons Company was maintained by three of John A. Roebling's great-grandsons. Joseph Metcalf Roebling (1907–1980), son of Ferdinand William Jr. and grandson of Ferdinand William I, was chairman of the board of directors. Joseph is shown *c.* 1944. (Courtesy Louis Borbi.)

Two

Early Beginnings

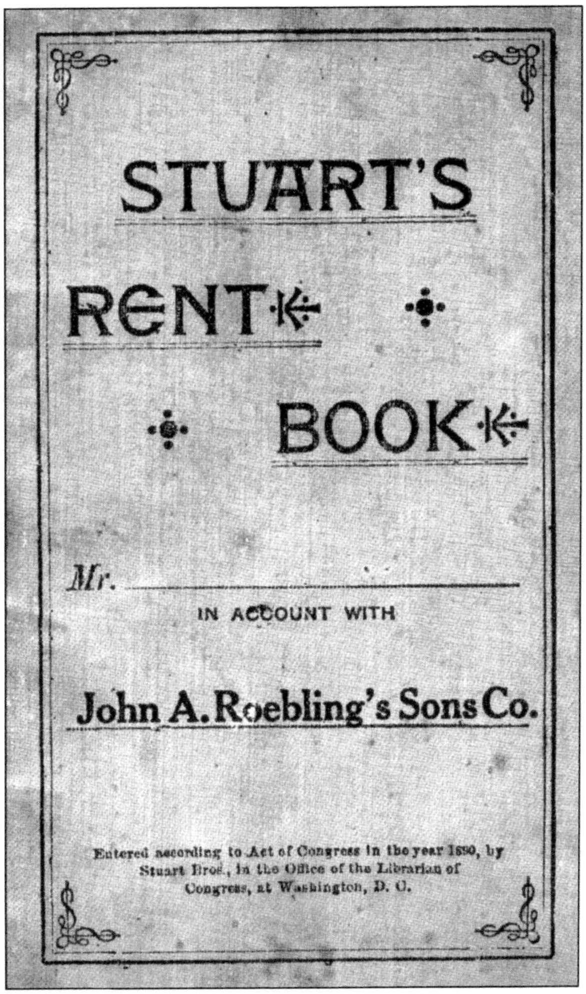
STUART'S RENT BOOK

Mr. ______________________

IN ACCOUNT WITH

John A. Roebling's Sons Co.

Entered according to Act of Congress in the year 1890, by Stuart Bros., in the Office of the Librarian of Congress, at Washington, D. C.

Shown is a copy of *Stuart's Rent Book for Landlord and Tenants* from 1919. L. Barbeley was the tenant. R.H. Thompson, who was in charge of the entire village operation and maintenance, stamped it. Up until the time the homes were sold in 1947, Thompson was the only real estate agent that the John A. Roebling's Sons Company ever had. (Courtesy Louis Borbi.)

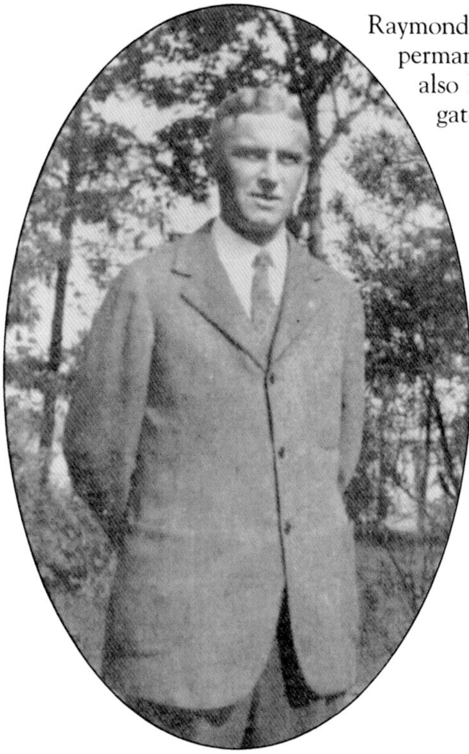

Raymond Hill Thompson is considered to be the first permanent occupant of Roebling because his office was also living quarters. It stood where the No. 2 railroad gate was located. (Courtesy Ray Thompson.)

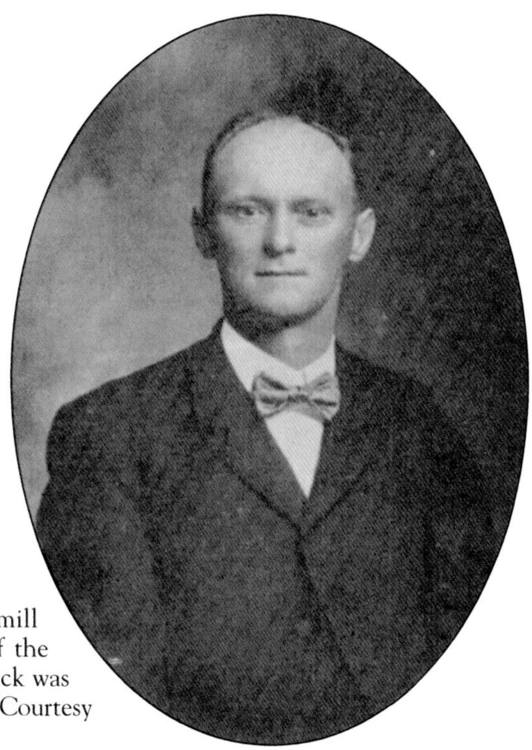

George Gauck was in charge of all mill construction, including the construction of the water supply tunnel and receiving well. Gauck was responsible for all of the mill construction. (Courtesy Ray Thompson.)

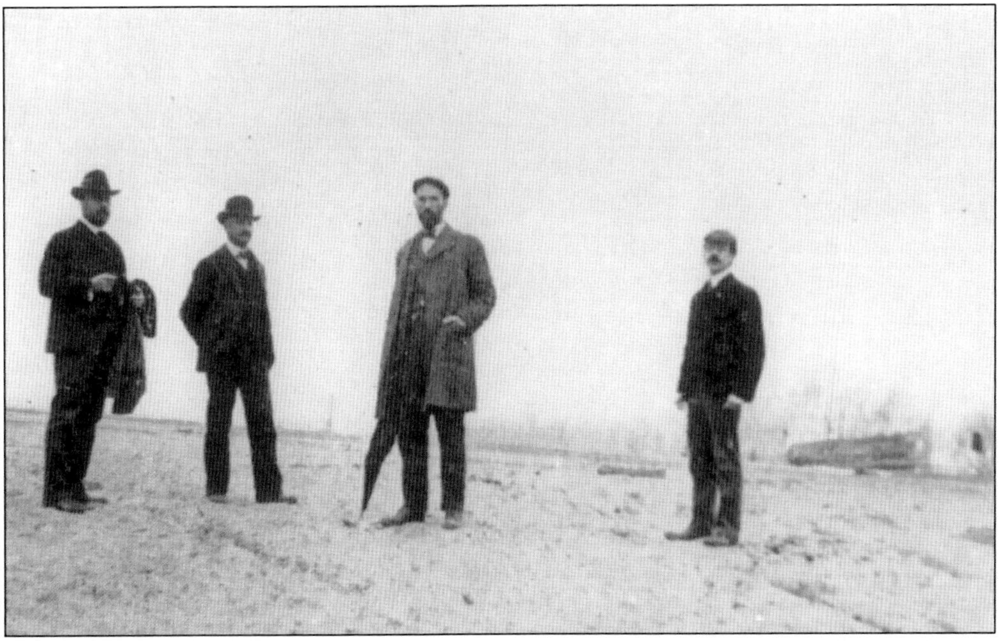

Seen in this photograph are J.H. Janeway Jr., Ferdinand Monard, A.D. Carnagy, and A.C. Cooley at the site of the Roebling works in November 1904. (Courtesy Ray Thompson.)

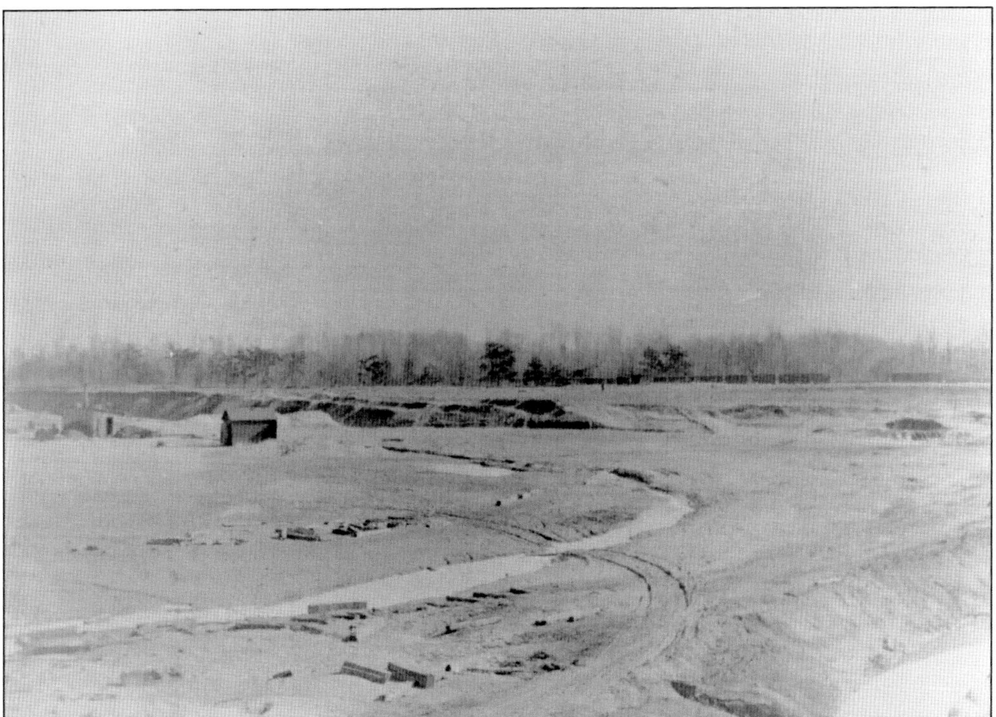

This photograph shows the start of the excavation of the land in the construction of the John A. Roebling's Sons plant in 1904–1905. (Courtesy Louis Borbi.)

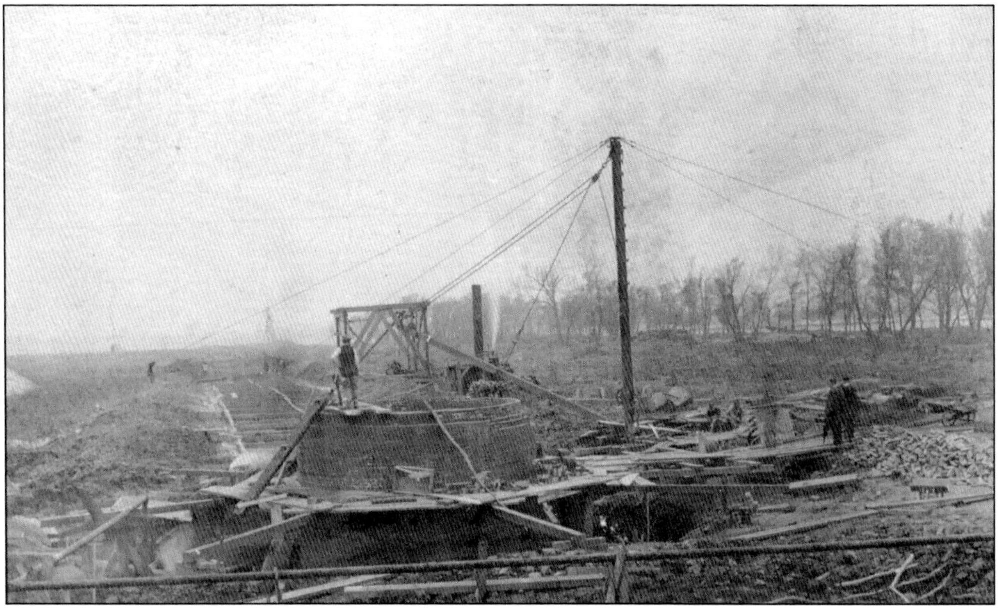

Seen here is the construction of the well at the Kinkora Works (John A. Roebling's Sons Company) on November 5, 1904. (Courtesy Louis Borbi.)

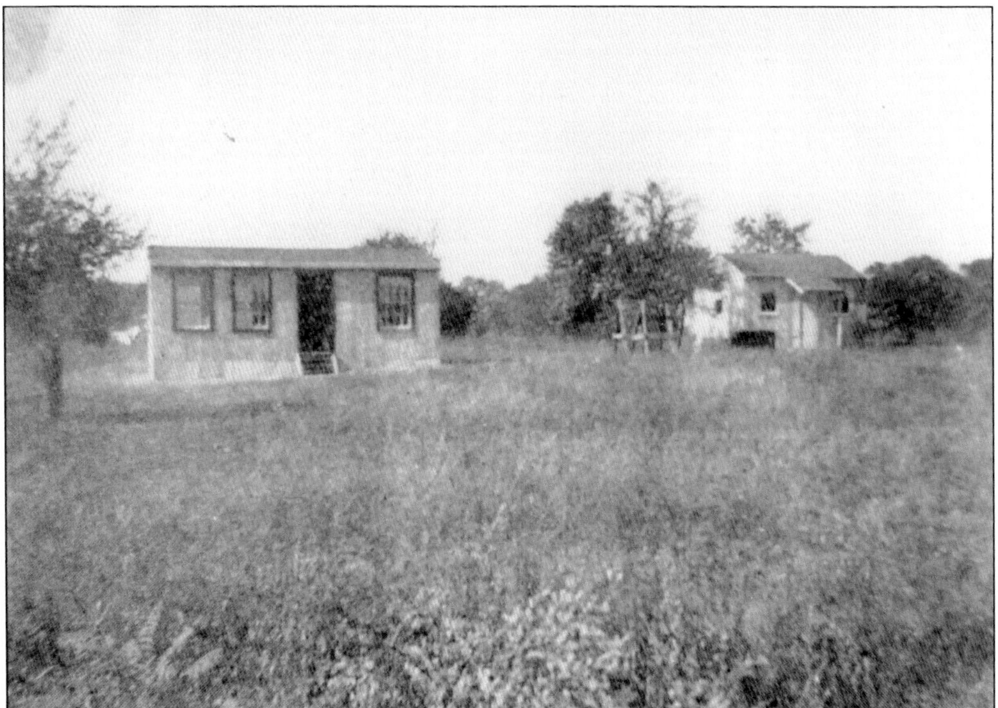

The "First Shack," located on the site of the original Pennsylvania Railroad Station, housed the office and living quarter. In September 1904, Raymond H. Thompson was the first resident of the village. (Courtesy Louis Borbi.)

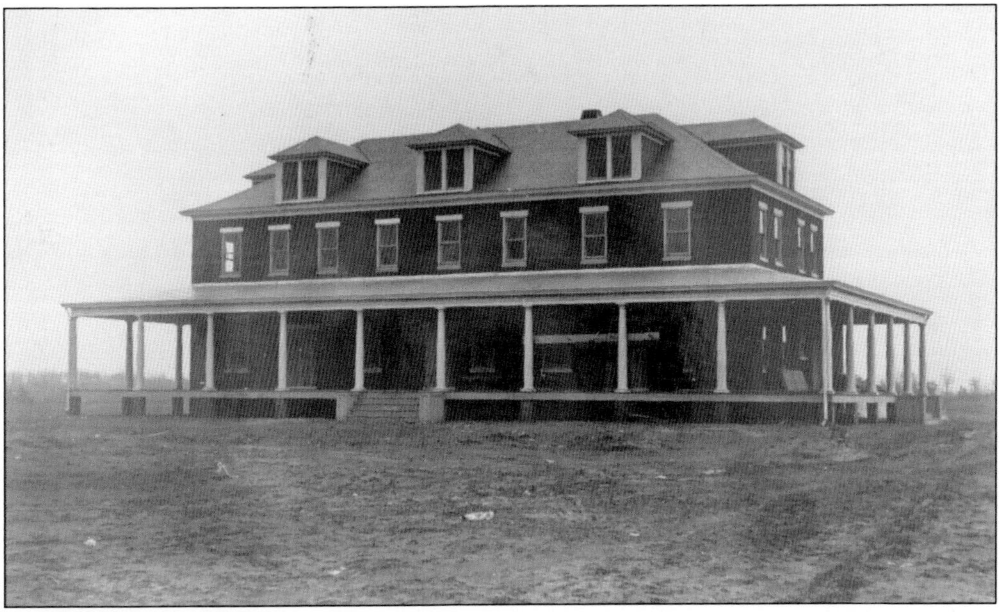

Pictured is the Roebling Inn, built in 1905. Men working in the construction of the plant and village paid $2 a week for room and board. In 1910, the Roeblings hired John W. Stone from Frackville, Pennsylvania, to manage the hotel and bar. It was referred to as "Stoney's Inn." He sold quality whiskey and bottled his own beer from kegs in the cellar. The Roebling Inn, the first permanent building constructed by the Roeblings is used today as low-income senior citizen housing. (Courtesy Louis Borbi.)

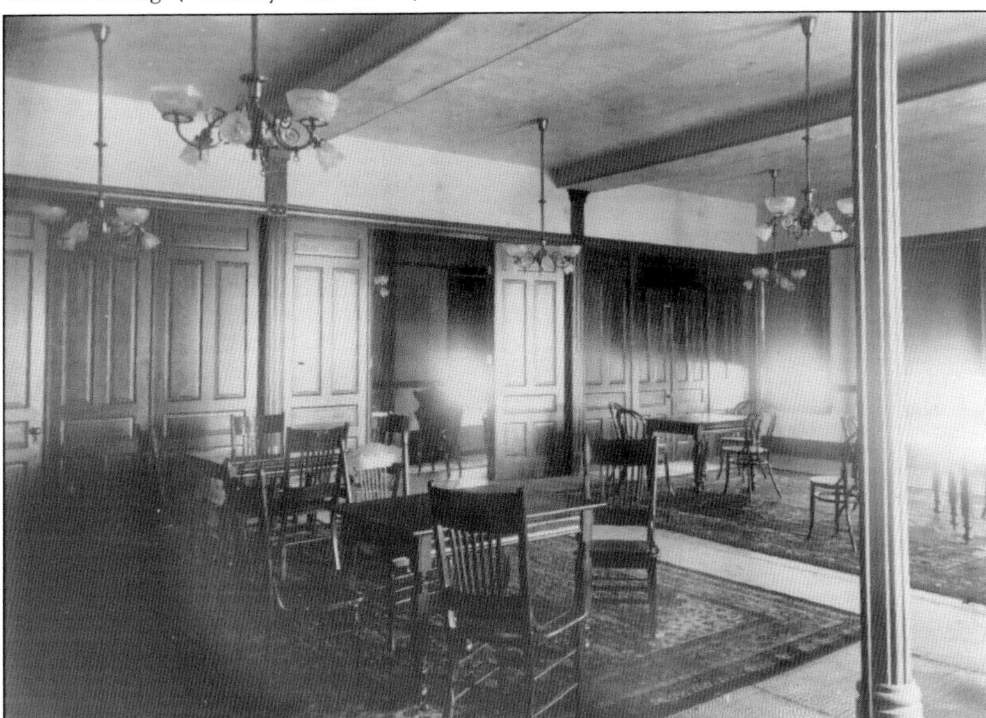

This *c.* 1912 view shows the dining room of the Roebling Inn. (Courtesy Louis Borbi.)

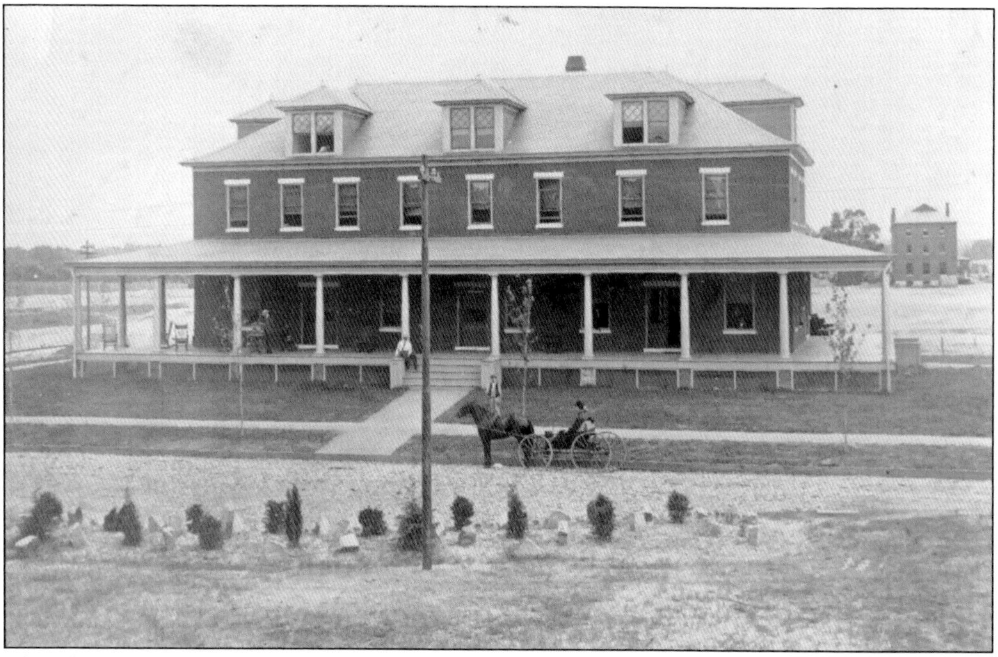

This photograph shows the Roebling Inn *c.* 1906. This was the very first building constructed in the village. The inn was built so workers building the mill and the village had a place to eat and sleep. After the construction was completed, the inn was used to house the single men working at the mill. (Courtesy Louis Borbi.)

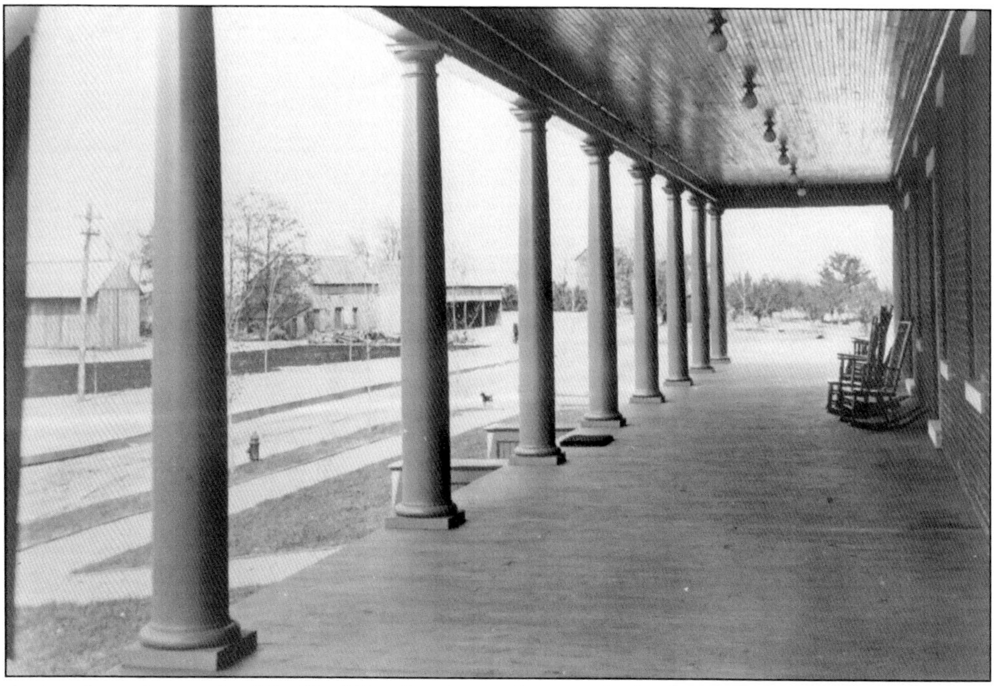

A view from the porch of the Roebling Inn shows the straight-back wooden rockers that residents could sit in. Across from the porch to the left are barns. Eventually two water towers would be put up where the barns stood on Second and Riverside Avenues. (Courtesy Louis Borbi.)

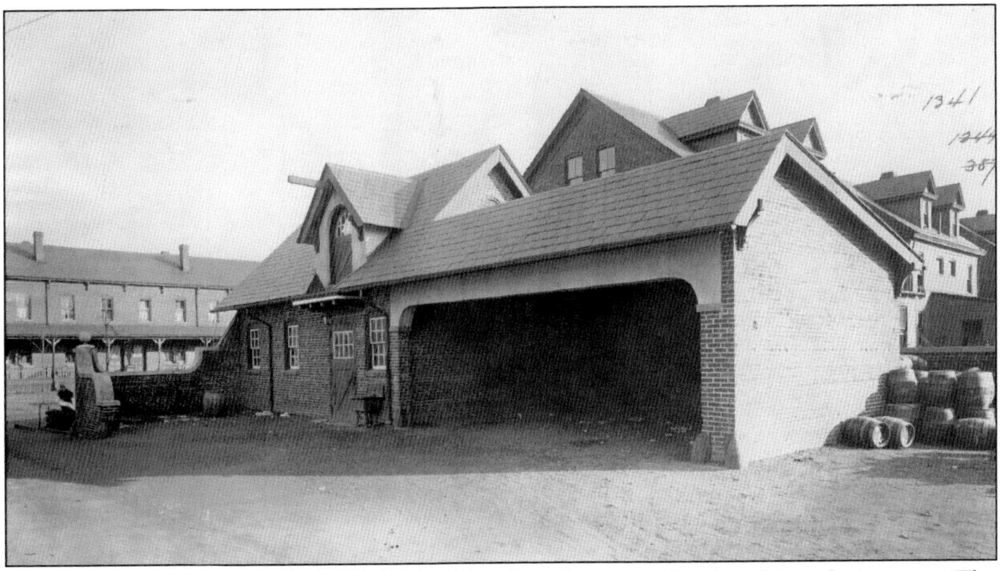

These stables were located behind the Roebling Inn, between Third and Fourth Avenues. The stables are now used as efficiency apartments. In the background are the Third Avenue row homes. This picture was taken when these homes were just two stories high. Later, third-floor dormers were added to the homes. (Courtesy Carol M. Sheaffer, M.D.)

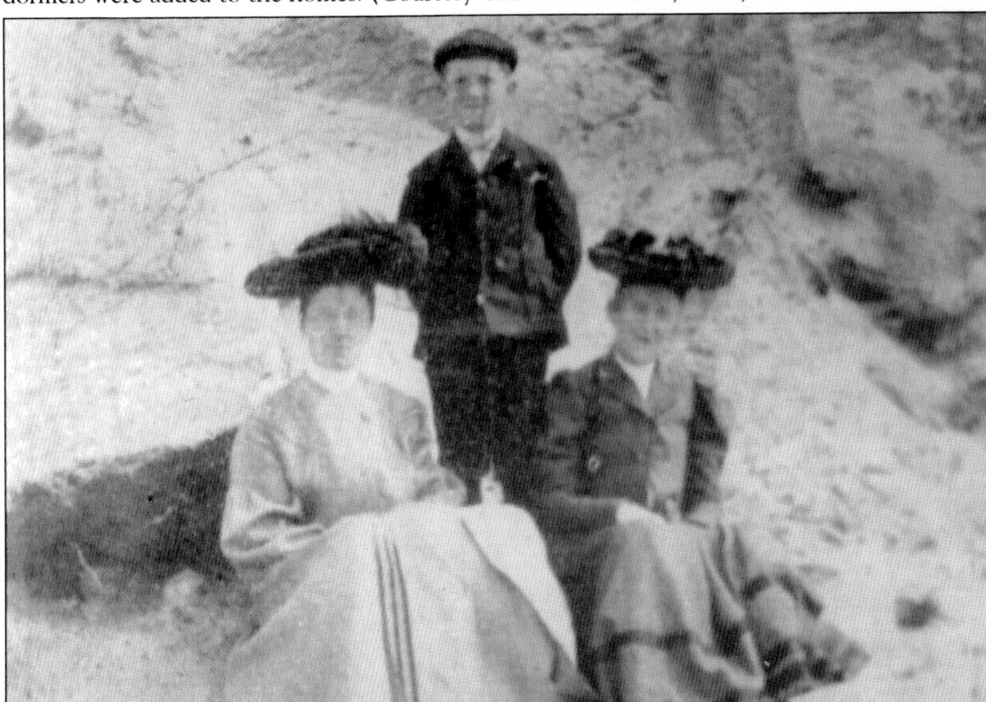

This photograph was taken in 1904. From left to right are Mrs. J.H. Cogill, daughter of Mrs. R.H. Carty; Norman C. Michalis, grandson of R.H. Carty; and Mrs. R.H. Carty. R.H. Carty was a mason contractor employed by the John A. Roebling's Sons Company for the erection of houses and stores. Carty will be remembered as having laid the first bricks in the houses of the village. The general store at Fifth and Main Streets is now located on this site. (Courtesy Louis Borbi.)

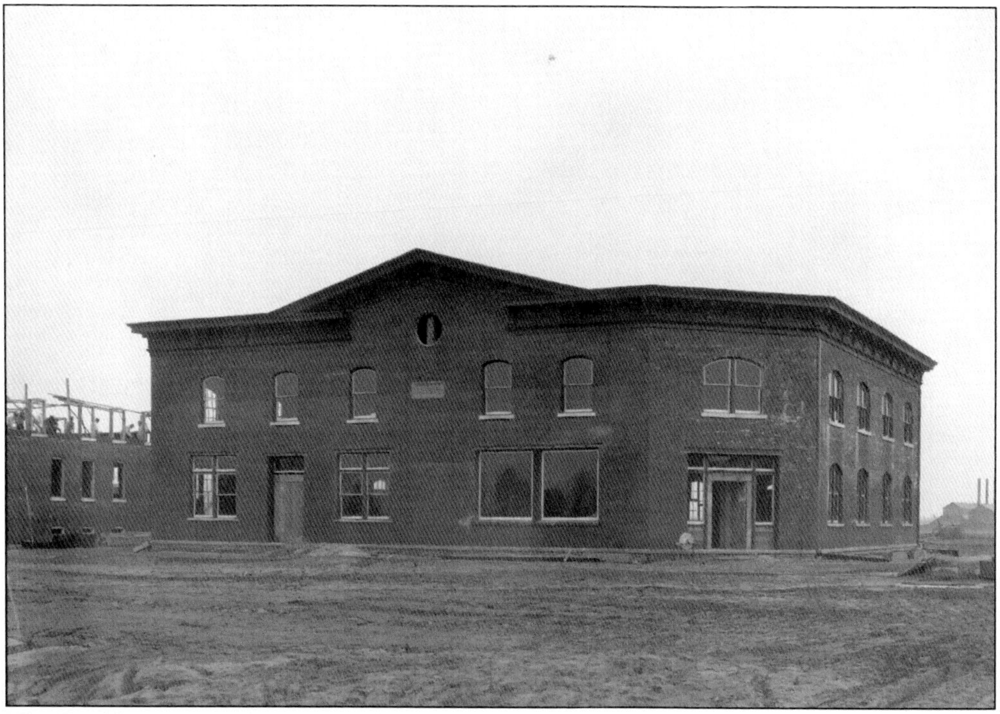

The Roebling General Store is shown under construction in 1905. (Courtesy Carol M. Scheaffer, M.D.)

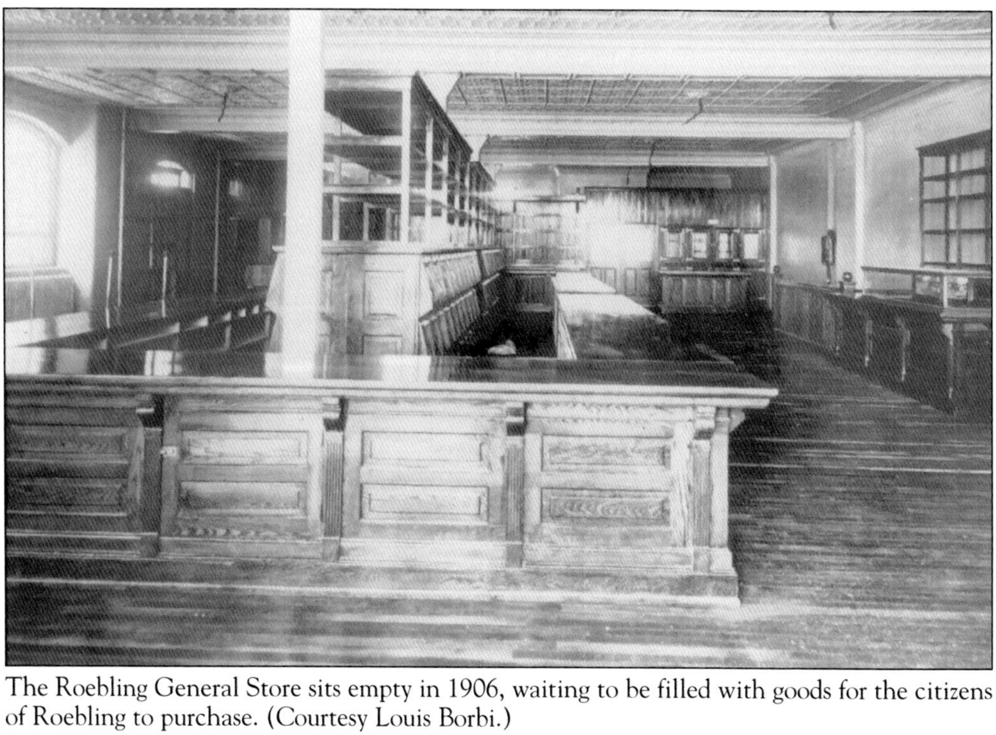

The Roebling General Store sits empty in 1906, waiting to be filled with goods for the citizens of Roebling to purchase. (Courtesy Louis Borbi.)

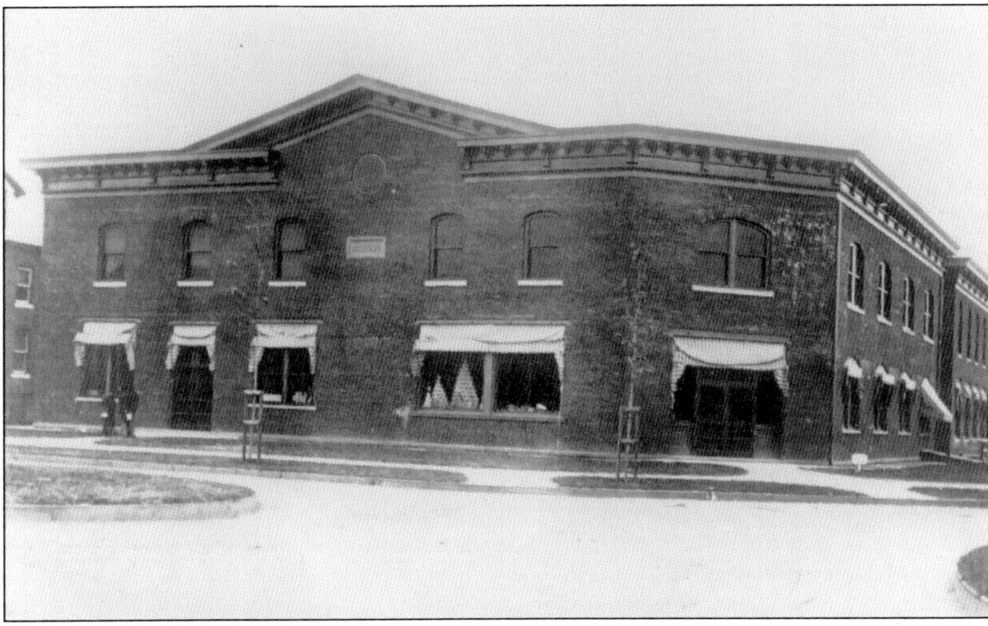

According to the August 6, 1908 edition of *Iron Age*, the construction of the Roebling General Store began in 1905. It opened for business on June 3, 1906, with Samuel L. Major in charge. The company maintained the store on a cash basis or, if preferred, accounts could be settled weekly, depending upon the credit of the customer. The company issued no script by its men, and no money was deducted from the pay envelope for store purchases. Men had the option to trade at the store or secure their supplies elsewhere. (Courtesy Louis Borbi.)

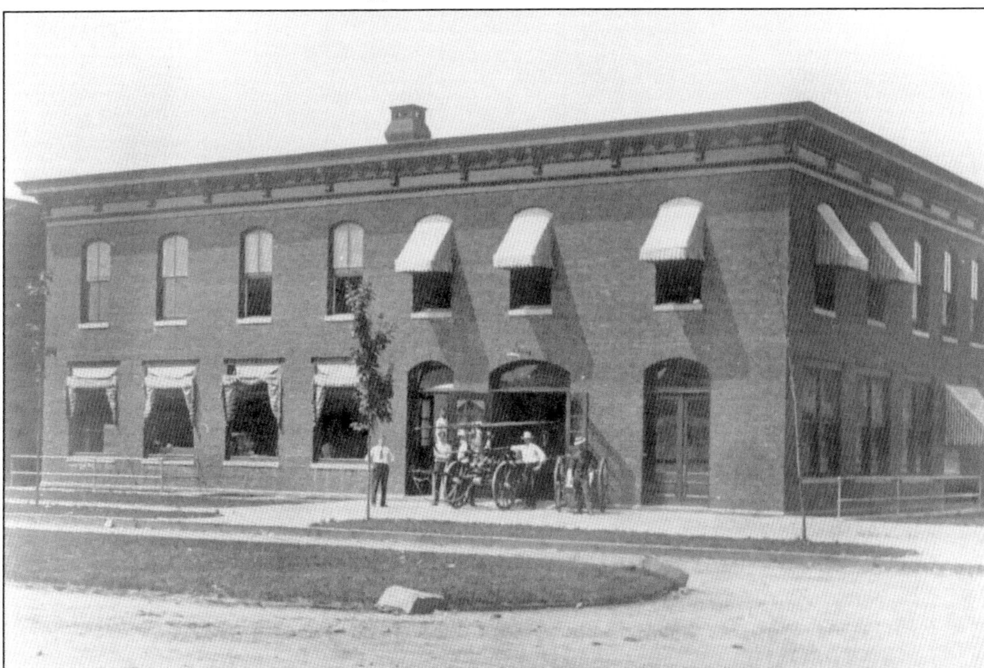

This *c.* 1907 photograph shows the drugstore at Fourth Avenue and Main Streets. The fire wagon was stored in the building. (Courtesy Louis Borbi.)

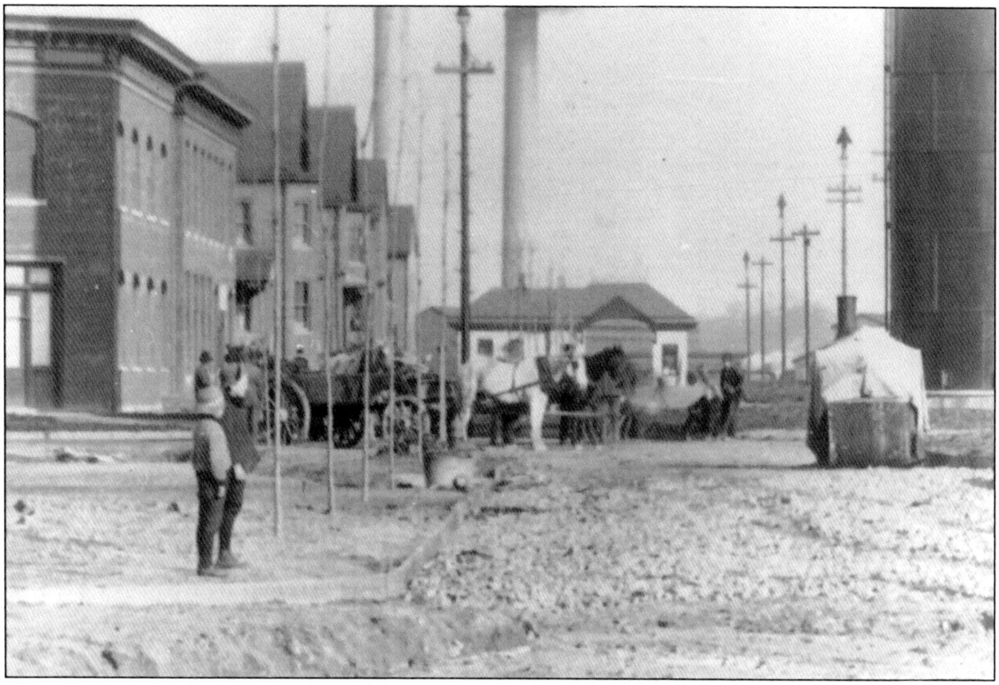

Construction of the village of Roebling started in June 1905. This view of Main Street shows the Roebling General Store in the left foreground, the water tower on the right, and the original Main Gate behind the horse-drawn wagon. The smokestack from the mill's power plant is visible in the background. (Courtesy Louis Borbi.)

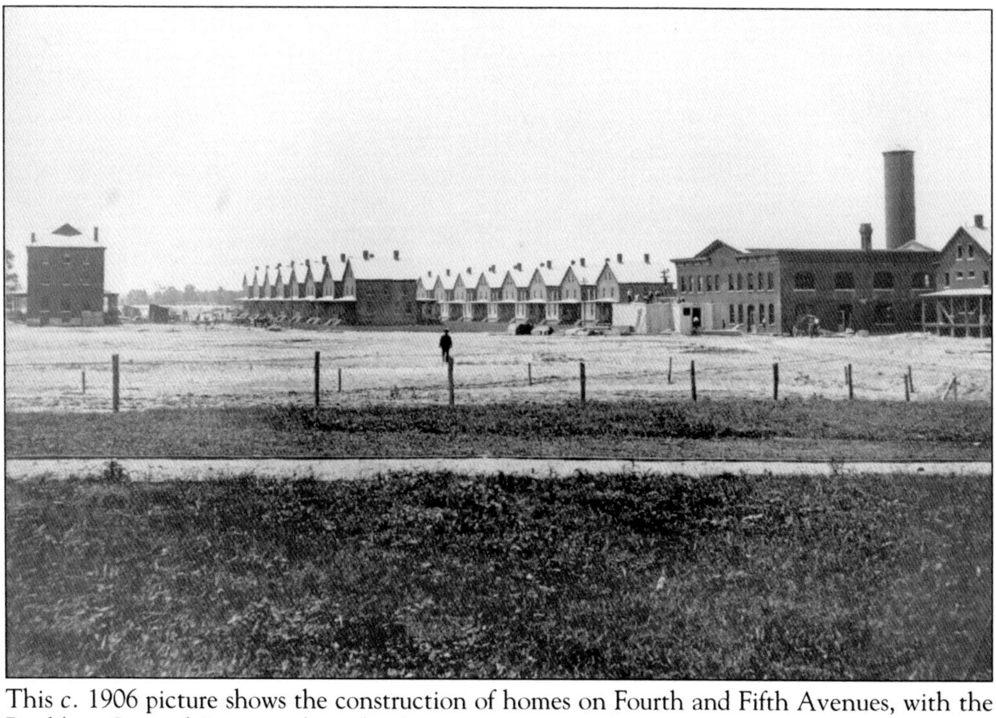

This *c.* 1906 picture shows the construction of homes on Fourth and Fifth Avenues, with the Roebling General Store on the right. (Courtesy Louis Borbi.)

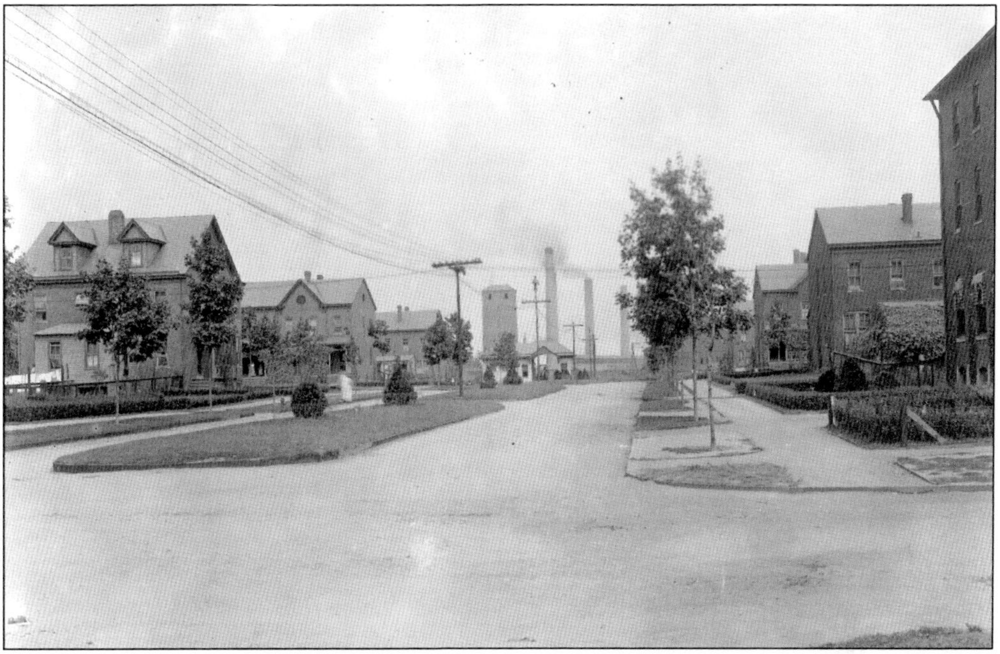

This view looks down Main Street from Fourth Avenue. Main Gate No. 1 and the smokestacks from the mill are in the background. (Courtesy Carol M. Sheaffer, M.D.)

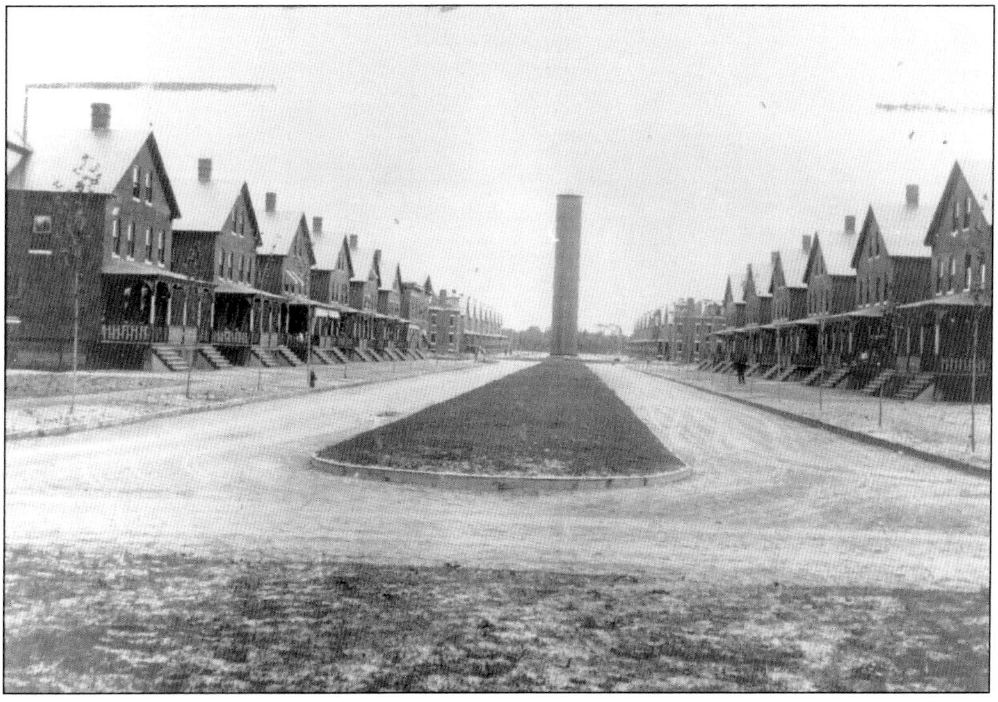

This is a view looking from Knickerbocker Avenue toward Main Street on Fifth Avenue c. 1908. (Courtesy Louis Borbi.)

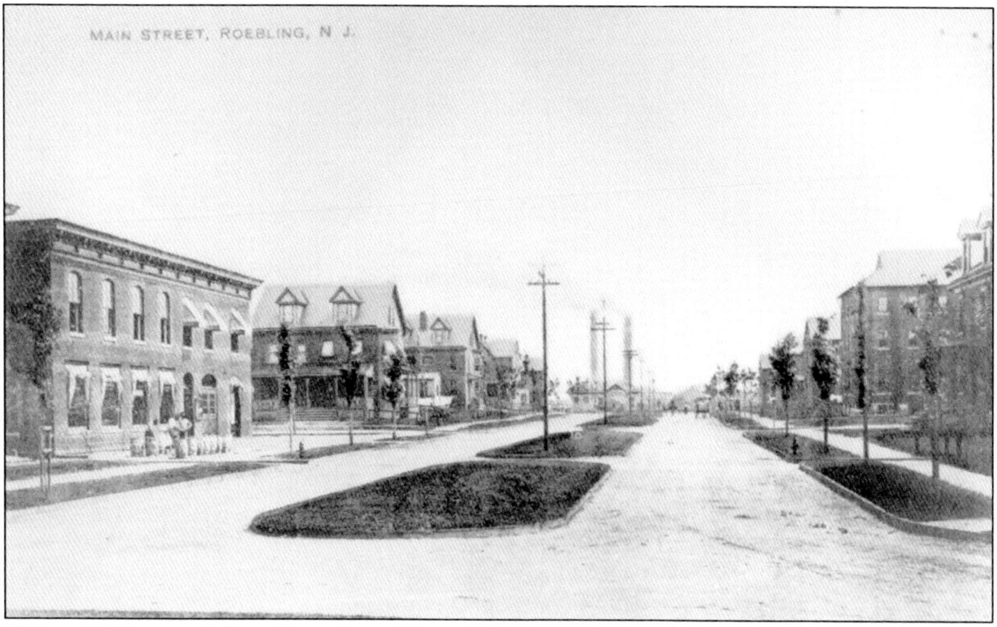

This *c.* 1910 view of the village shows Main Street from the circle, connecting Main Street and Fifth Avenue. Main Gate No. 1 is at the end of the street. (Courtesy Louis Borbi.)

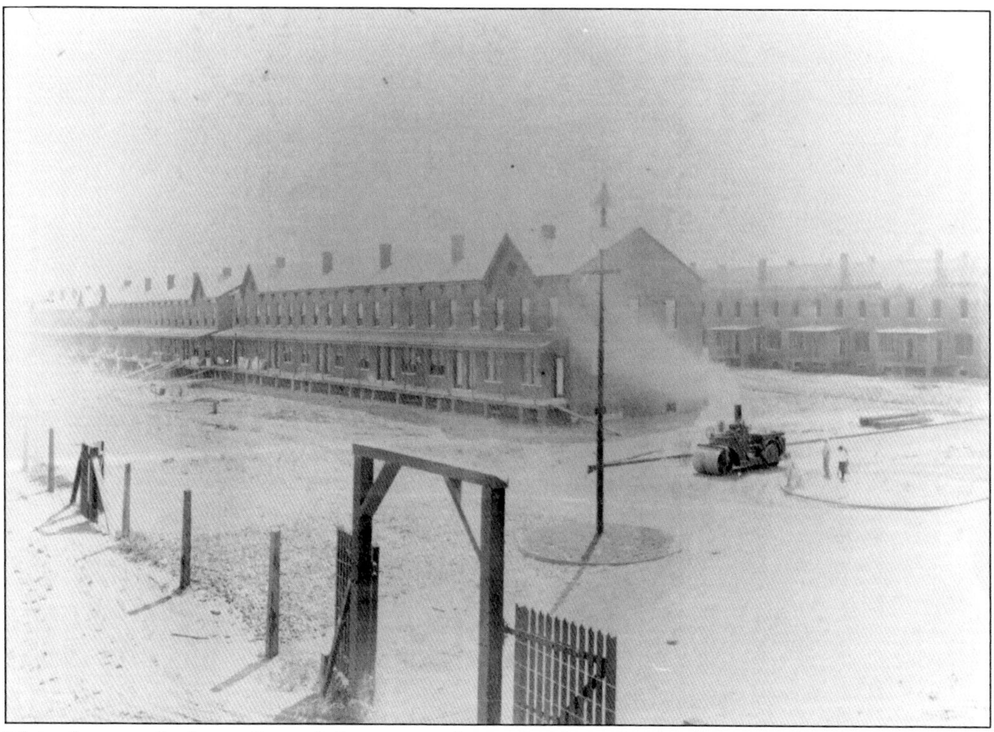

This photograph shows Second Avenue in the early 1900s. In the foreground is Main Gate No. 1 in the beginning stages of construction. In the background, homes are being constructed. The paver is located on Main Street. (Courtesy Louis Borbi.)

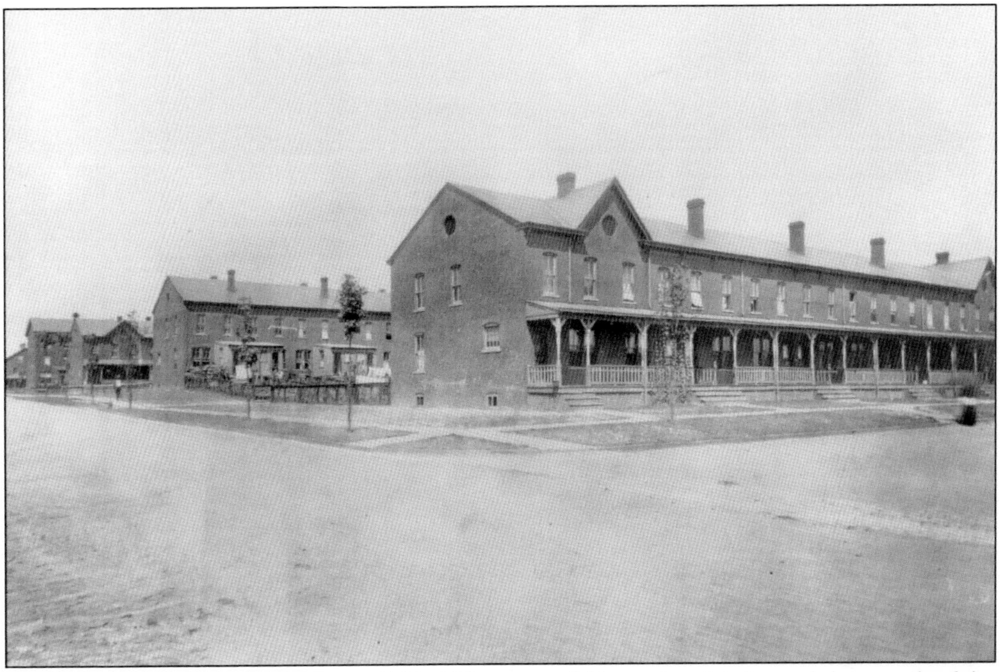

This is a view of Second Avenue in 1911. Villagers could hear the whistles and the sounds of the John A. Roebling's Sons Company, which was part of the everyday life. (Courtesy Louis Borbi.)

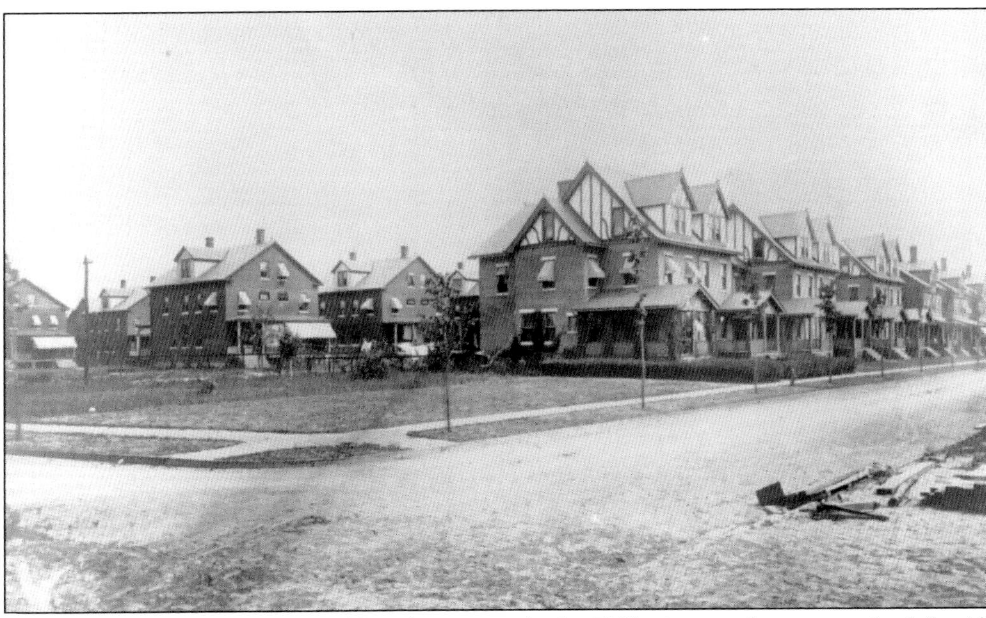

Pictured are Sixth Avenue Roebling homes, with the Fifth Avenue homes on the left. All backyards were enclosed on three sides by a fence. The 10-foot alleys were for the convenient collection of ashes and garbage. The delivery wagons also used the alley, and all materials entered and exited by way of the backyards. The front lawns were maintained by the company to keep the appearance neat and attractive. The tenant took care of the backyard. (Courtesy Louis Borbi; *Iron Age*, August 6, 1908.)

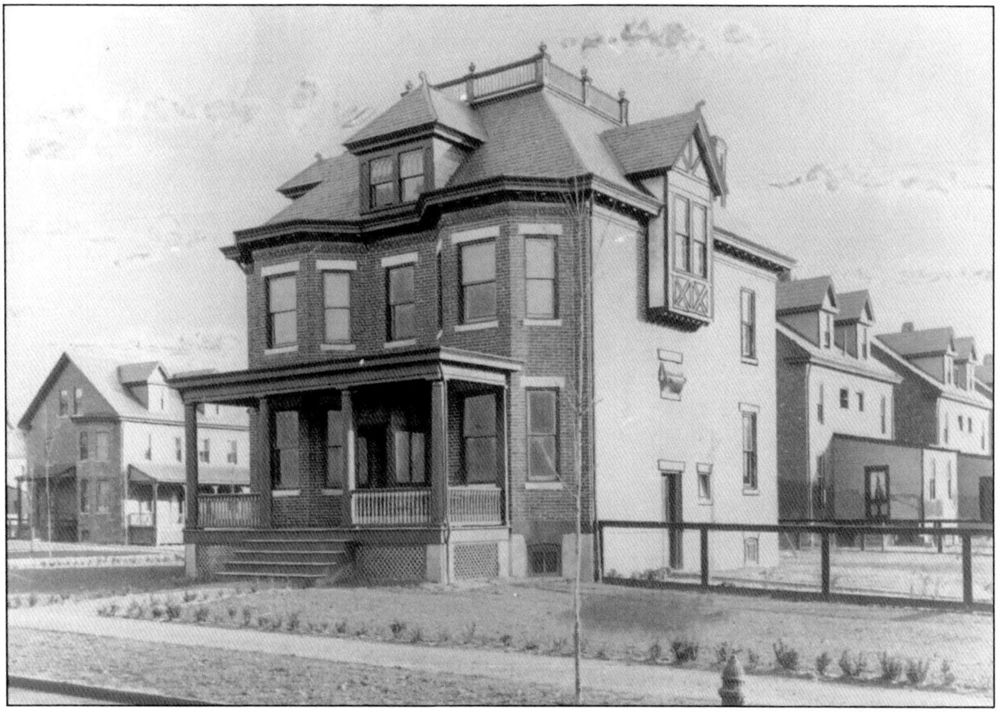

Shown are two views of 40 Riverside Avenue. The original blueprints, dated 1905, listed this as 10 Kinkora. Mill superintendent Frank Miller and his family occupied the house. Afterwards, various foreman and mill officials occupied it until 1920. That year, the house was remodeled and the wraparound porch was installed. Since 1947, the Theodore Mitre family has owned and lived in the house. (Above courtesy Ted Mitre; below courtesy Louis Borbi.)

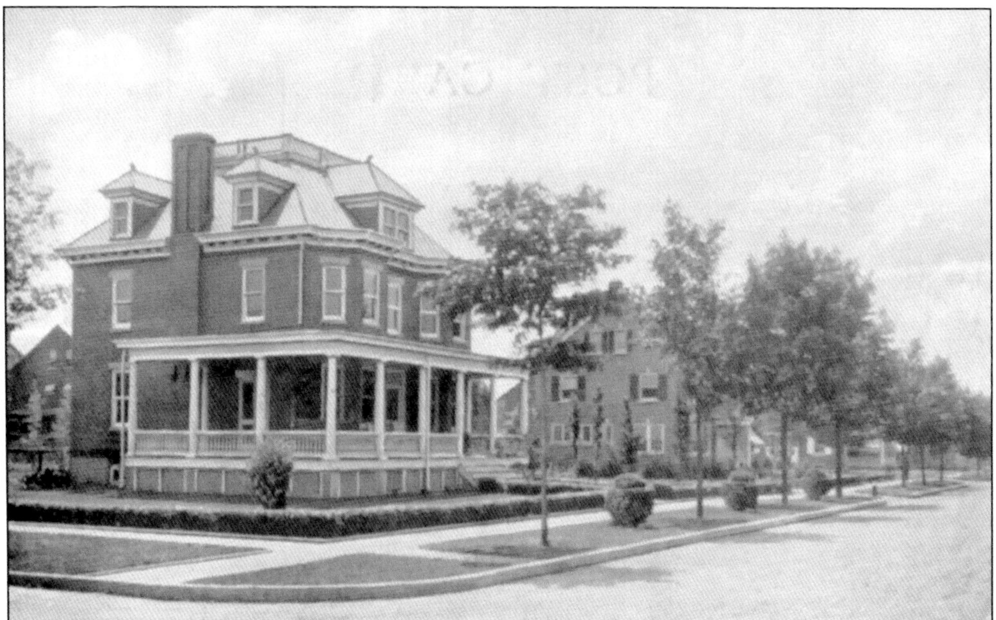

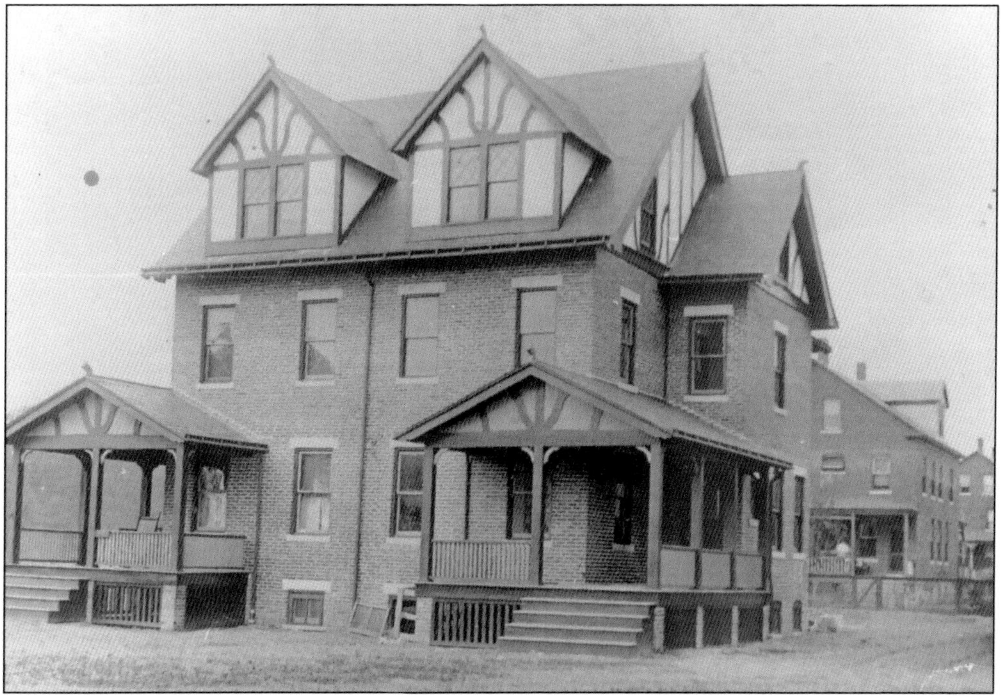

This Sixth Avenue duplex was three stories in height and contained six to nine rooms and a bath. It would rent for $20 a month. There were only three homes of this style built and it would house supervisors with large families. (Courtesy Louis Borbi; *Iron Age*, August 6, 1908.)

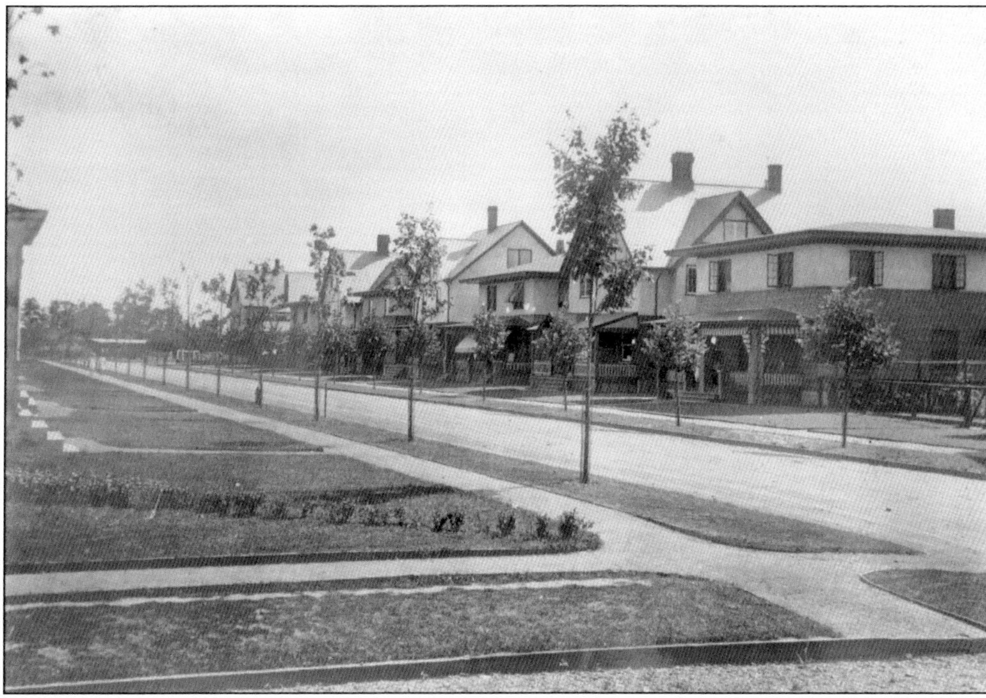

This *c.* 1910 view was taken from Sixth Avenue and Main Street. All the streets in Roebling were 80 feet wide, with Fifth and Main Streets measuring 100 feet wide. (Courtesy Louis Borbi.)

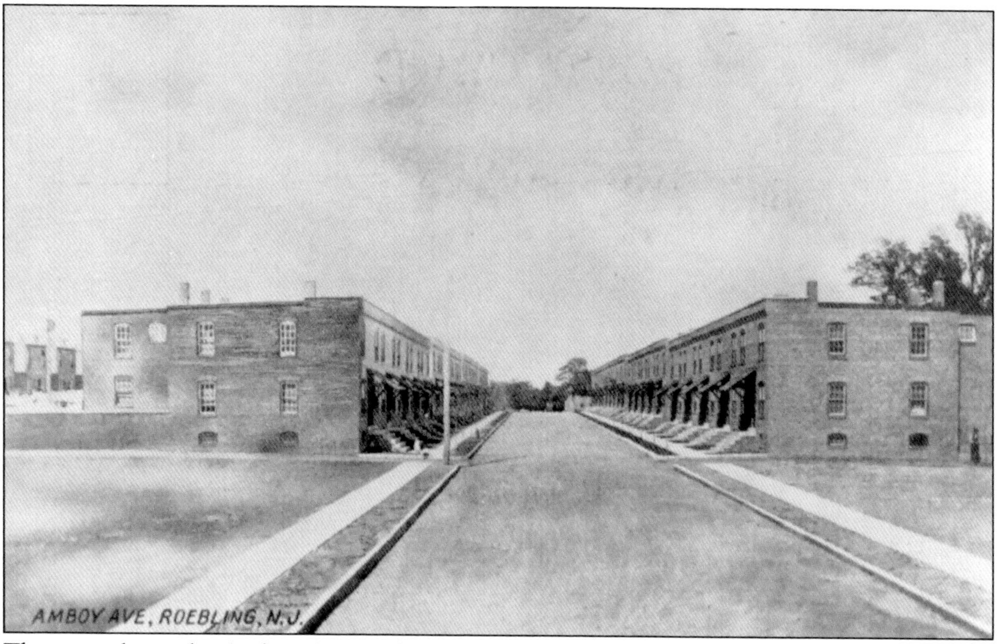

This view shows the Amboy Avenue homes constructed in late 1910. (Courtesy Louis Borbi.)

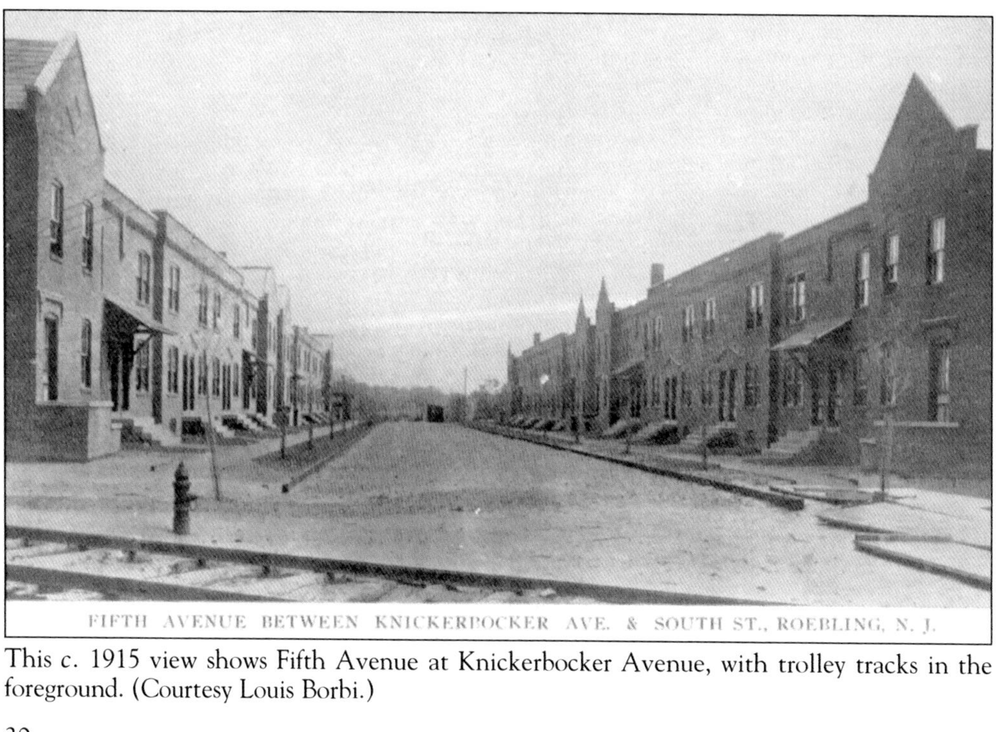

FIFTH AVENUE BETWEEN KNICKERBOCKER AVE. & SOUTH ST., ROEBLING, N. J.

This c. 1915 view shows Fifth Avenue at Knickerbocker Avenue, with trolley tracks in the foreground. (Courtesy Louis Borbi.)

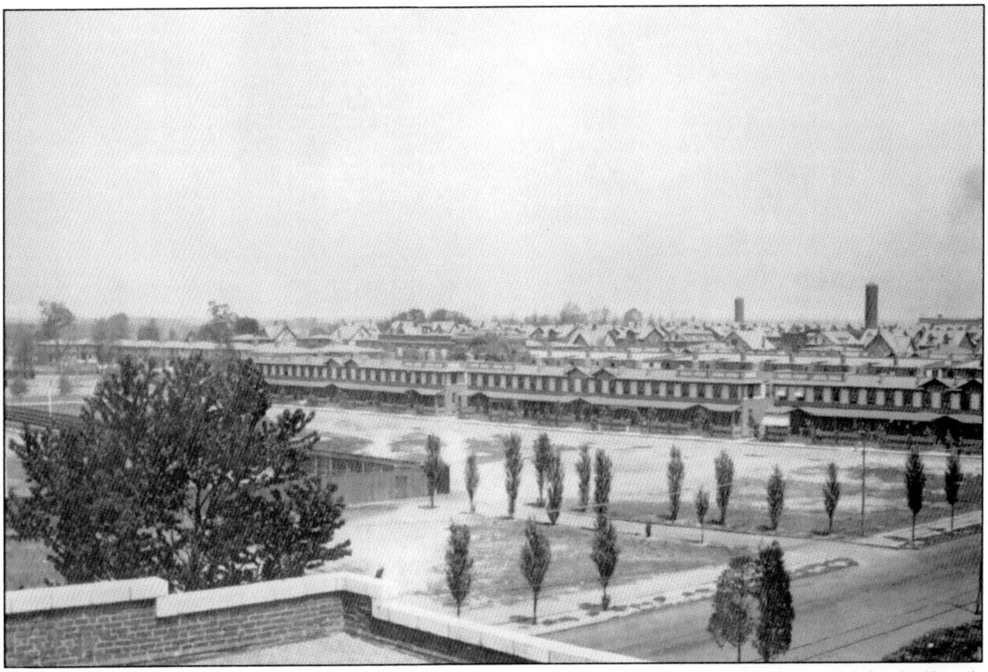

This view shows the village from the roof of the public school *c.* 1912. The fence of the ballpark is visible to the left center, and Eighth Avenue homes are visible in the center and to the right. (Courtesy Louis Borbi.)

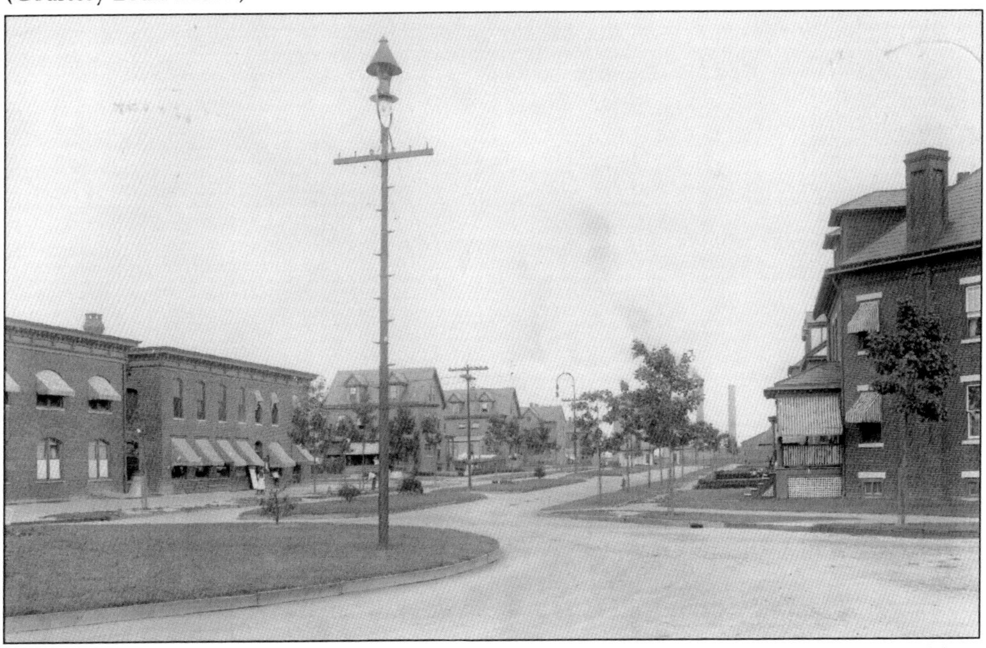

This picture shows the corner of Fifth Avenue and Main Street in Roebling. The Roebling General Store is in the left foreground and the bakery is behind it. The house shown on the right was moved and became known as the One Horse House. It has been said that one horse moved the house to its present location on Eighth Avenue and Main Street. (Courtesy Carol M. Scheaffer, M.D.)

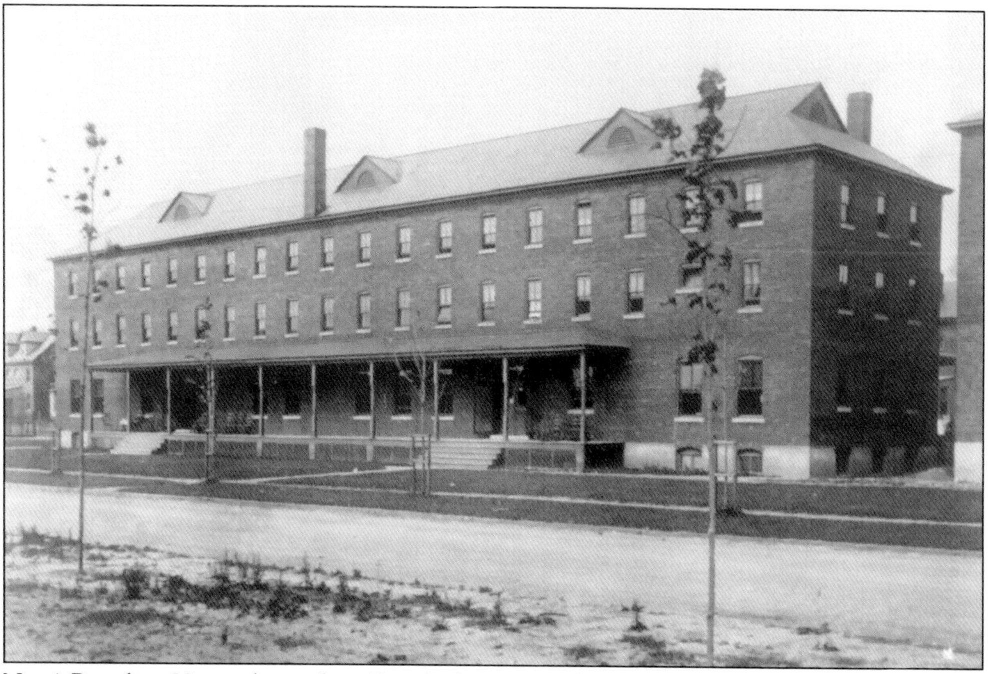

No. 1 Boarding House, located on Fourth Avenue, is shown in the early 1920s. It housed the post office, Booster Club, doctor's office, and hospital. (Courtesy Louis Borbi.)

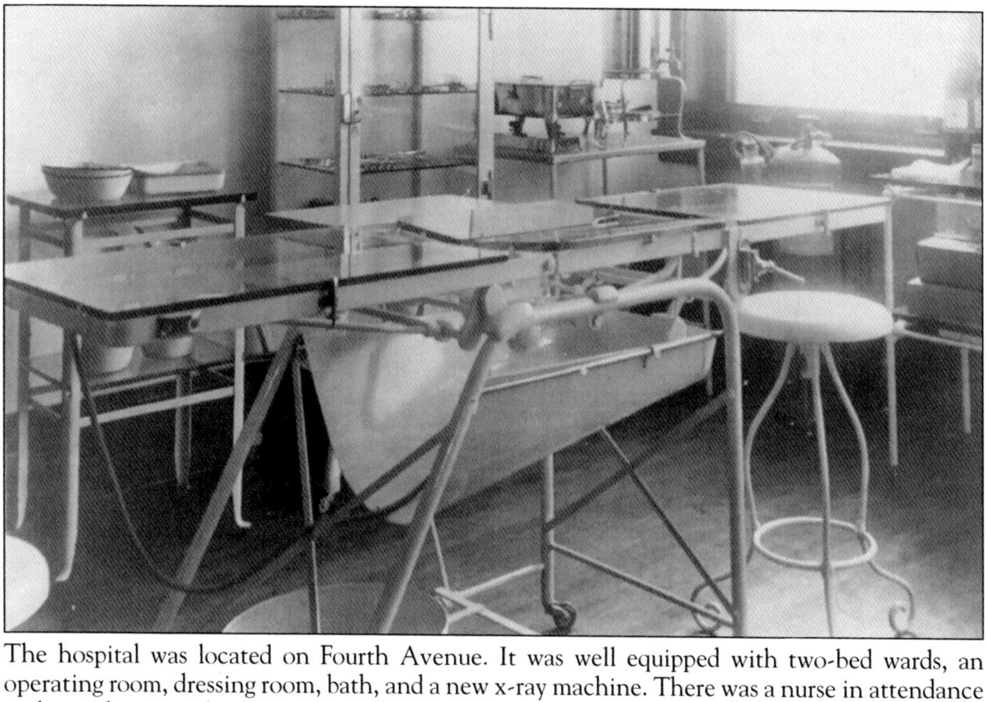

The hospital was located on Fourth Avenue. It was well equipped with two-bed wards, an operating room, dressing room, bath, and a new x-ray machine. There was a nurse in attendance and two doctors. The workers and their families were encouraged to use the facility. Because it was an emergency hospital, cases requiring extended treatment were taken in the company's ambulance to St. Francis Hospital in Trenton, New Jersey. (Courtesy Louis Borbi; *Iron Age*, January 3, 1924.)

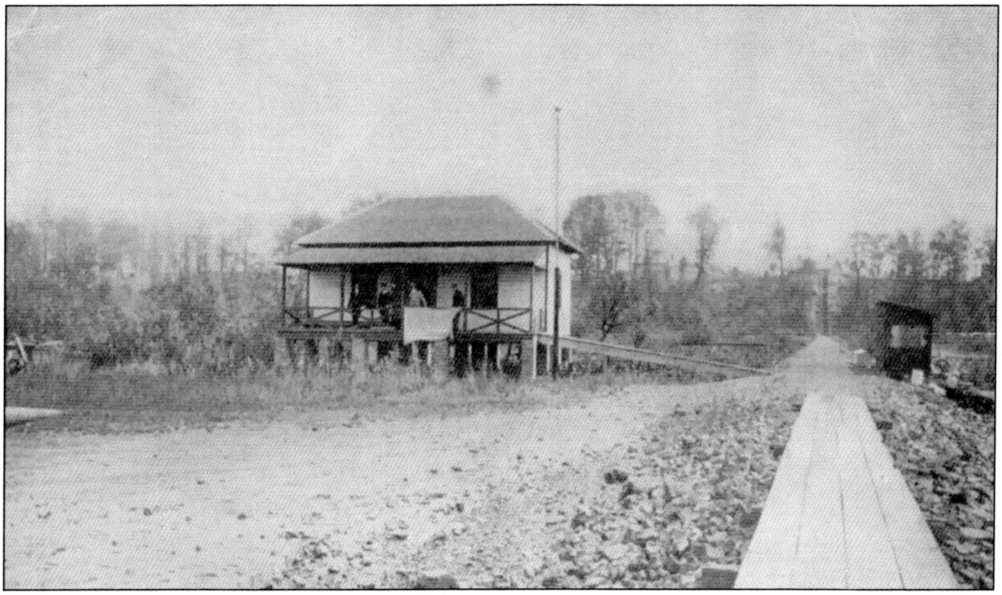

Pictured on July 3, 1912, is the boathouse that was located between Fifth and Sixth Avenue. (Courtesy Louis Borbi.)

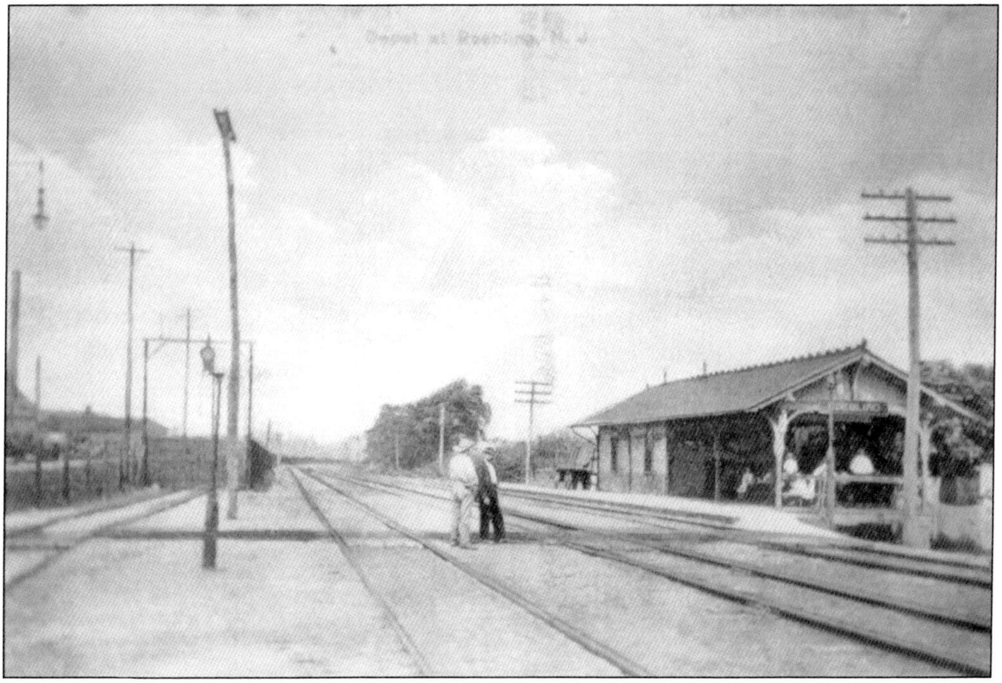

In this c. 1910 view of the Roebling Depot, the Pennsylvania Railroad tracks are pictured on the right. (Courtesy Louis Borbi.)

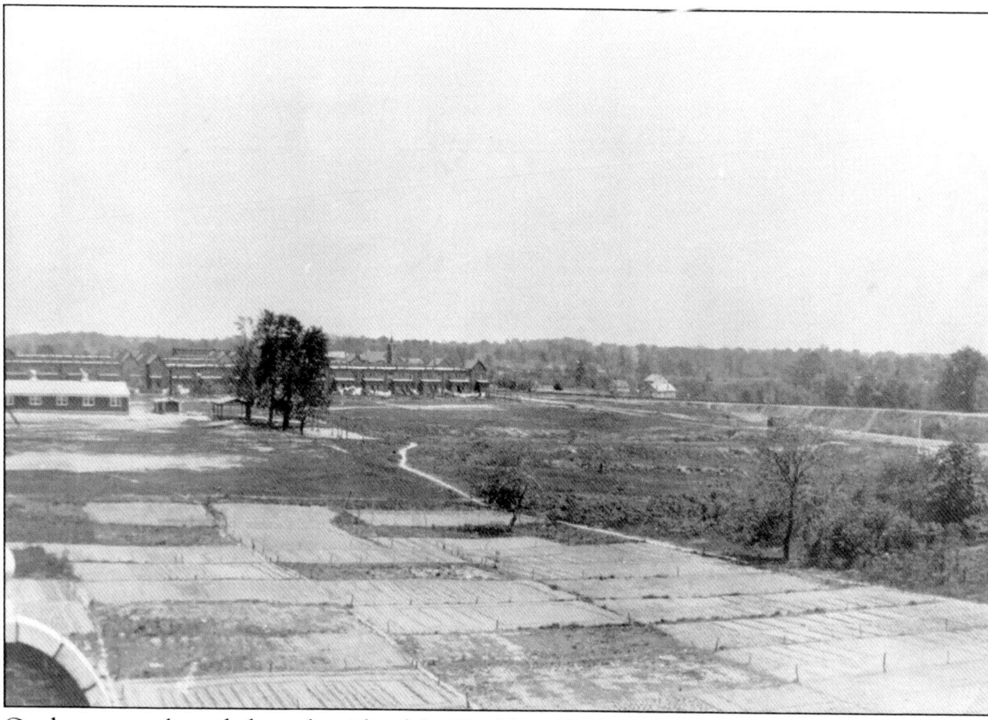

Gardens were planted along the side of the Roebling Public School in the mid-1920s. Near the trees is a playground, and to the right of the center is the first dump. (Courtesy Louis Borbi.)

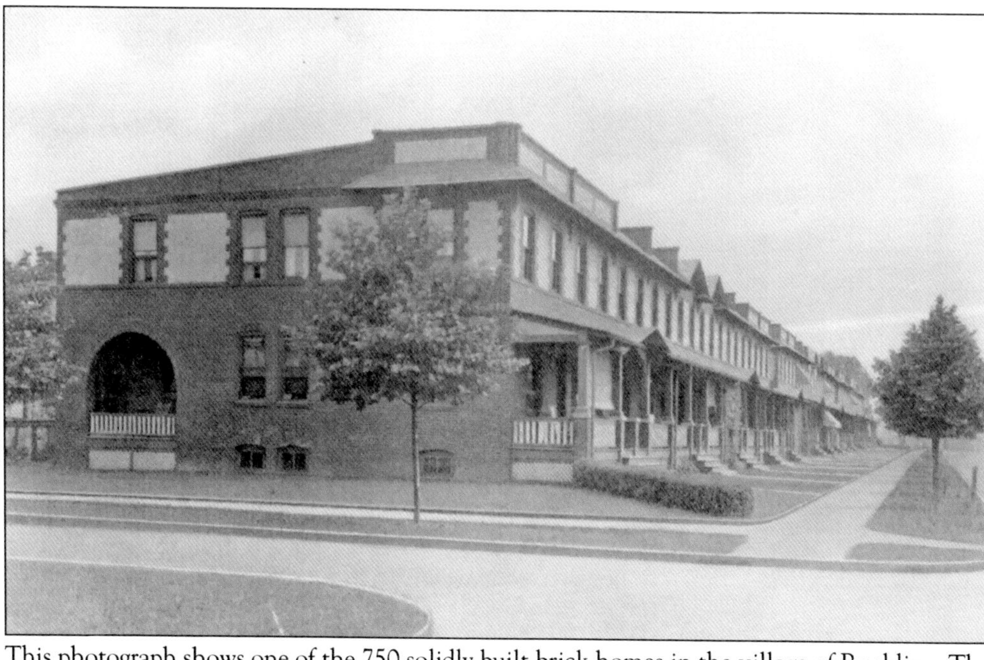

This photograph shows one of the 750 solidly built brick homes in the village of Roebling. The company maintained the workers' homes inside and out until 1947, when the company sold the homes to the mill workers. This home, located on the corner of Seventh Avenue and Main Street, still has the original arch on the side porch. (Courtesy Louis Borbi.)

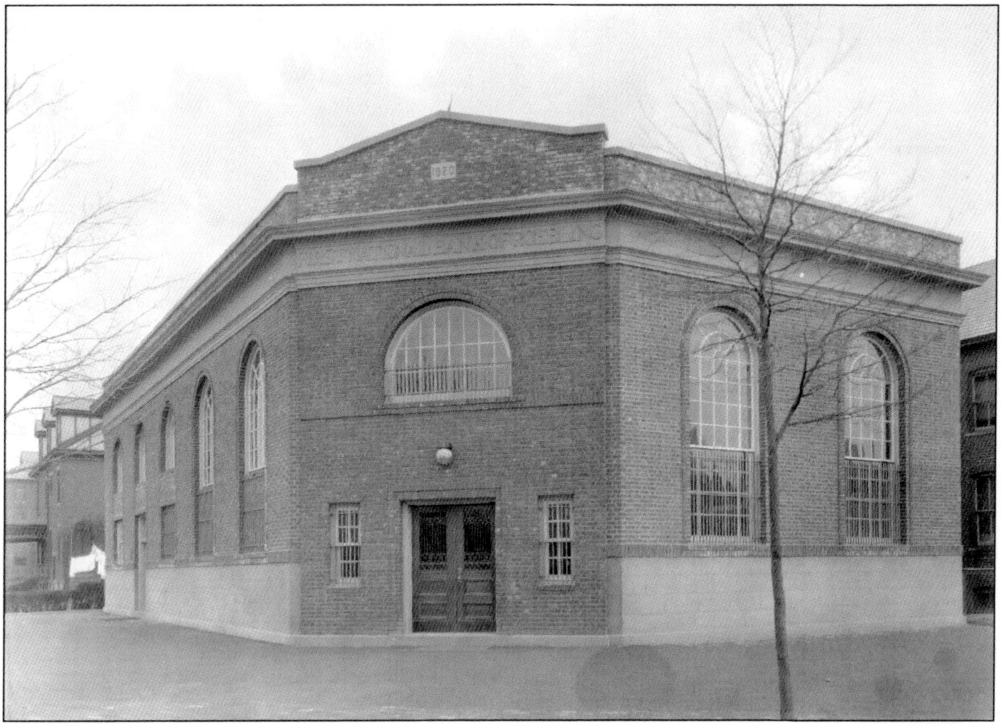

This is the First National Bank of Roebling in 1920. (Courtesy Carol M. Scheaffer, M.D.)

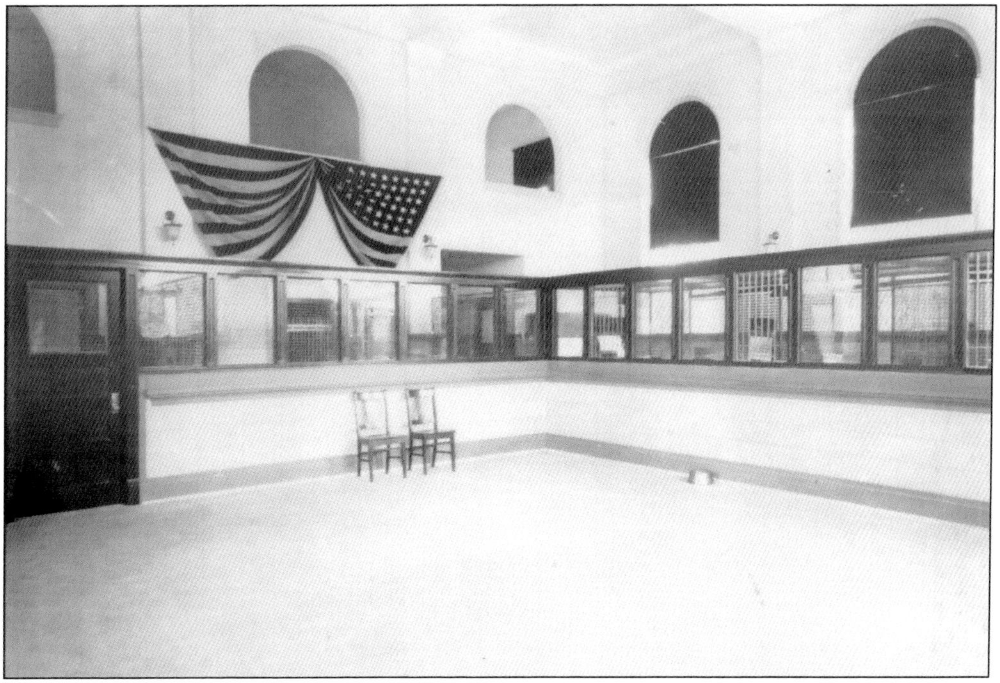

W.L. Wilson, from Lambertville, New Jersey, started the First National Bank of Roebling. The bank's first location was inside Main Gate No. 1. In 1920, the new building was opened on Fifth Avenue and Main Street. (Courtesy Louis Borbi.)

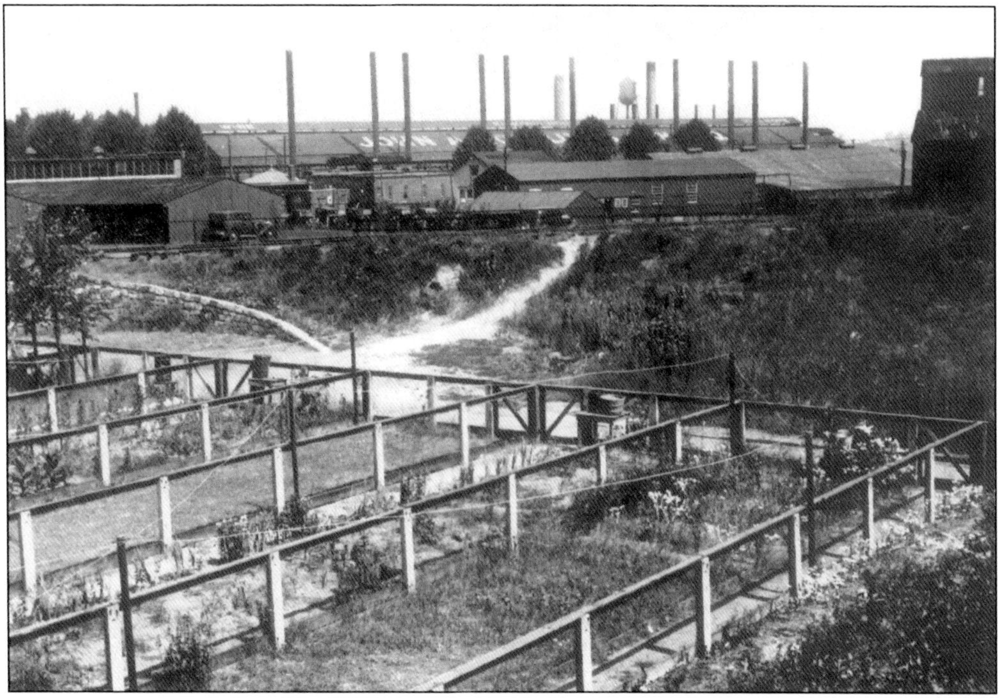

This *c.* 1928 view of the mill was taken from the Fourth Avenue alley. On the right is the coal silo, which stored coal for heating of the village homes. (Courtesy Louis Borbi.)

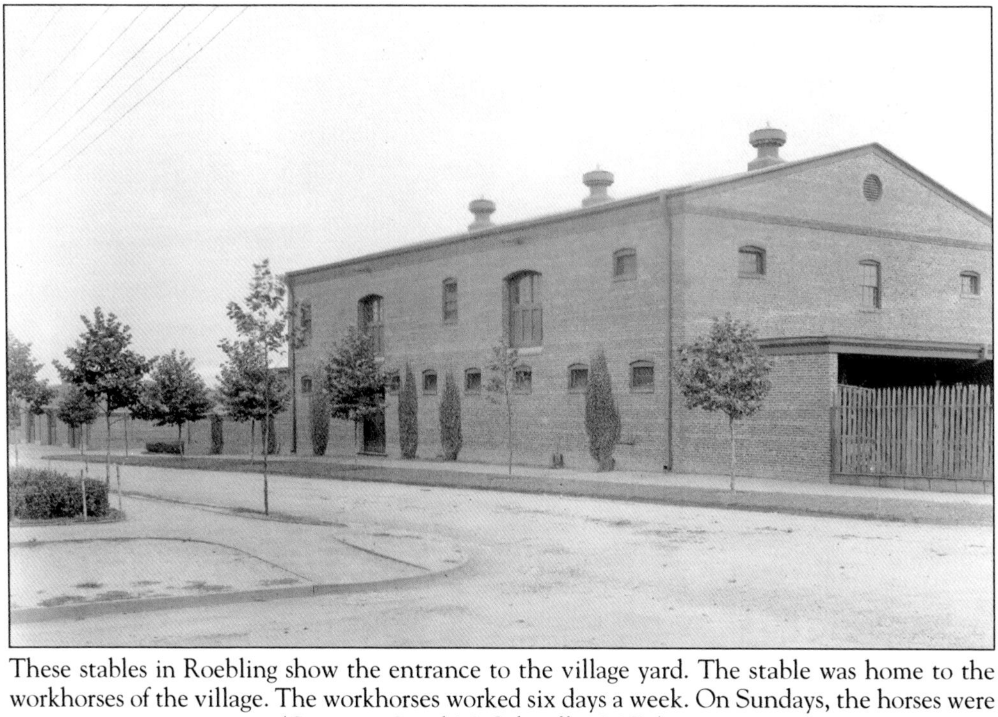

These stables in Roebling show the entrance to the village yard. The stable was home to the workhorses of the village. The workhorses worked six days a week. On Sundays, the horses were put out to pasture to rest. (Courtesy Carol M. Scheaffer, M.D.)

Three

The Mill and Its Workers

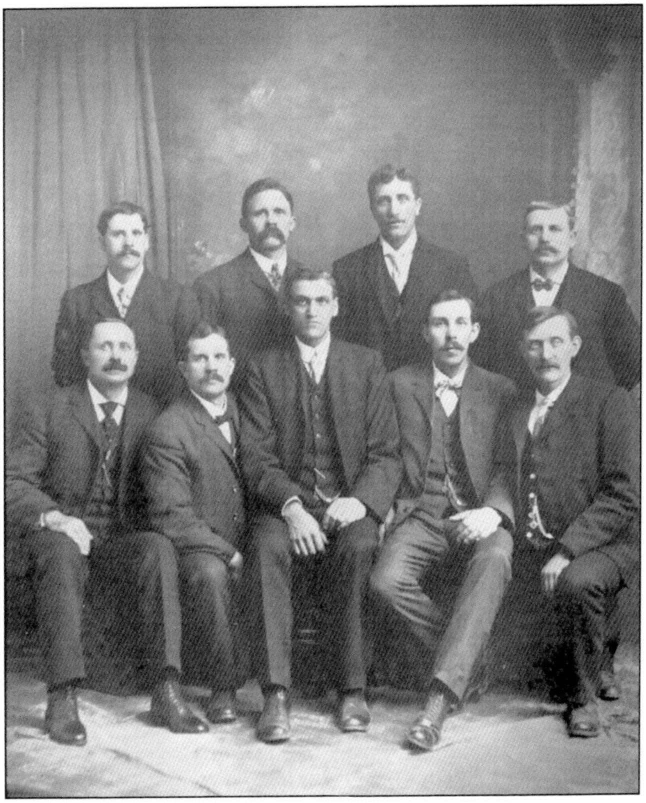

Late in 1906, the steel mill was nearing completion. Charles Roebling and Bill Gummere went to the Quinsegamond Works of the U.S. Steel Company in Worcester, Massachusetts, to seek experienced manpower with expertise to make and roll steel. Roebling and Gummere contacted Carl Lybeck. Lybeck approached eight other Swedes with the idea of moving to Roebling. Shown from left to right are the following: (front row) John Johnson, Fred Ullman, Oscar Larson, Andrew Fors, and Oscar Carlson; (back row) Oscar Lundin, Carl Lybeck, Carl Englund, and August Larson. (Courtesy Ray Thompson.)

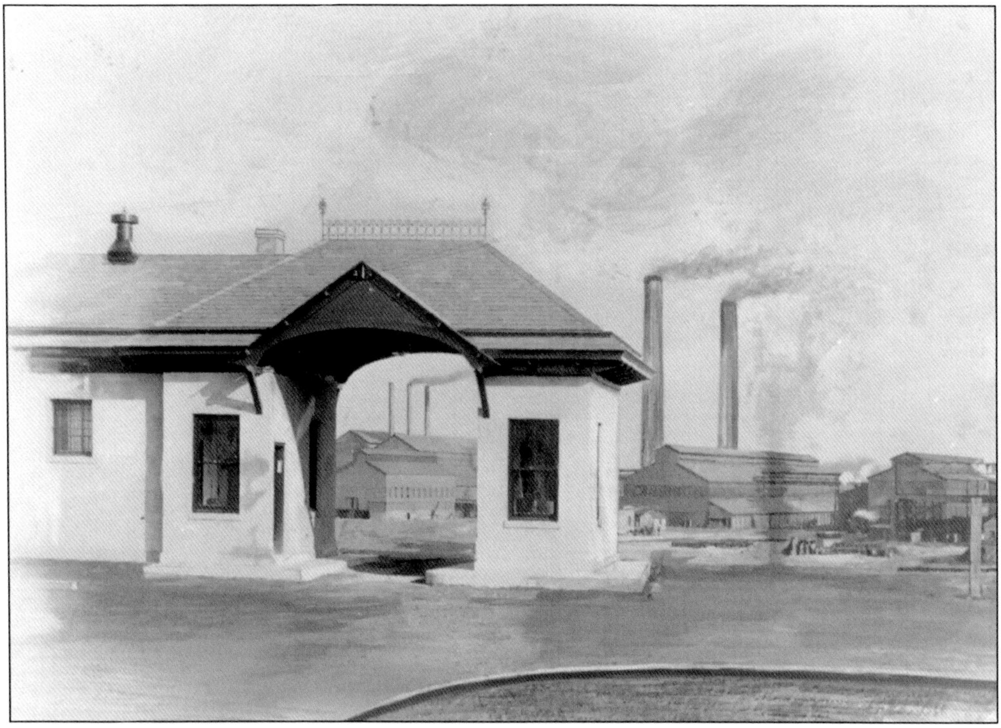

Shown *c.* 1906 is a portion of Main Gate No. 1 on Second Avenue. (Courtesy Louis Borbi.)

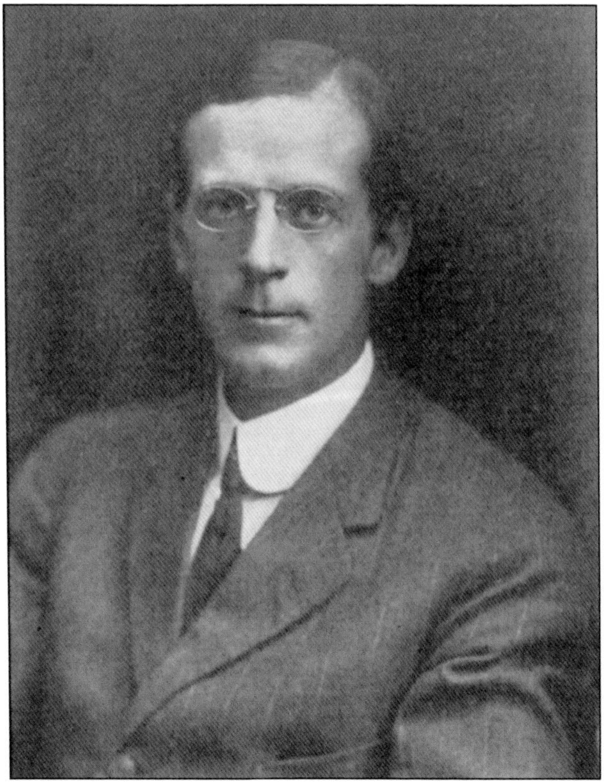

The steel-making equipment consisted of 12 open-hearth furnaces that were under the supervision of William Gummere. He was also a member of the board of directors and served the community as president of the Roebling National Bank. (Courtesy Ray Thompson.)

Charles G. Roebling (left) and Washington A. Roebling are pictured taking part in the dedication of the flagpole and flag unfurling on June 2, 1917. (Courtesy Mary Arnold Montalto.)

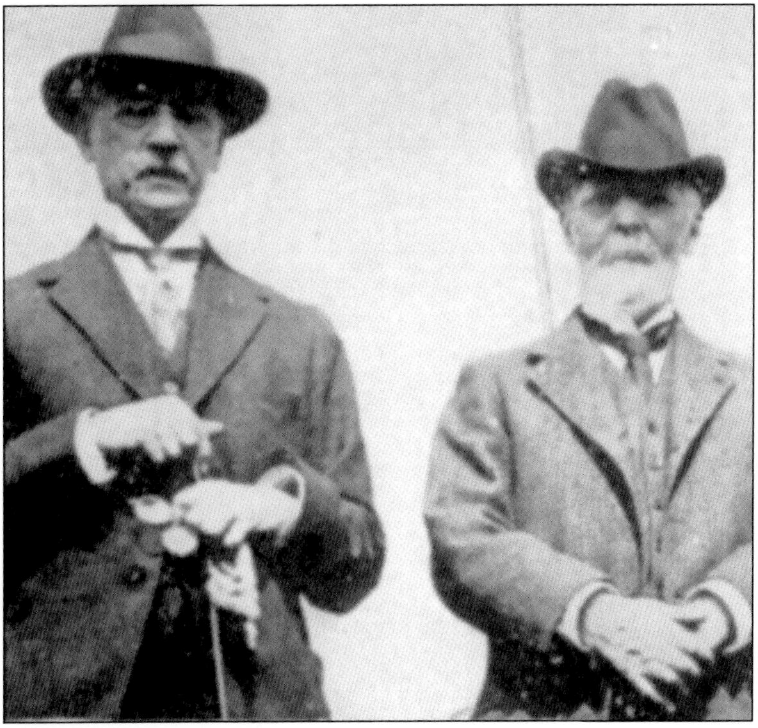

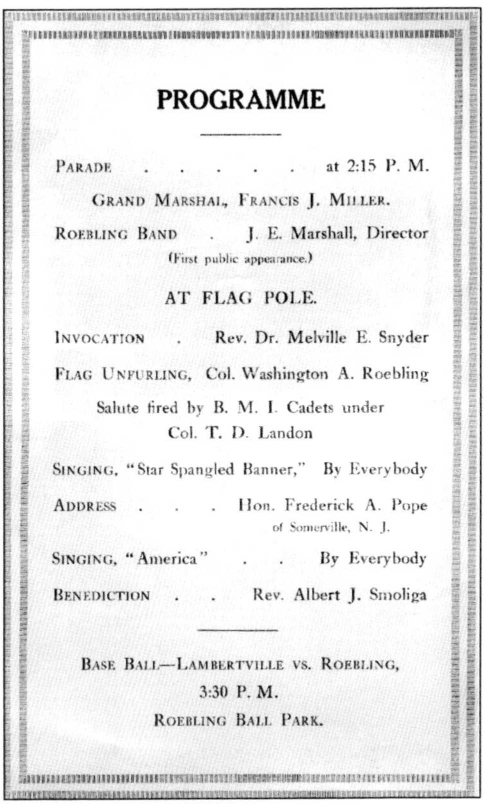

PROGRAMME

PARADE . . . . . . at 2:15 P. M.

GRAND MARSHAL, FRANCIS J. MILLER.

ROEBLING BAND . J. E. Marshall, Director
(First public appearance.)

AT FLAG POLE.

INVOCATION . Rev. Dr. Melville E. Snyder

FLAG UNFURLING, Col. Washington A. Roebling

Salute fired by B. M. I. Cadets under Col. T. D. Landon

SINGING, "Star Spangled Banner," By Everybody

ADDRESS . . . Hon. Frederick A. Pope
of Somerville, N. J.

SINGING, "America" . . By Everybody

BENEDICTION . . Rev. Albert J. Smoliga

BASE BALL—LAMBERTVILLE VS. ROEBLING,
3:30 P. M.
ROEBLING BALL PARK.

Pictured is the program of exercises at the flag unfurling ceremony on Saturday, June 2, 1917. J.E. Marshall, in his first public appearance, directed the Roebling Band. The flag unfurling was done by Col. Washington A. Roebling, with a salute fired by the Bordentown Military Institute cadets. (Courtesy Ray Thompson.)

Blue Center

VOLUME I. TRENTON, N. J., November, 1925. NUMBER

To the Employees of the John A. Roebling's Sons Company:

We are a large family, scattered from the Atlantic to the Pacific—some eight thousand of us—each laboring with the problems which have fallen to our lot, but at the same time sincerely interested in the great human organization bearing the name of the John A. Roebling's Sons Company, and in what is being done by our fellow-employees around us and across the continent.

In issuing the "Blue Center," it will be our earnest endeavor to make it a periodical of outstanding quality in character, such as its name would naturally inspire. We shall try to make it helpful and interesting, and if it succeeds in bringing our organization into closer understanding and harmony our efforts shall not have been in vain.

EDITORIAL COMMITTEE.

Named after the company's trademark blue fiber core in its wire rope, the *Blue Center* magazine was published by the John A. Roebling's Sons Company, expressly for the interests of its workers and families. Pictured is the cover of the very first *Blue Center*, published in November 1925. (Courtesy Ray Thompson.)

This is the program from the Seventh Annual Dinner of the Superintendents and Foreman of the Kinkora Works, which was held at the Roebling Inn on February 10, 1915. Dr. Paul A. Traub, surgeon for the John A. Roebling's Sons Company, served as toastmaster. (Courtesy Ray Thompson.)

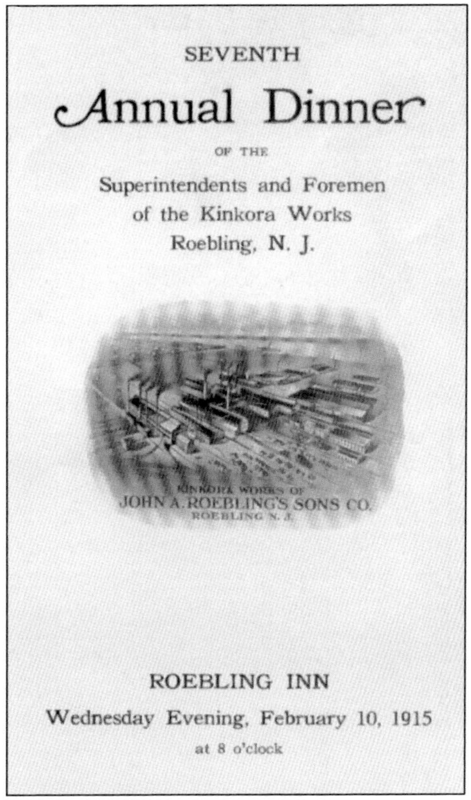

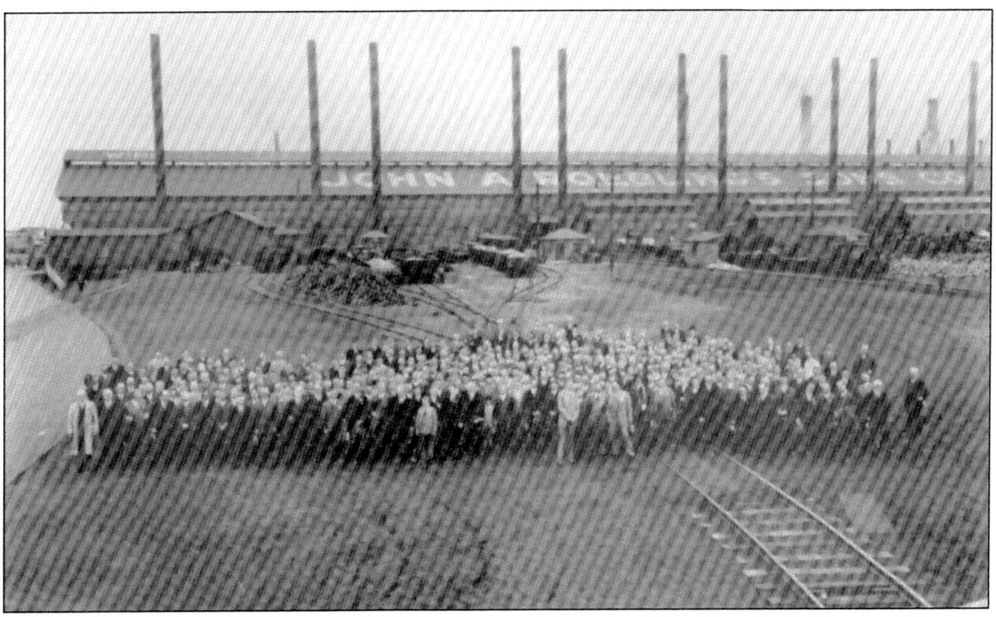

On Thursday, May 2, 1929, some 300 members and friends of the New York Electrical Society arrived for an inspection tour of the Roebling plant. At noon, a group picture was taken, after which a luncheon was served in the Roebling Auditorium. (Courtesy Carl G. Friday.)

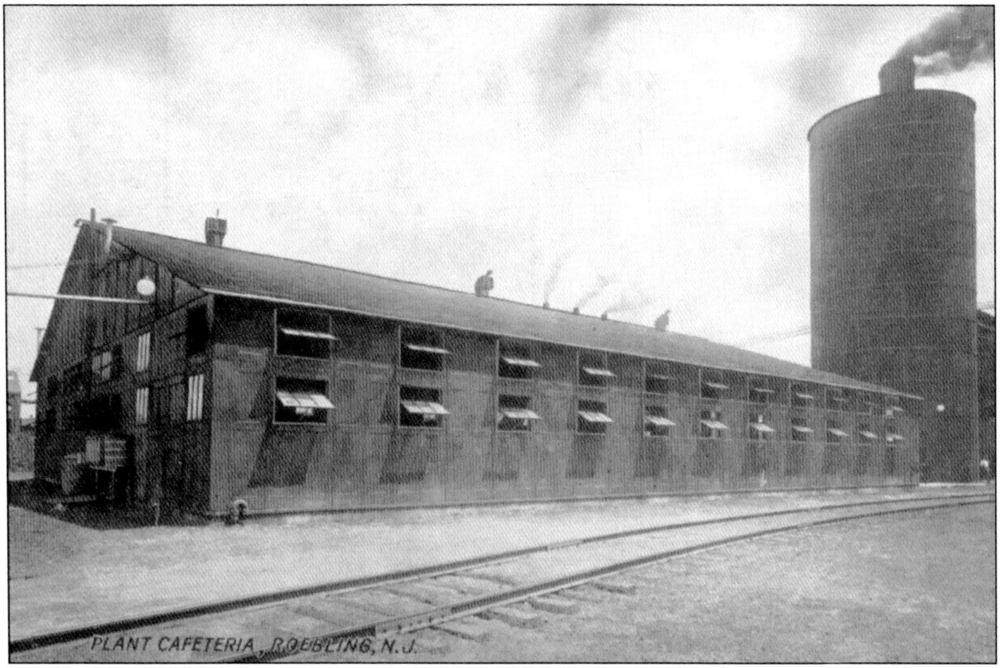

This photograph is of the John A. Roebling's Sons Company cafeteria, located on the mill site. (Courtesy Louis Borbi.)

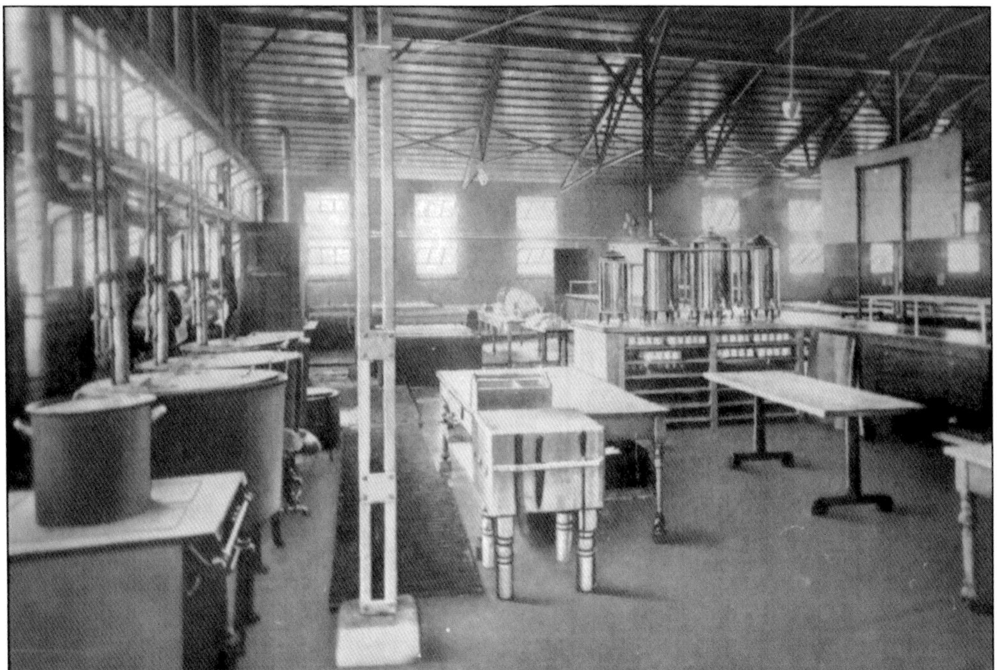

Pictured is the kitchen of the John A. Roebling's Sons Company cafeteria. (Courtesy Louis Borbi.)

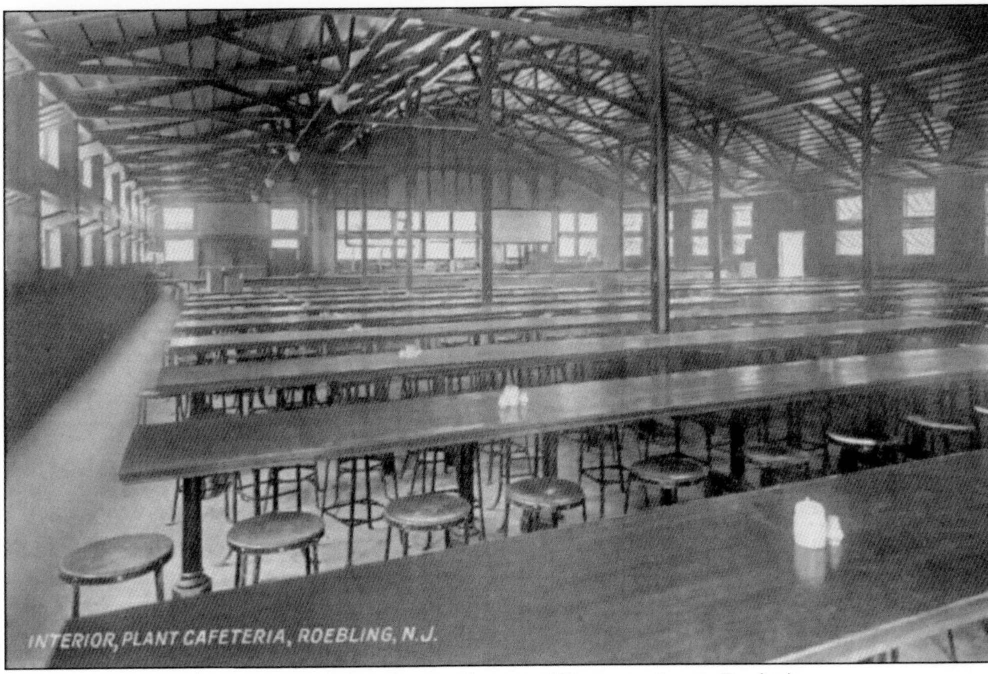

This view shows the interior of the plant cafeteria. (Courtesy Louis Borbi.)

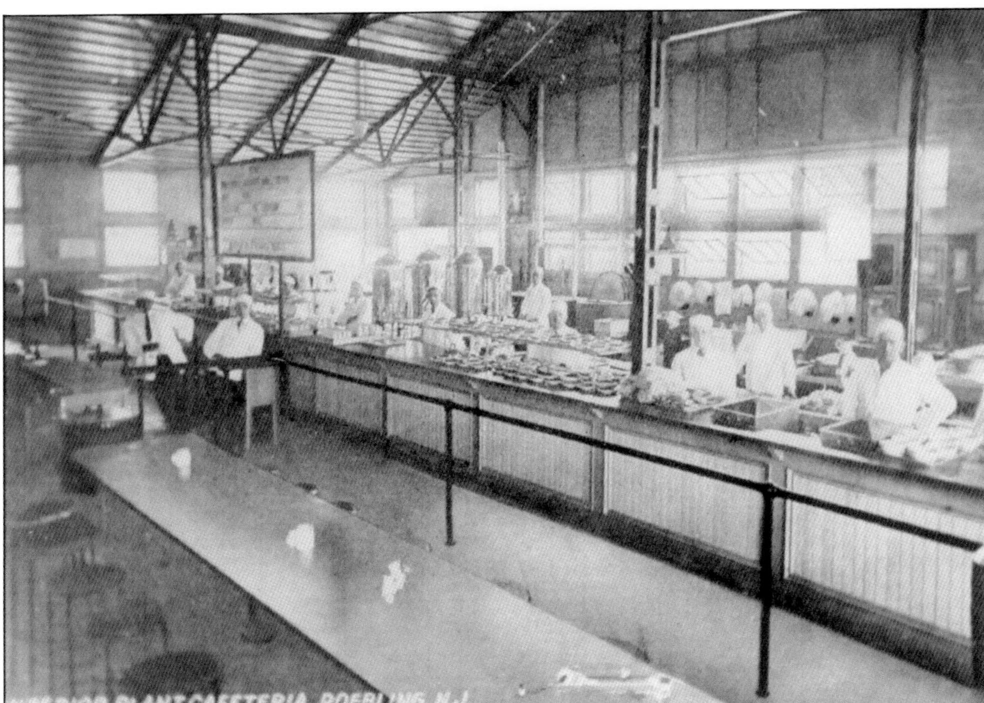

This is an interior view of the plant cafeteria, which was only in existence for several years during the 1920s. (Courtesy Louis Borbi.)

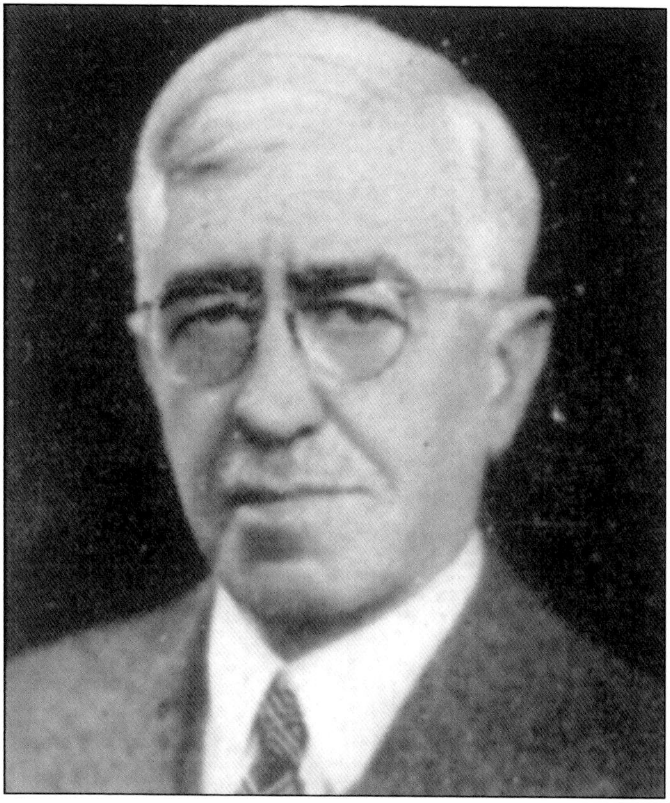

William A. Anderson, a Roebling employee for 56 years and a first cousin to Ferdinand W. Roebling Jr., became president of the company in 1936 upon his cousin's death. (Courtesy Mary Arnold Montalto.)

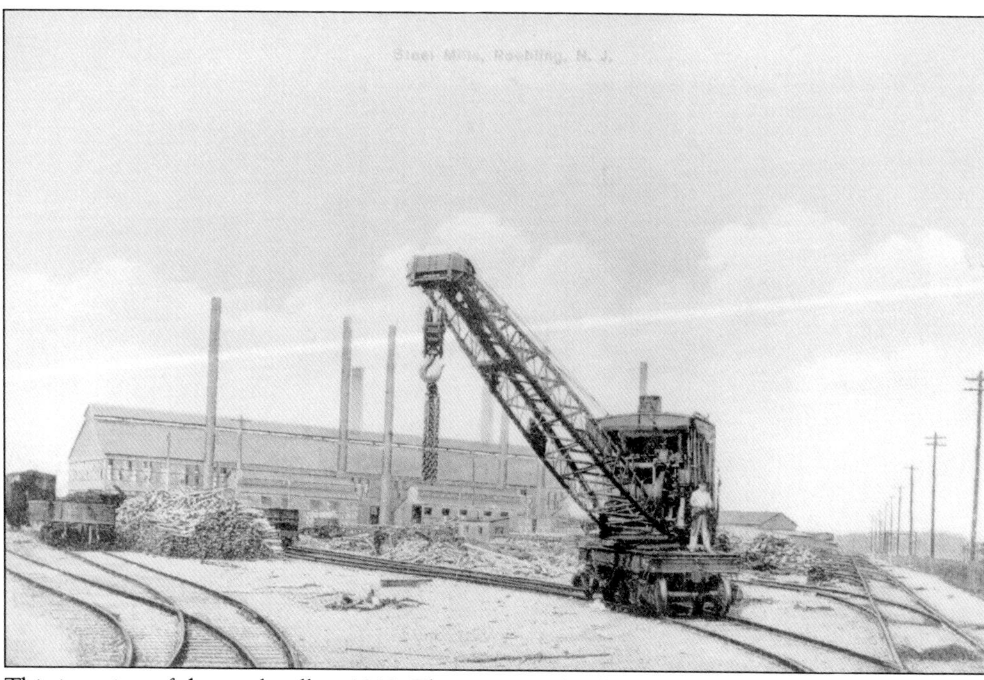

This is a view of the steel mill in 1910. The crane in the foreground will move scrap metal. The crane was used prior to the construction of the Second Avenue craneway. (Courtesy Louis Borbi.)

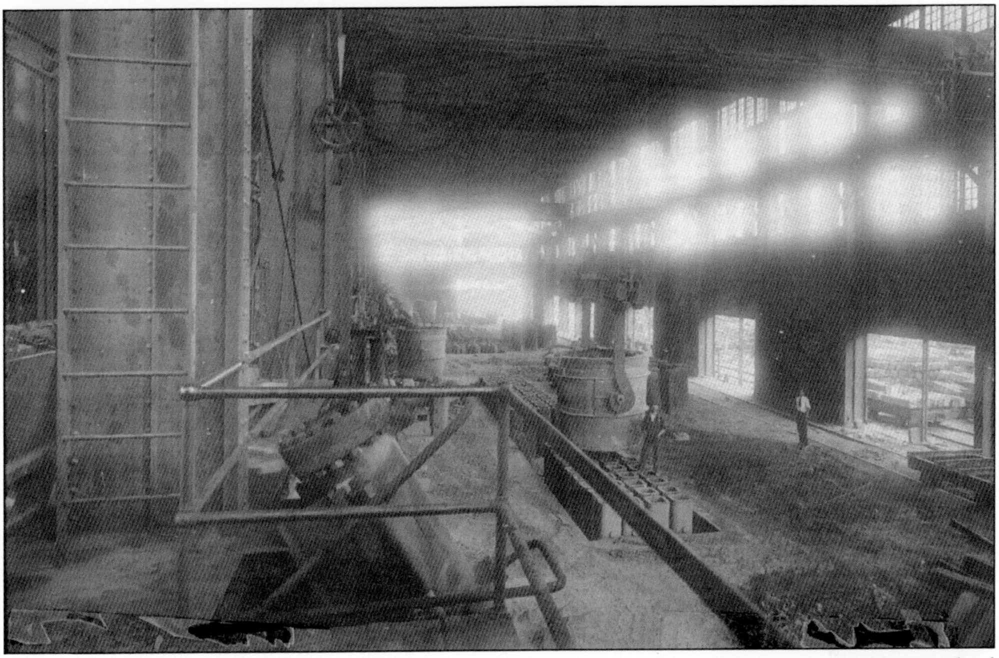

Pictured *c.* 1918 is the pit side of the steel mill. The ladle in the center contained hot melted steel. The bottom of the ladle had a two-inch opening that enabled the liquid steel to be poured into the molds. When cooled, the molds were extracted by using the machine pictured on the left. At that point, the extracted steel ingot was put on a railroad car for its next processing. (Courtesy Louis Borbi.)

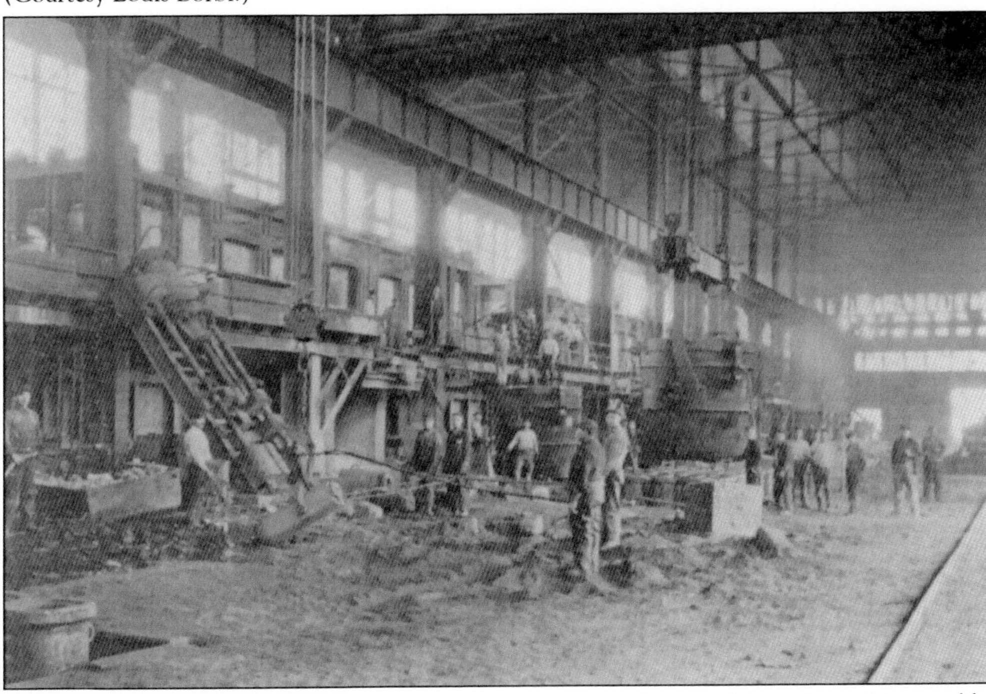

Pictured at the pit side in 1926 are men preparing to pour hot steel into the waiting molds. (Courtesy Ray Thompson.)

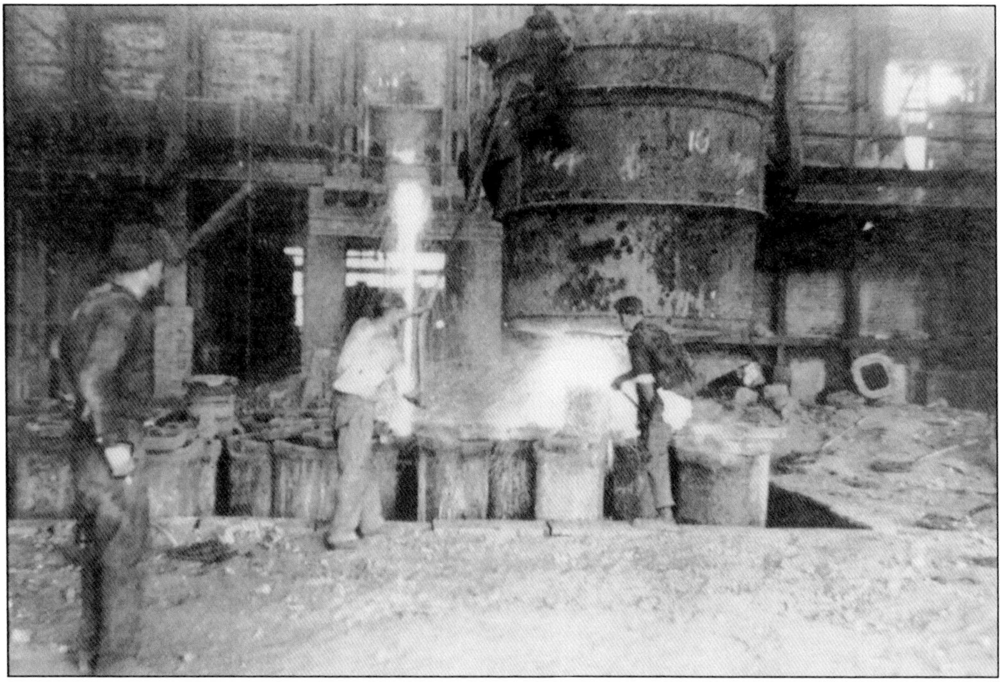

In this 1926 photograph, steelworkers pour a soft-heat into molds. (Courtesy Ray Thompson.)

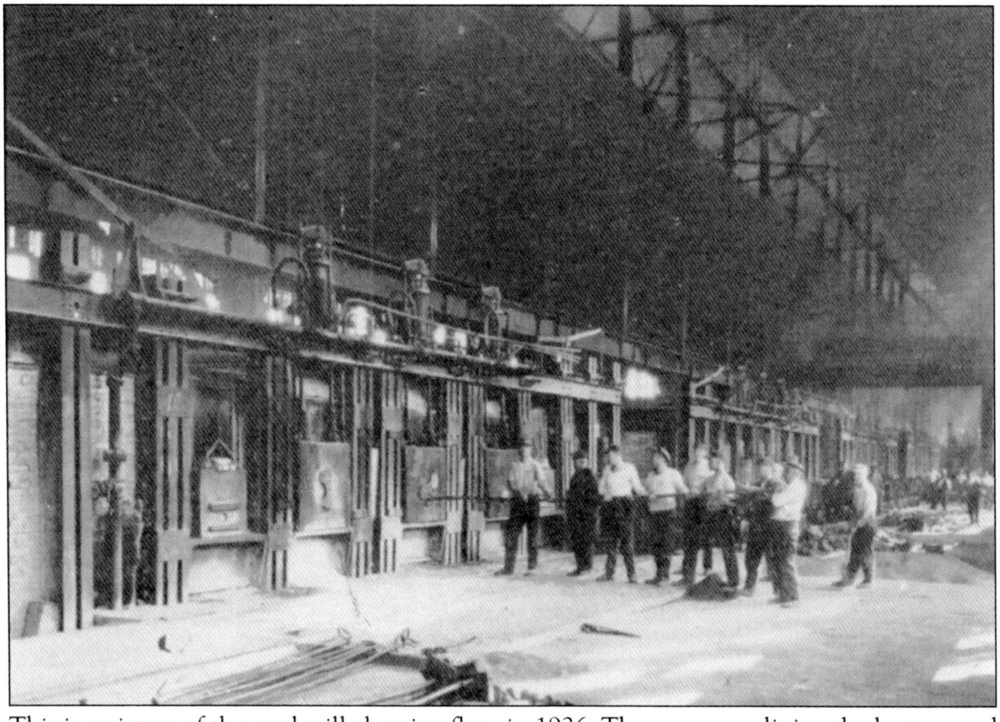

This is a picture of the steel mill charging floor in 1926. The men are relining the bottom and sides of the open hearth with a mixture of claylike sand to repair the open hearth. (Courtesy Ray Thompson.)

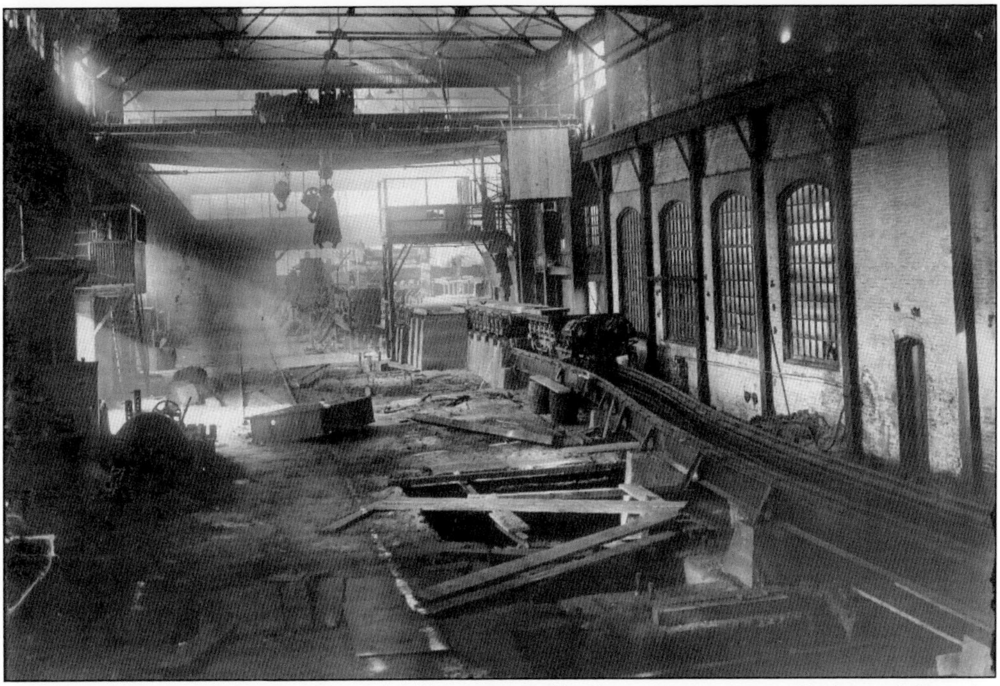

Shown in this 1915 photograph is the blooming mill, where ingots were rolled into billets for preparation for the rod mill. (Courtesy Louis Borbi.)

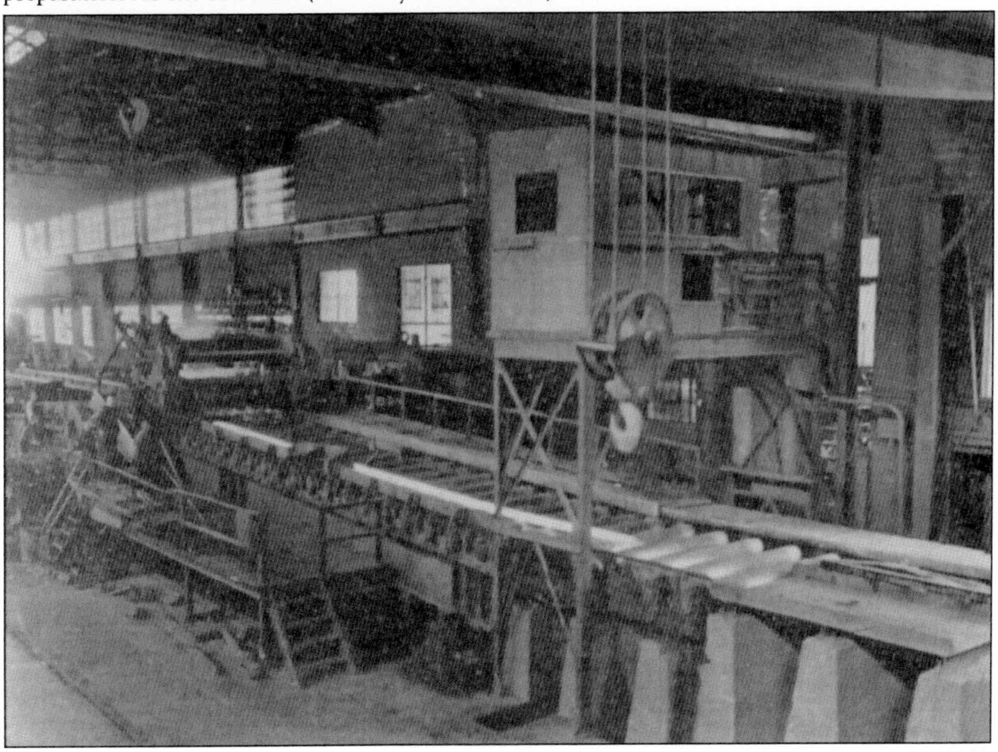

This is a picture of the blooming mill in 1926, where ingots were rolled into four-and-a-half-inch cubes in preparation to be put down to the two-inch mill. (Courtesy Ray Thompson.)

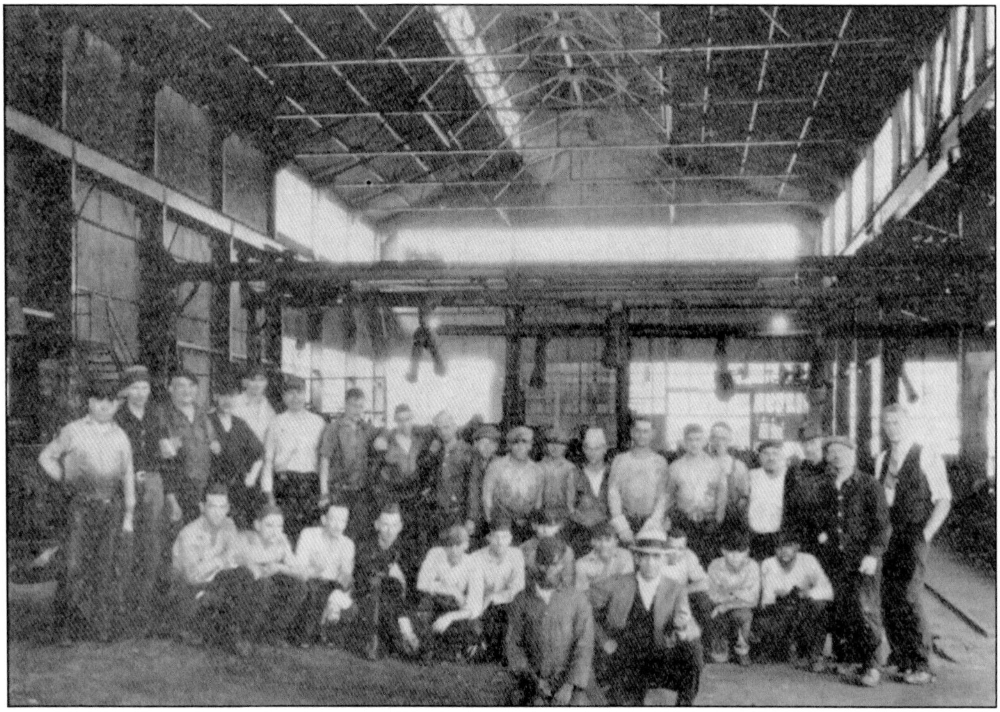

Pictured in 1926 is the rolling mill force in Rod Mill No. 1. (Courtesy Ray Thompson.)

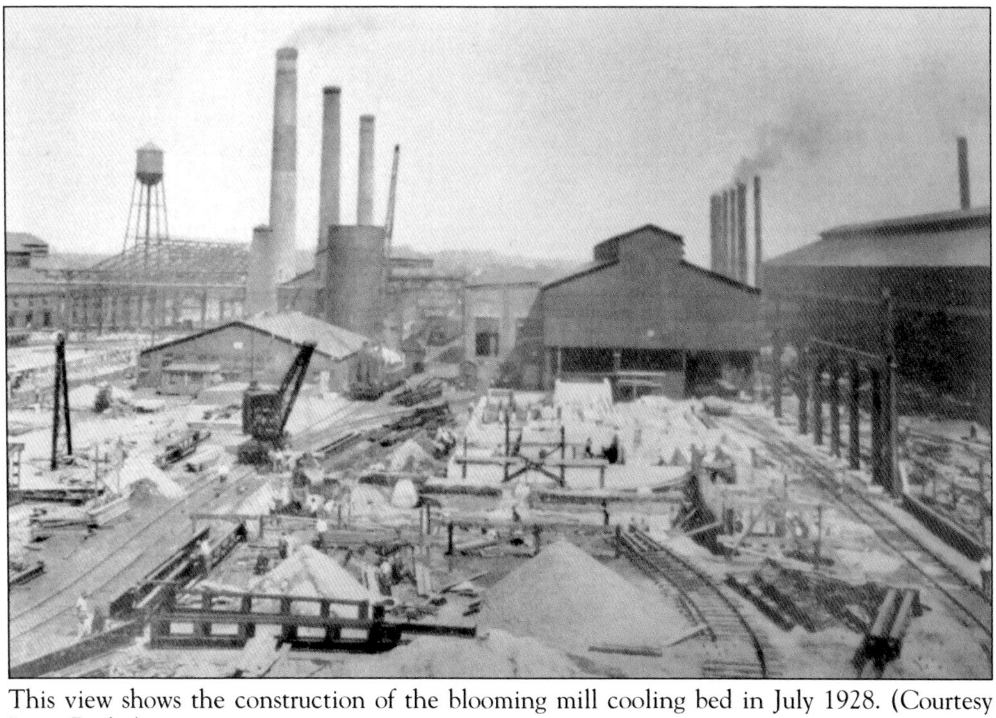

This view shows the construction of the blooming mill cooling bed in July 1928. (Courtesy Louis Borbi.)

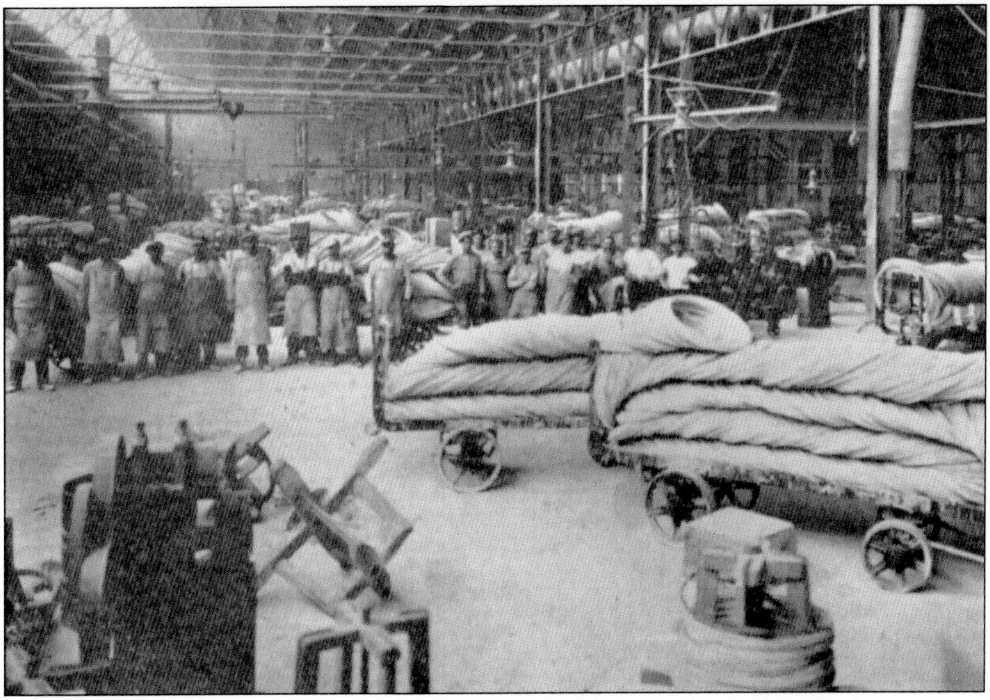

Wire Mill No. 1, shown in 1926, was where the wire product was drawn through the machines to the desired size. (Courtesy Ray Thompson.)

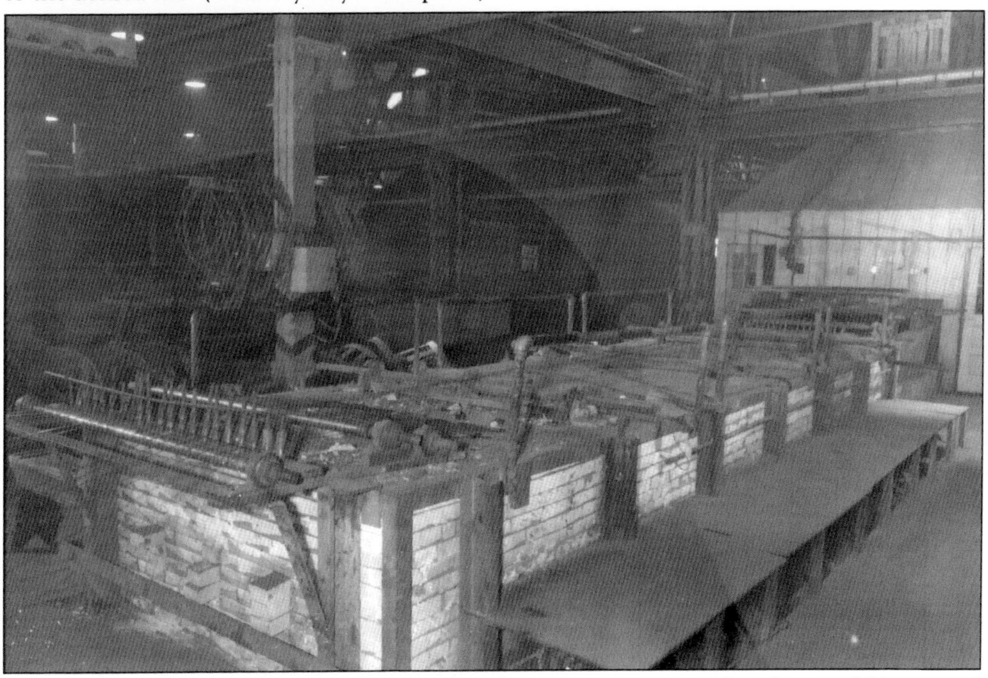

The galvanizing shop is shown c. 1940. After the wire rope was produced, it could be coated in a hot bath of zinc and lead. This process, called galvanizing, would prevent the wire rope from rusting. This wire was used not only in bridge building but also for clotheslines. (Courtesy Louis Borbi.)

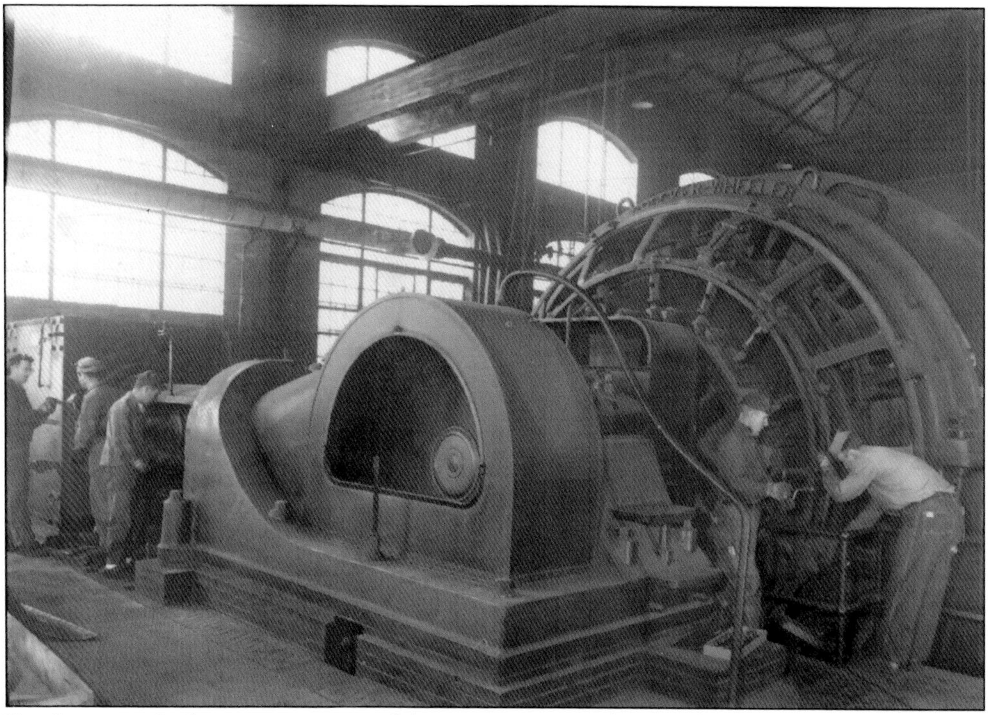

Employees worked to maintain one of the two generators that supplied power to the entire mill c. late 1940s. (Courtesy Louis Borbi.)

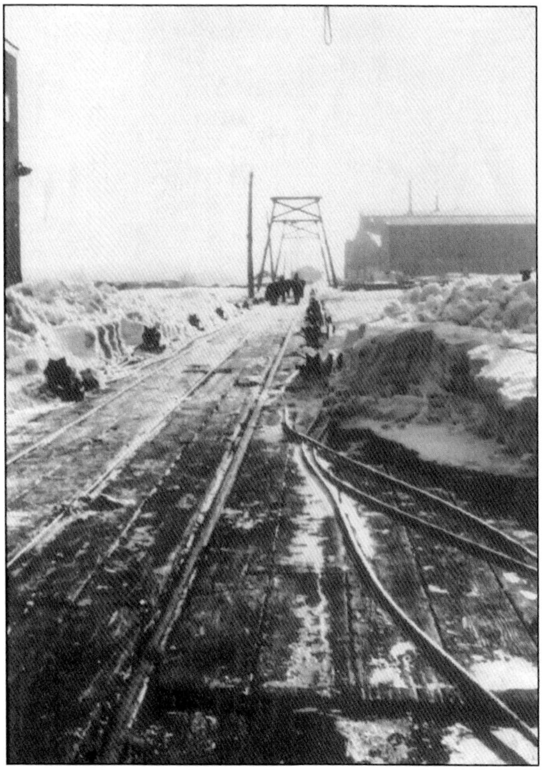

Pictured c. 1935 are the rope stretchers that were used to stretch both elevator wire as well as suspender wire ropes for bridges. All suspender ropes that were to be used in bridge construction were stretched on this machine, including those of the Golden Gate Bridge suspenders. (Courtesy Louis Borbi.)

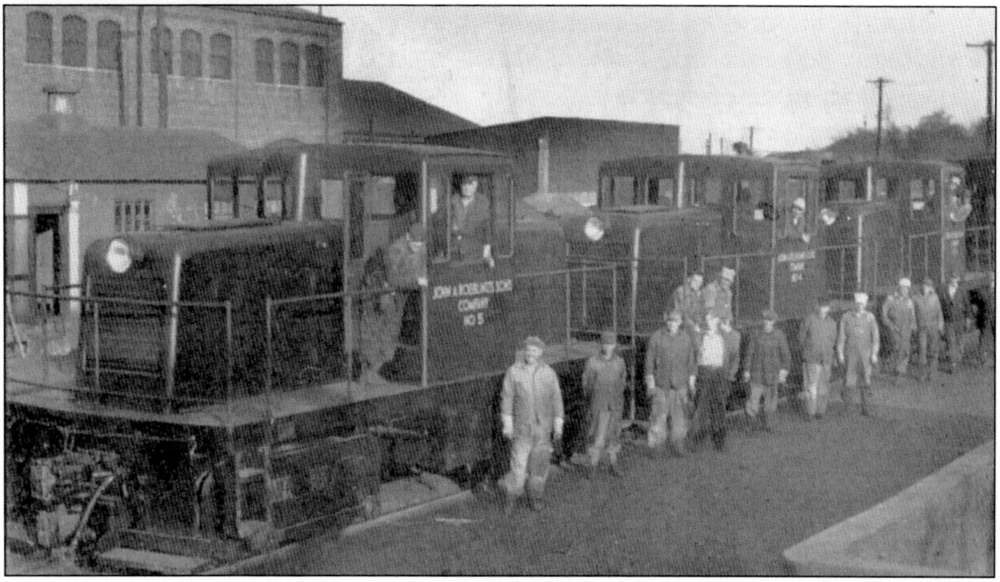

Pictured is a 1947 Roebling locomotive crew with three diesel electric engines. The railway system operated under the John A. Roebling's Sons Company Transportation Division. Running over 14 miles of winding track, the railway system was the primary method of transporting materials, as the production process required within the mill. All raw materials were moved in via the Pennsylvania Railroad interchange track to the internal railway system. Final products were moved out via the Pennsylvania Railroad. (Courtesy Mary Arnold Montalto.)

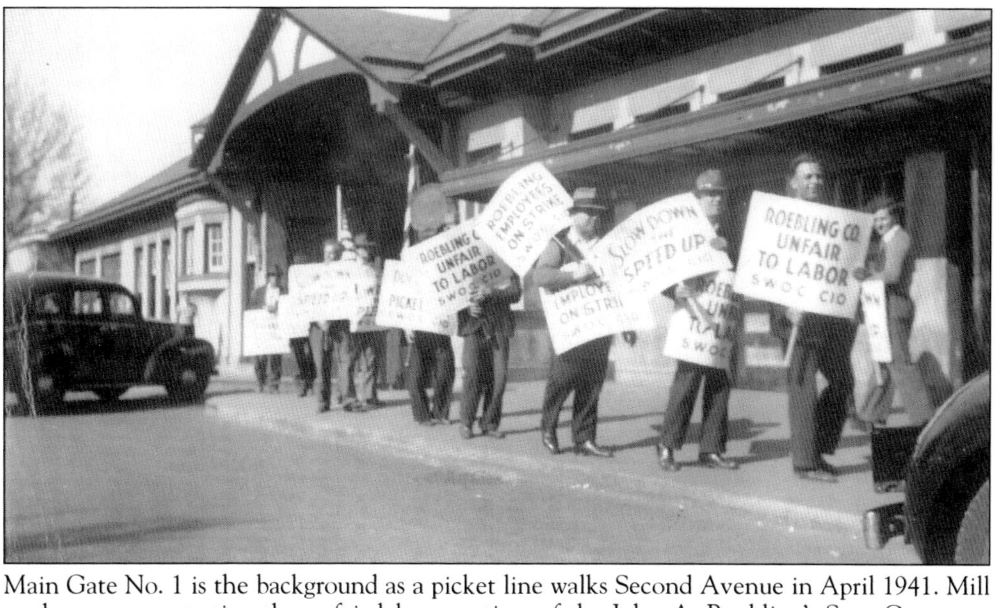

Main Gate No. 1 is the background as a picket line walks Second Avenue in April 1941. Mill workers were protesting the unfair labor practices of the John A. Roebling's Sons Company. The 13-day strike ended when the company agreed to recognize the Steel Workers Organizing Committee (SWOC) to represent the employees and granted them a 10-percent wage increase. (Courtesy Louis Borbi.)

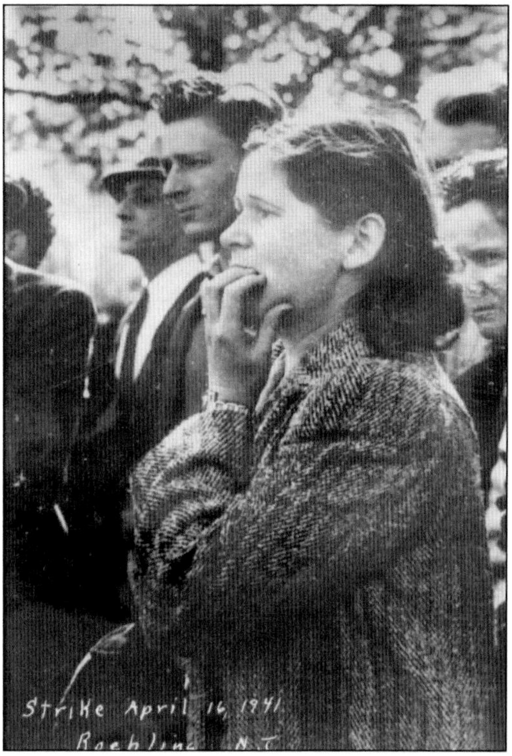

Mrs. Brantmayer, in the foreground, and Malvina Sav watch the events of the strike on April 16, 1941. (Courtesy Louis Borbi.)

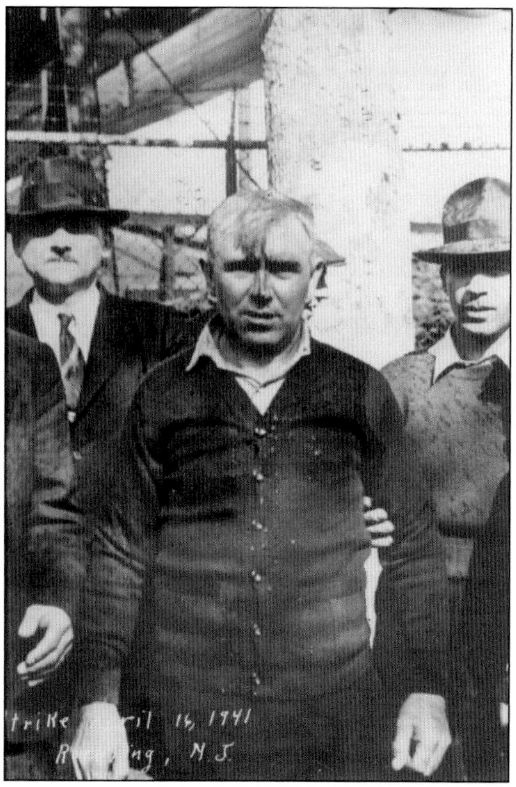

The worker's strike of 1941 takes a violent turn. Shown from left to right are Louis Kocsis Sr., Andrew Kollar, and Ely Pop. (Courtesy Louis Borbi.)

Police Chief Bellerjeau mans a fire hose aimed at the striking workers during the 1941 strike. Ray Arnold, on the left, observes the scene. (Courtesy Louis Borbi.)

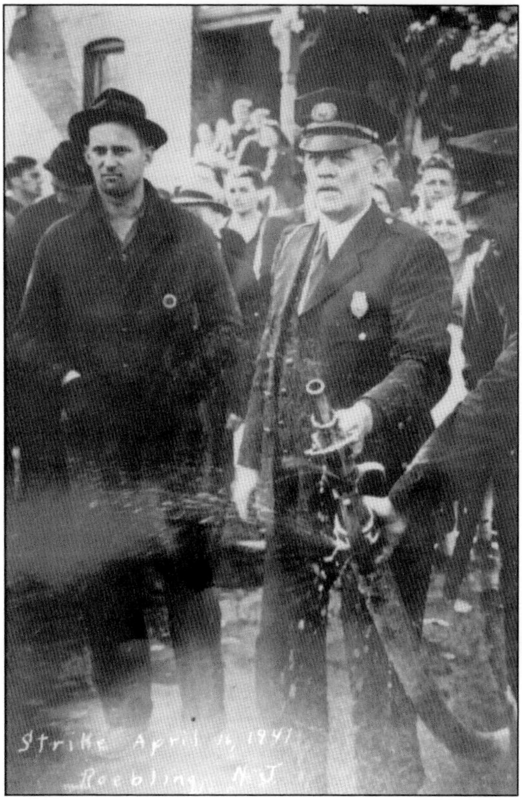

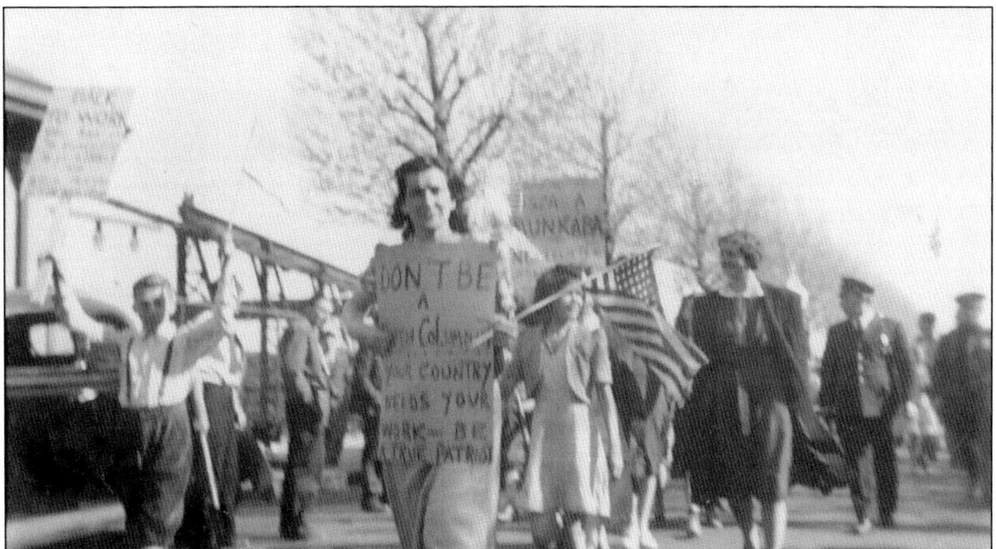

Women had their own picket line against the striking workers. The woman in the foreground is carrying a sign that states, "Don't Be A Fifth Columnist. Your country needs your work— Be A True Patriot." This photograph was taken in April 1941. (Courtesy Joseph D. Zahorsky and Donna Orfe.)

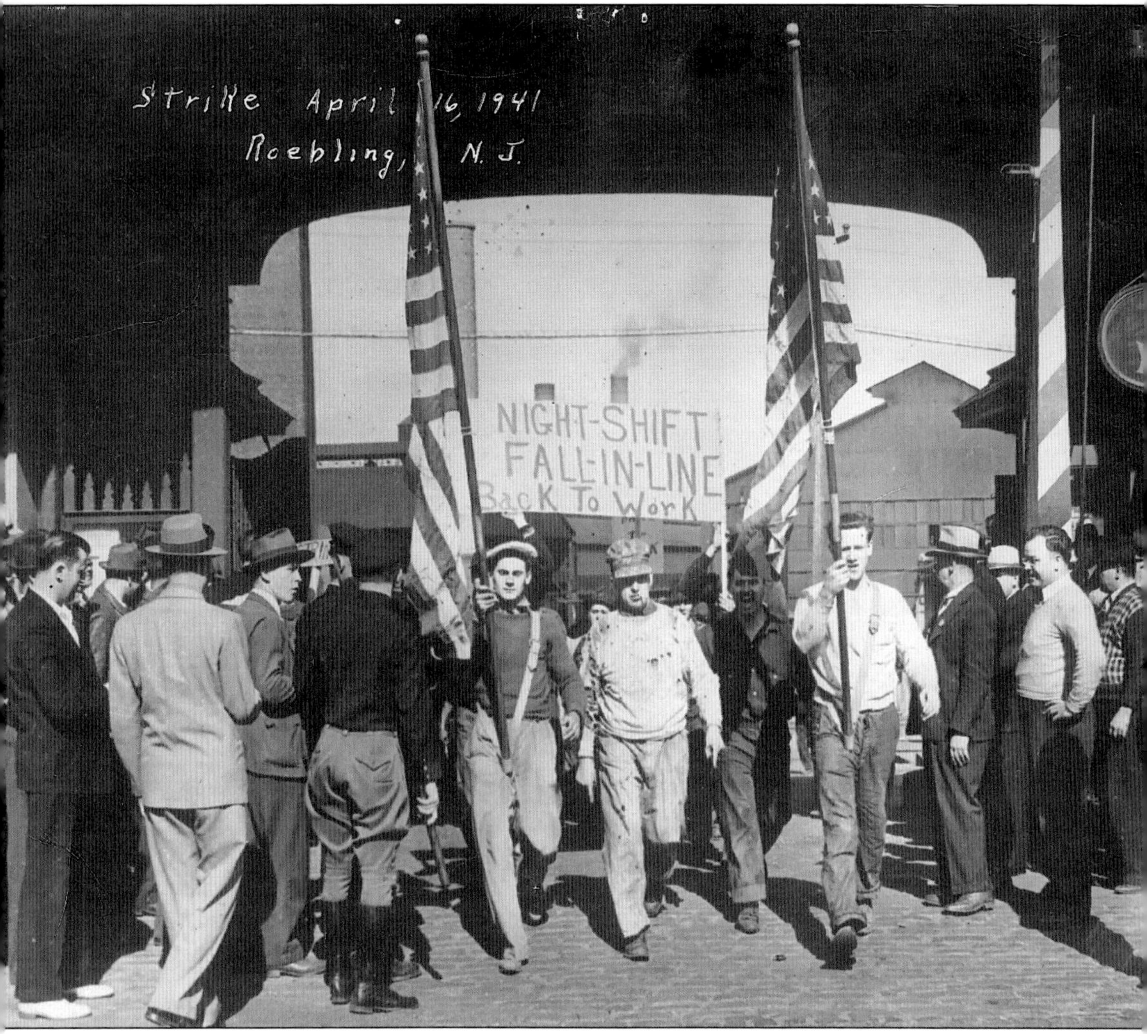

During the strike of 1941, not all workers were in agreement. Pictured is the night shift crew urging strikers to fall in line and get back to work. The flag bearer on the left is George Zahorsky, and Lester Danley is on the right. (Courtesy Joseph Yeager.)

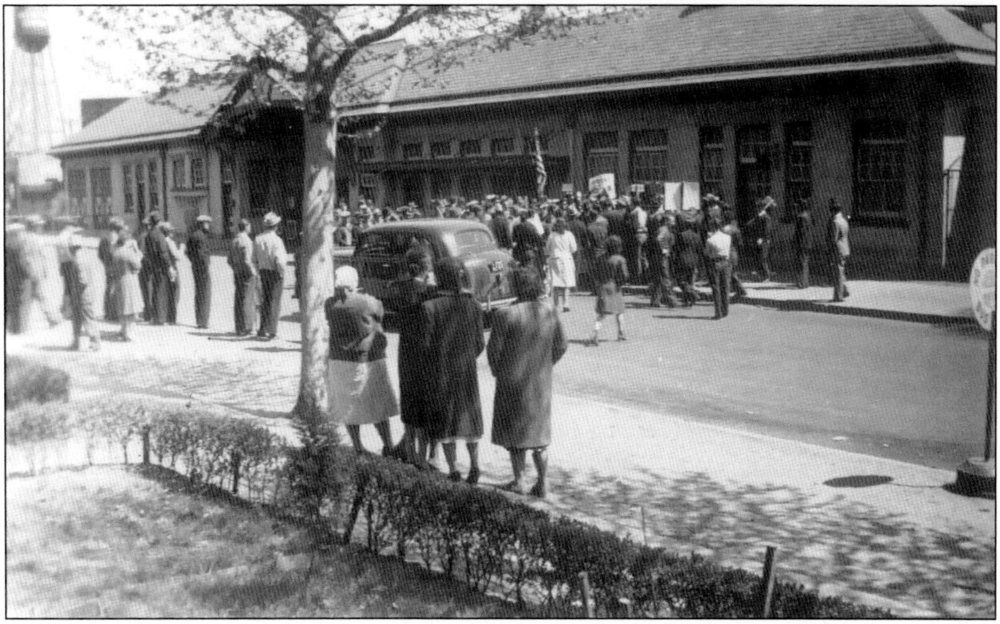

Workers and curious onlookers are shown during the April 1941 strike. The building in the background is Main Gate No. 1. (Courtesy Joseph D. Zahorsky and Donna Orfe.)

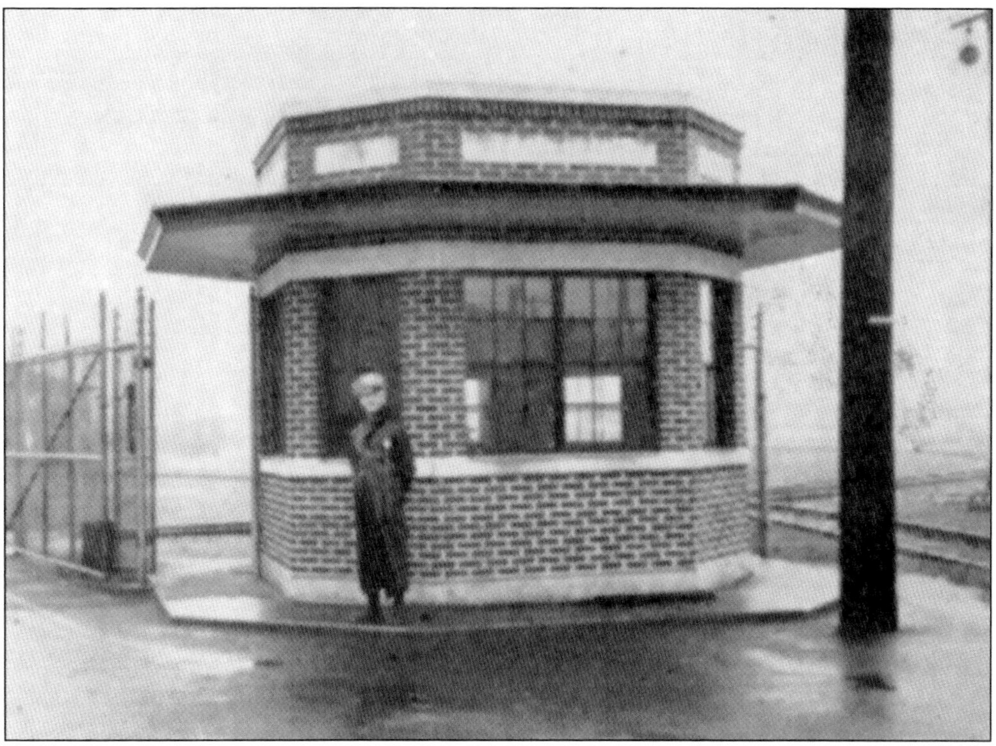

A guard stands in front of Gate No. 2 of the mill c. 1949. (Courtesy Mary Arnold Montalto.)

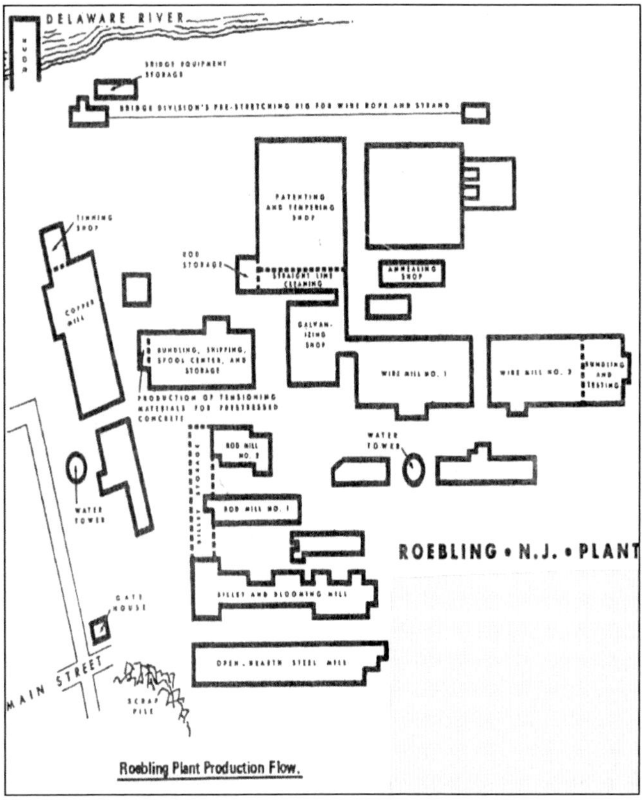

This c. 1930 map shows the John A. Roebling's Sons Company, where steel was produced and converted into wire. Some of the more important buildings in this group house the open-hearth shop, blooming mill, rod mills, cleaning houses, wire mills, the annealing and tempering department, the galvanizing shop, and copper mill. Also located here were the bridge shop and the production facilities for manufacturing tensioning materials for prestressed concrete. (Courtesy Louis Borbi.)

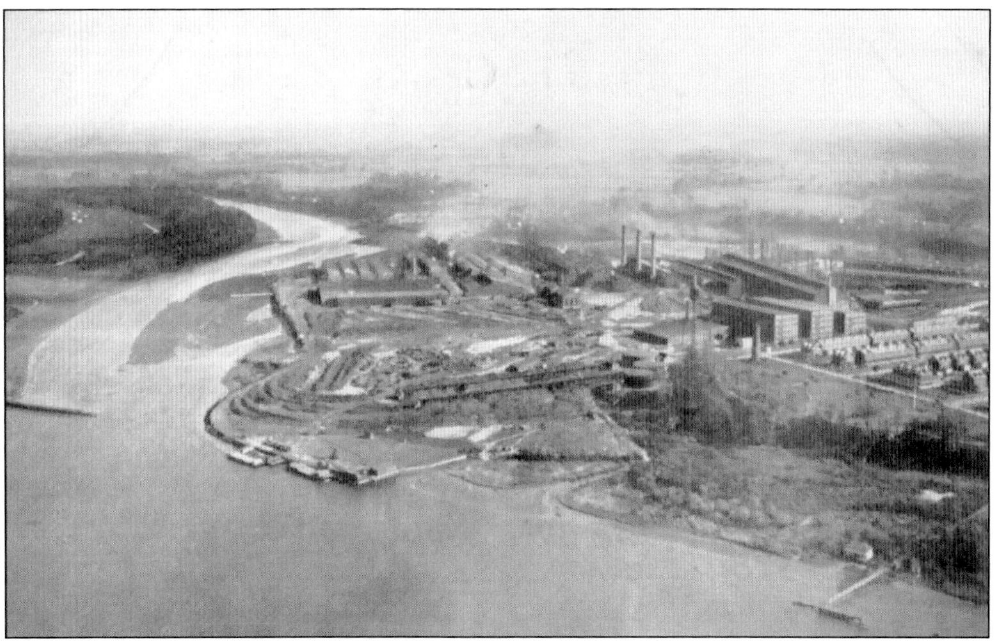

Some homes can be seen on the right in this 1912 view of the John A. Roebling's Sons Company. (Courtesy Louis Borbi.)

Four

The War Effort

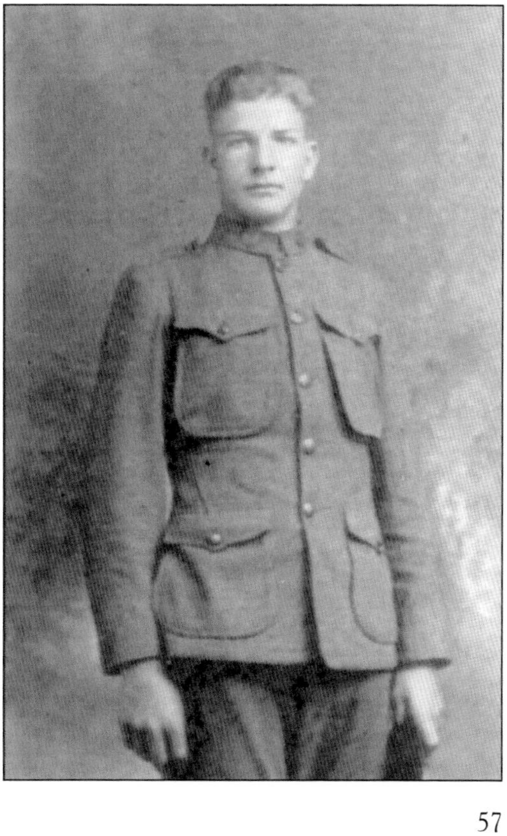

Paul Willitts was one of the two young men who died while serving in World War I. The Willitts-Hogan Post No. 39 American Legion was organized in 1927 with John G. Kennan as commander. Later, the name Tonne was added to honor James R. Tonne, who died in World War II. (Courtesy Louis Borbi.)

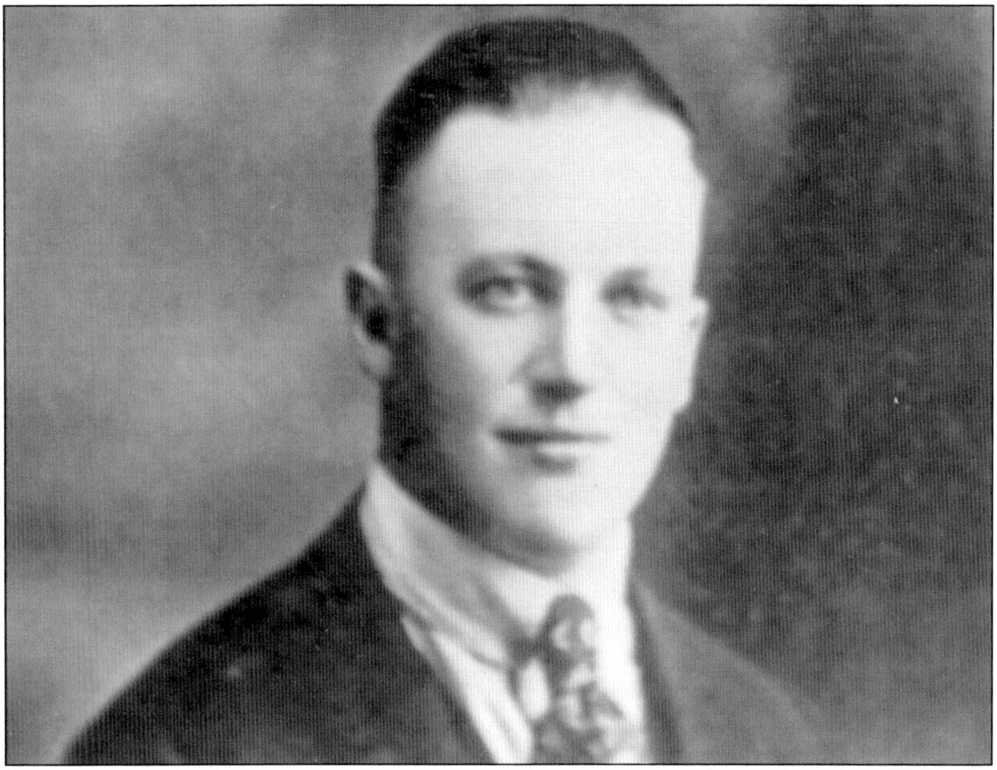

Pictured is William Hogan, who died while serving his country in World War I. (Courtesy Louis Borbi.)

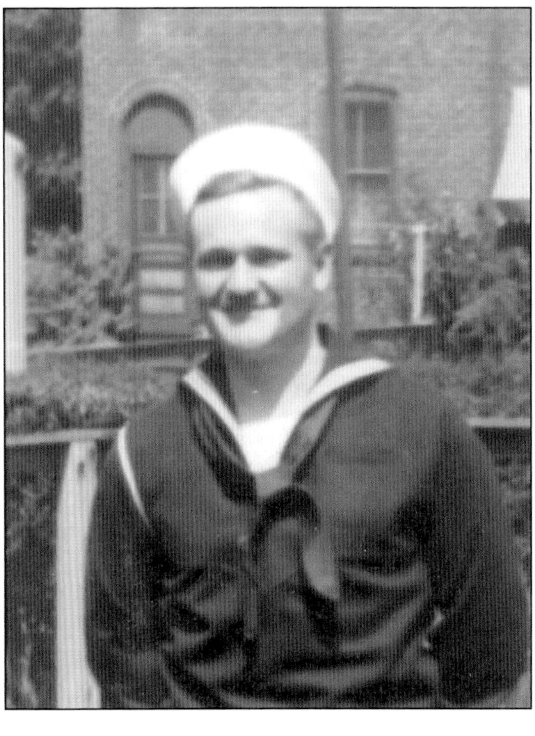

Seen in this photograph is James R. Tonne, the first Roebling resident to make the ultimate sacrifice in World War II. His name was added to the Willitts-Hogan-Tonne Post No. 39. (Courtesy Steven and Dorothy Tonne Buzash.)

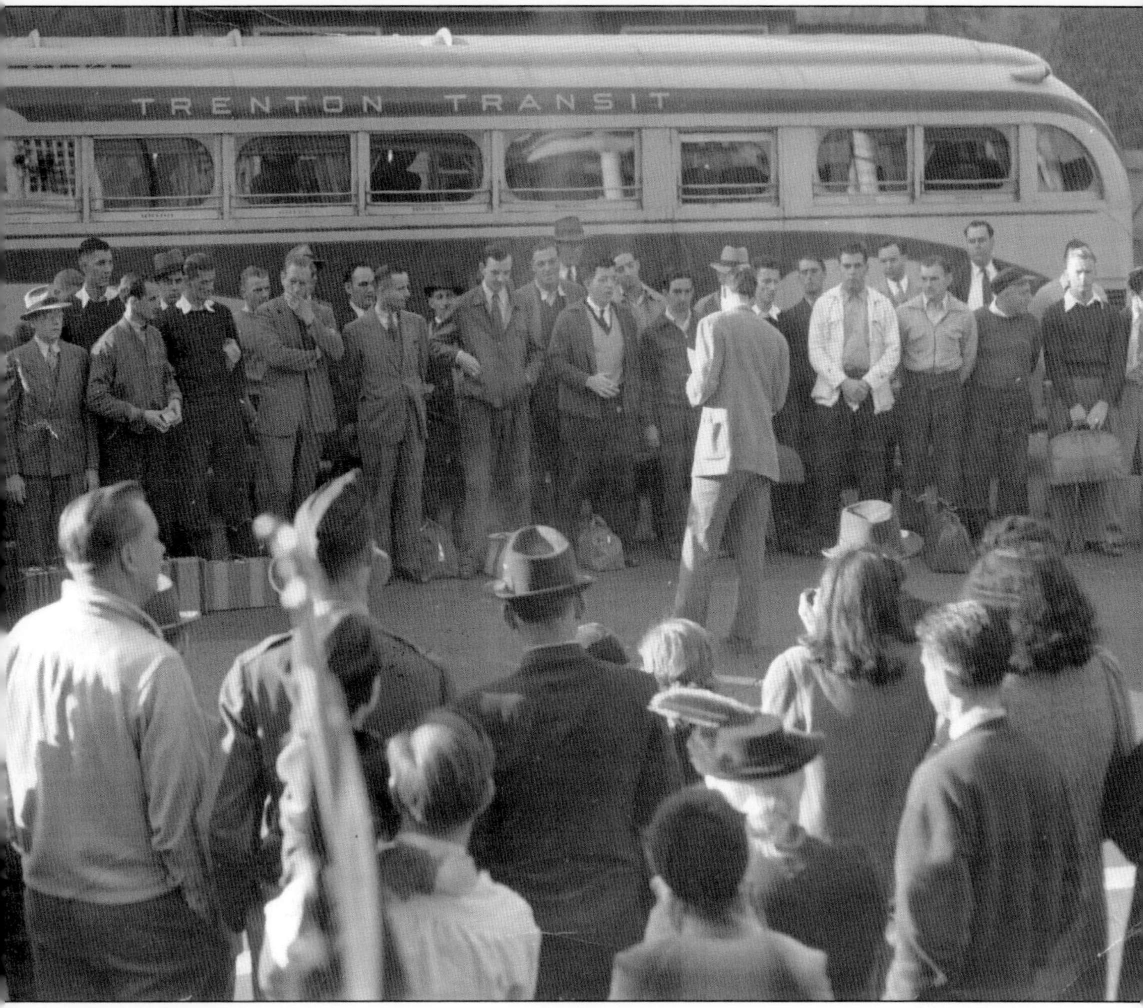

Some Roebling residents are waiting to board a bus to go to basic training at Fort Dix on October 20, 1942. (Courtesy Joseph D. Zahorsky and Donna Orfe.)

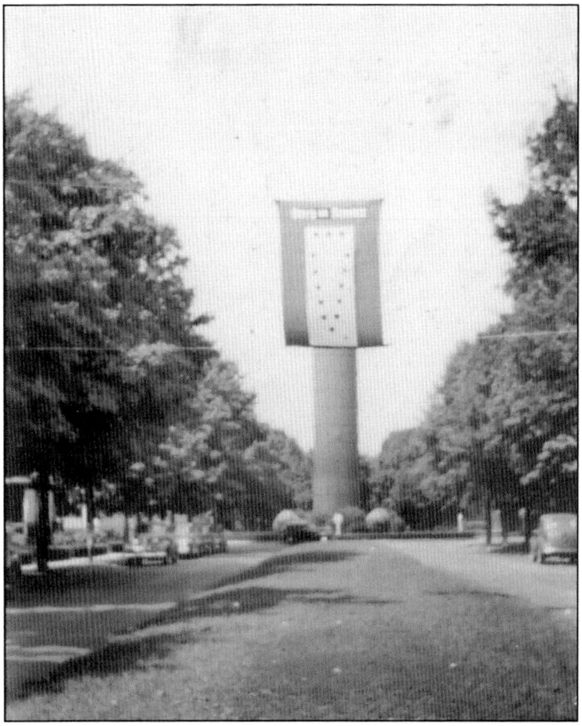

Pictured in August 1942 is the Roebling Water Tower, located at Fifth Avenue and Main Street. The banner shows the mill's support of the war effort during World War II. (Courtesy Louis Borbi.)

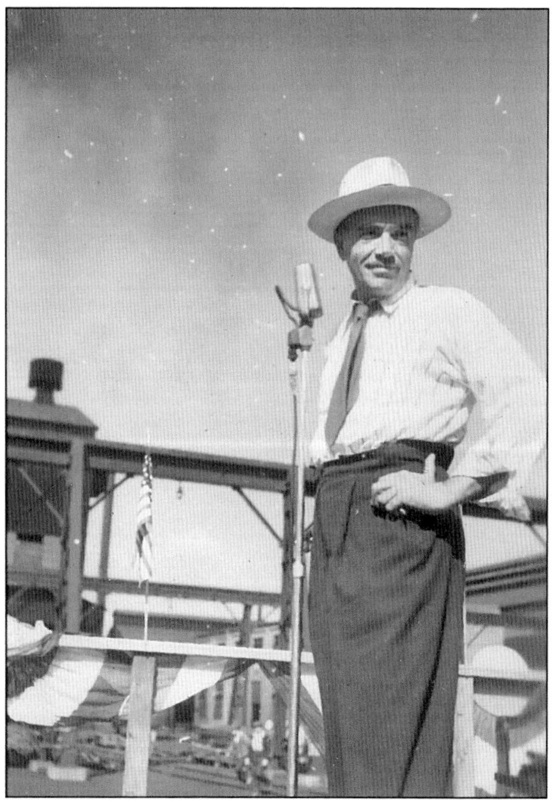

Character actor Walter Abel is shown at the John A. Roebling's Sons Company on September 2, 1942. Abel and actress Hedy Lamarr visited the town to promote the sale of war bonds. (Courtesy Louis Borbi.)

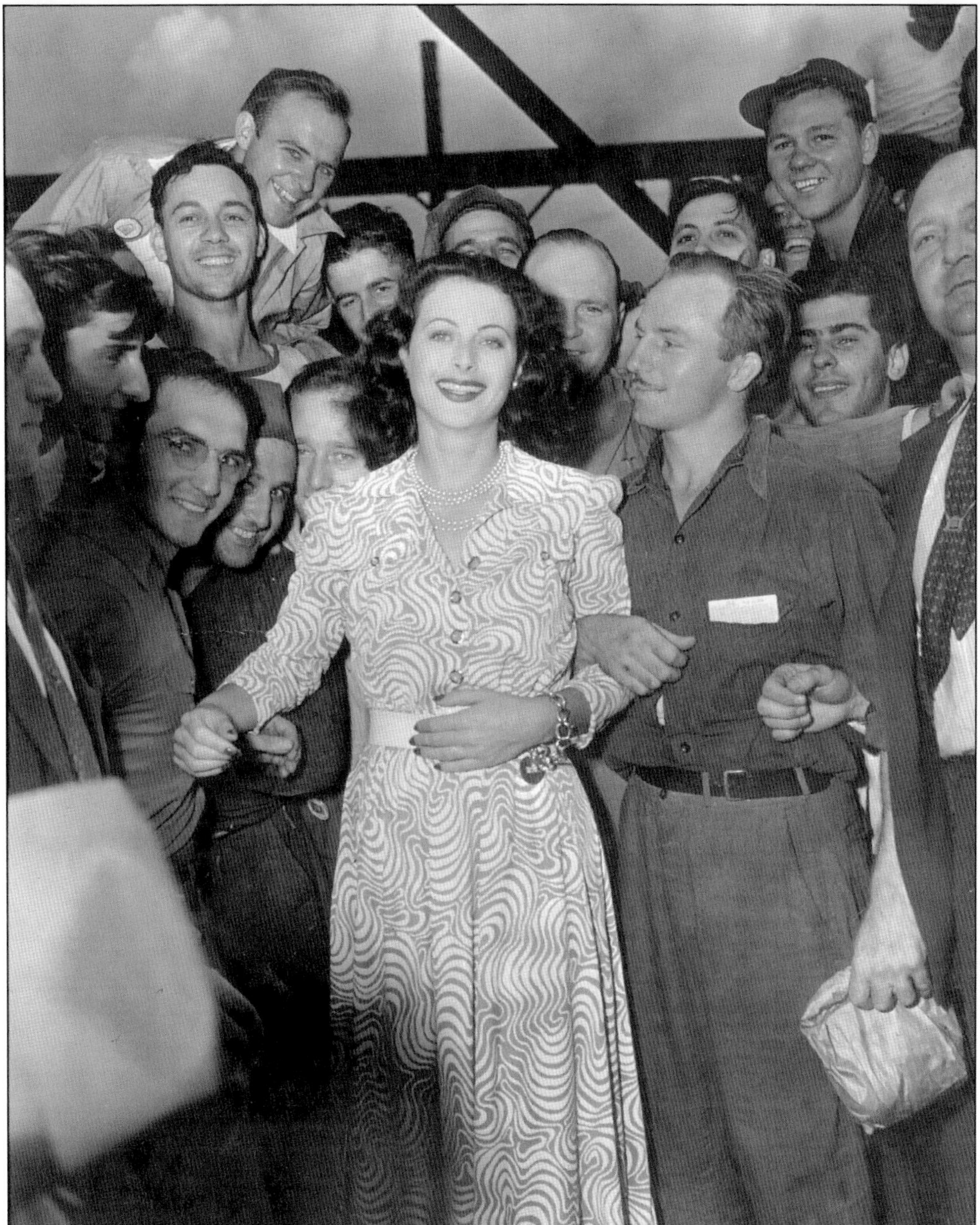

Film actress Hedy Lamarr visited the village in 1942 to inspire the residents to buy war bonds. Although many excited mill workers surrounded Lamarr for the photograph, cleaning house worker Stephen Yetko was the lucky one to link arms with the movie star. On the far right is Lamarr's bodyguard, who is making sure Yetko doesn't get too close. (Courtesy Yolanda Simko and Mary Yetko.)

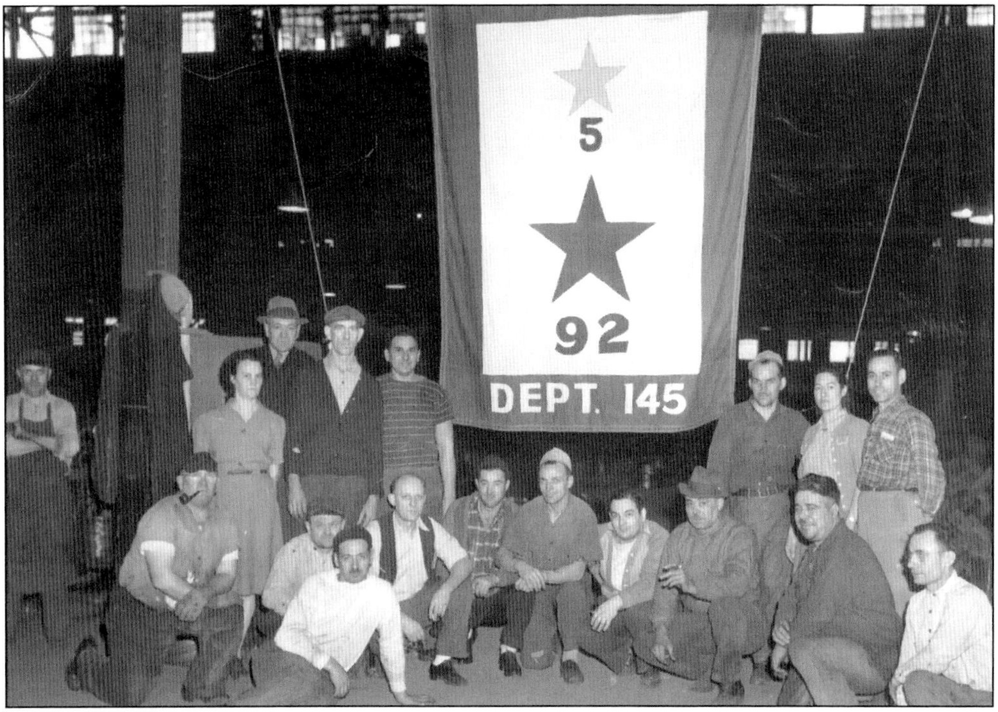

Department 145 of the John A. Roebling's Sons Company tempering shop is pictured c. 1942. The banner signifies that five members of the tempering department were lost in World War II and 92 workers served their country. (Courtesy Louis Borbi.)

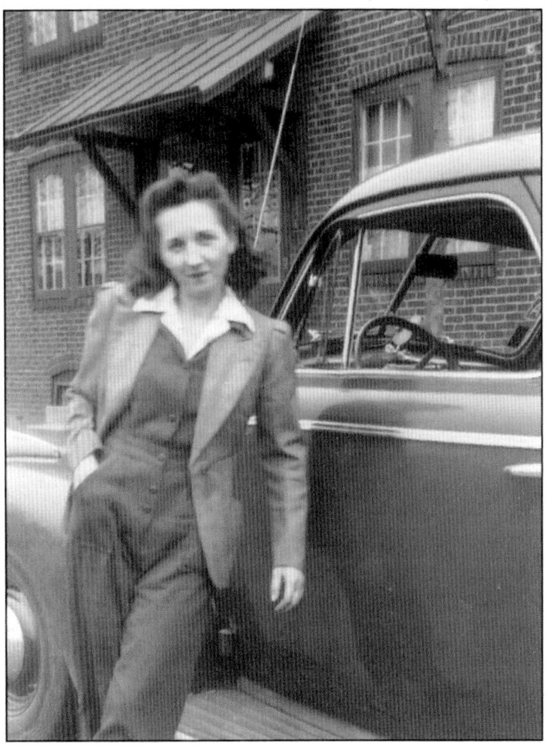

A female mill worker strikes a pose on Amboy Avenue in 1943. Since many men were drafted into military service during World War II, women filled the vacant positions. (Courtesy Louis Borbi.)

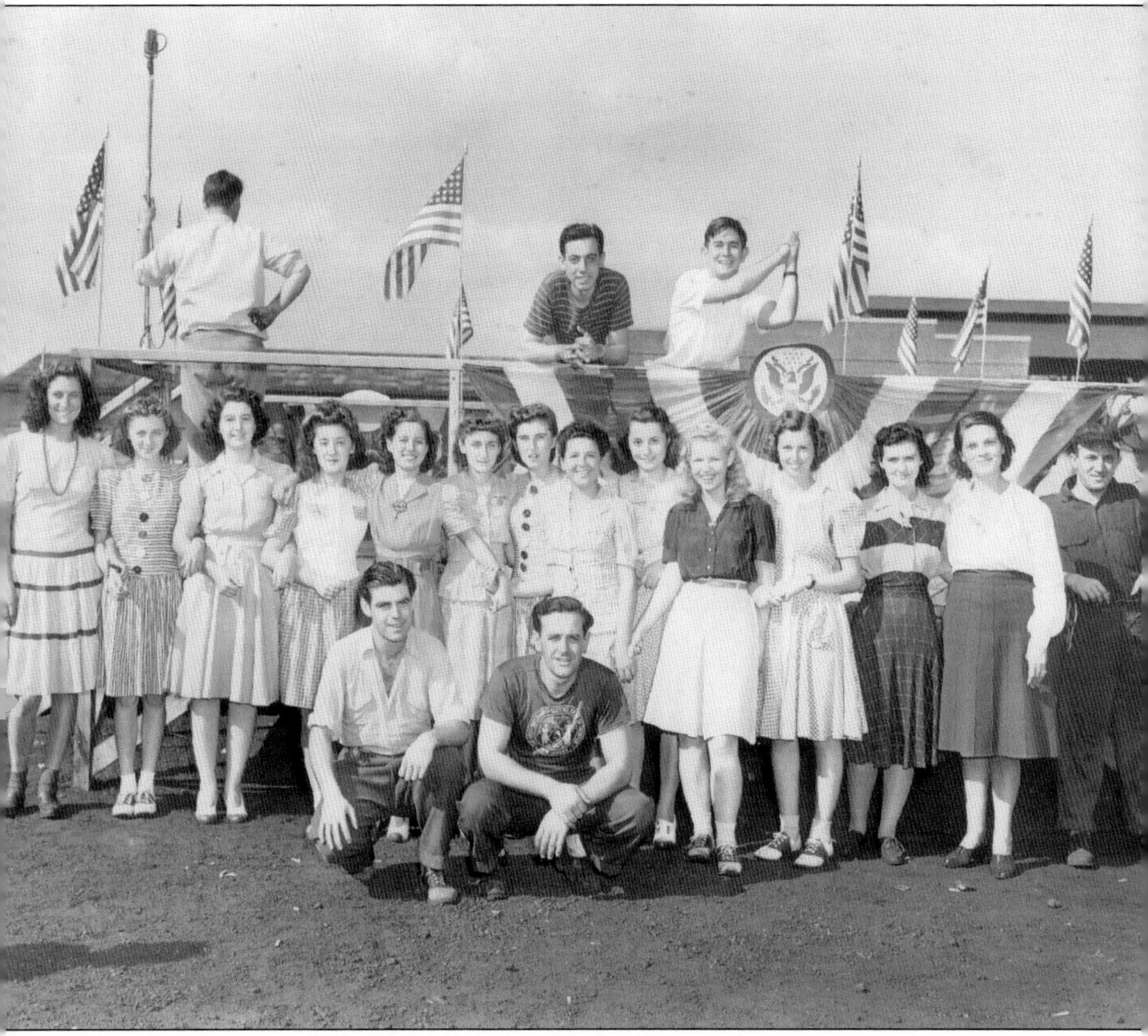

Workers celebrate the visit of Hedy Lamarr and Walter Abel on September 2, 1942. Standing from left to right are Verna Stefanoni Chance, Lillian Matlack Jedryk, Lettia Crochran, Tillie Steiner Kushner, Doris Jones, Virginia Chamberlain Brown, Betty Lichvarcik Basarab, Doris Selenak Paykos, Mary Simkovich Chanti, Alice Smythe, Loretta Weast, Helen Clancey Molnar, Pearl English, and John Borbi. (Courtesy Mary Arnold Montalto.)

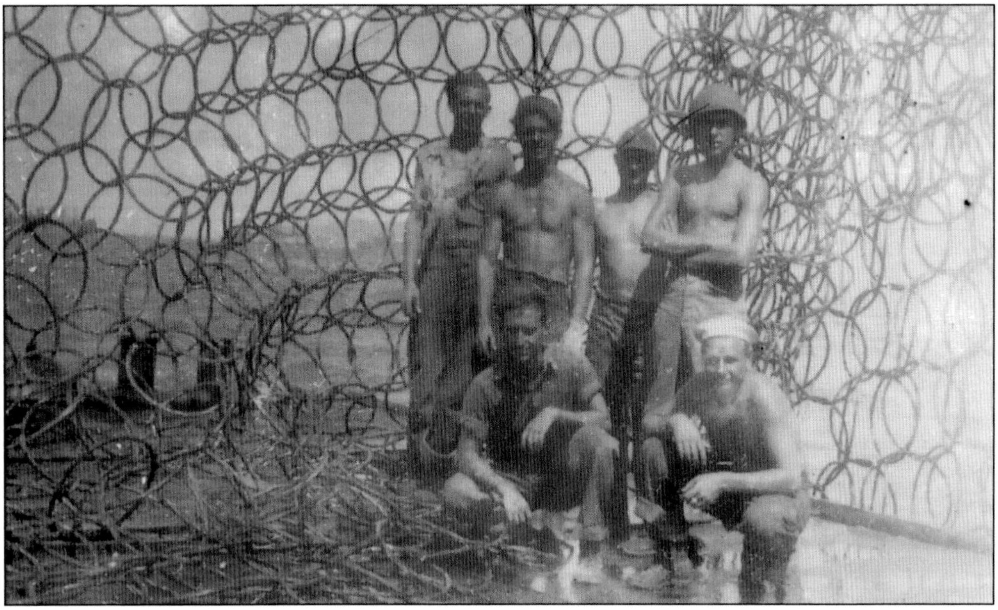

Submarine nets and harbor-defense nets were two of the many products the company produced. These underwater wire nets functioned as a line of defense against enemy submarines. Pictured is Roebling resident Bill Gyenge (back row, second from left) displaying a John A. Roebling submarine net that was handmade at the plant. This picture was taken when Bill Gyenge was stationed in the South Pacific during World War II. Bill was a second-class petty officer and served as a boatswain mate. (Courtesy Bill Gyenge.)

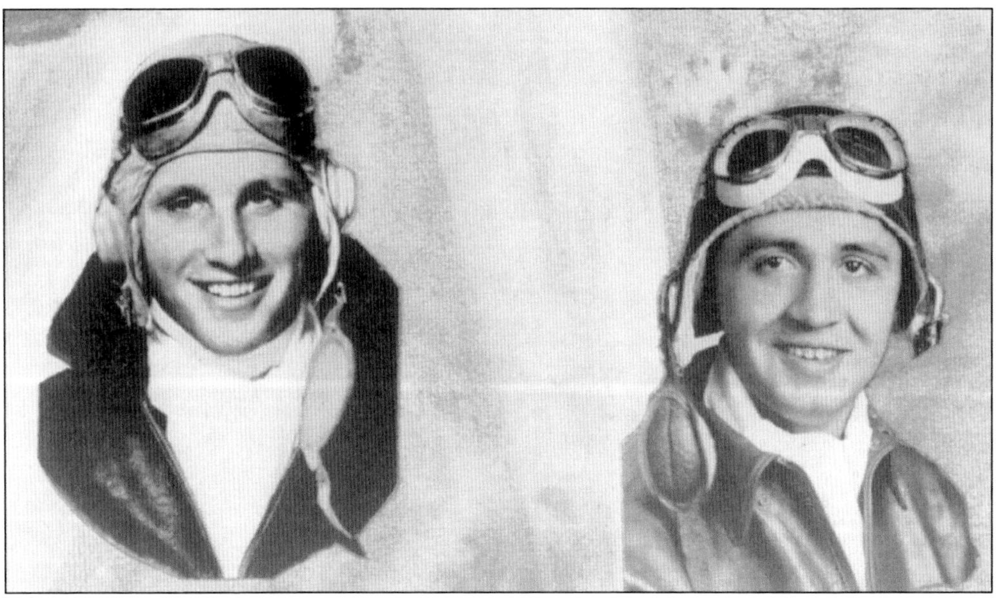

Featured in the 1949–1950 edition of *Roebling* magazine were these two "Roebling boys," Thomas Pierson and John A. Karpac Jr. The article, entitled "Tribute to Valor," acknowledged the thousands of gallant individuals who served their country with distinction. Thomas Pierson worked in the Bridge Division and was a radio gunner in the U.S.Navy in World War II. John A. Karpac Jr. was a B-24 navigator in the U.S. Army in World War II. (Courtesy Mary Arnold Montalto.)

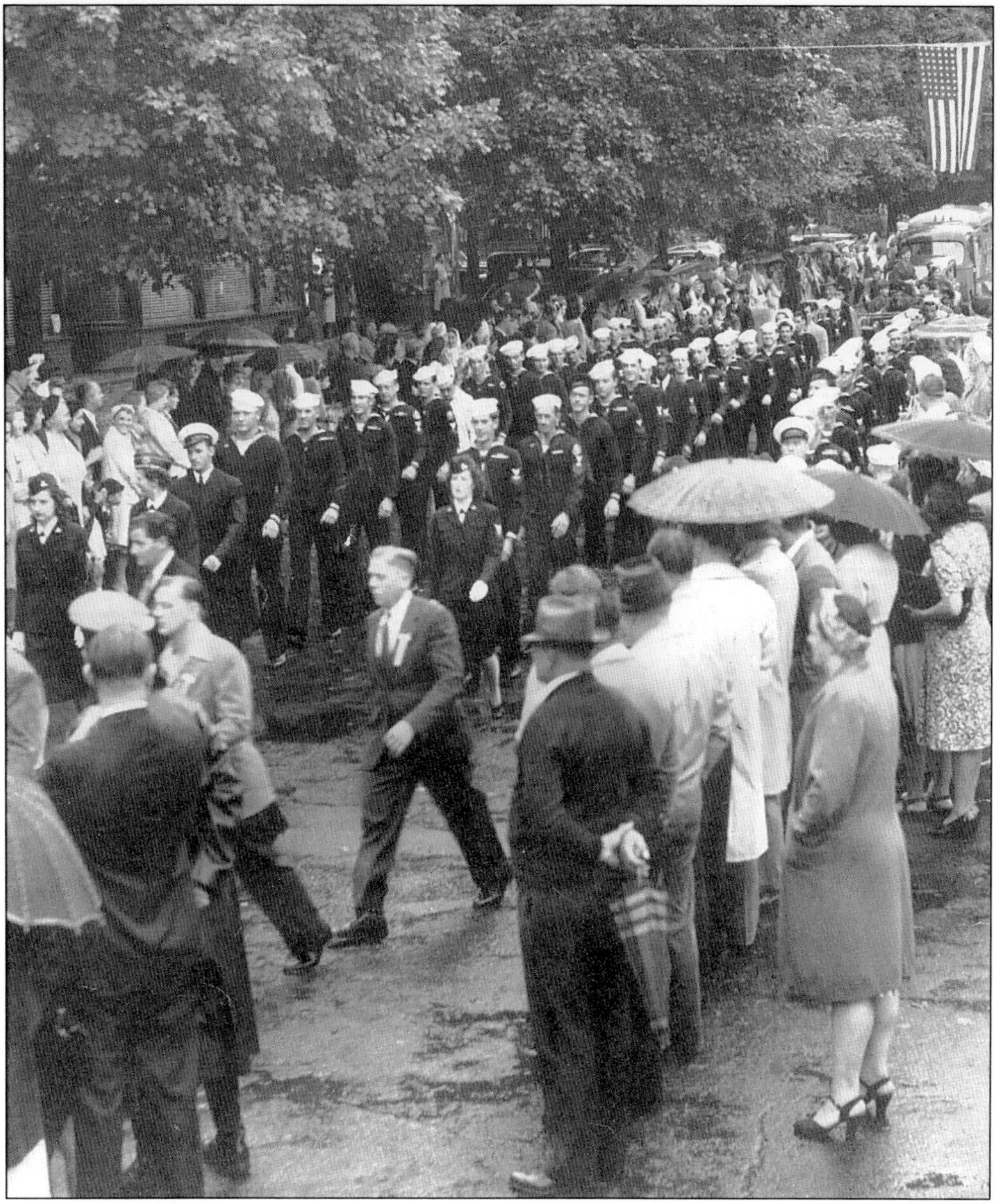

A two-day reception and memorial program was held by the citizens of the town honoring the men and women of Roebling who wore uniforms of their country during the war years. Despite a drenching rain that fell during most of the ceremony, it was to the credit of Roebling folks that they watched the lengthy parade, exhibiting a praiseworthy sense of community responsibility and a pride in community achievements. (Courtesy Mary Arnold Montalto; *Roebling*, January 1948.)

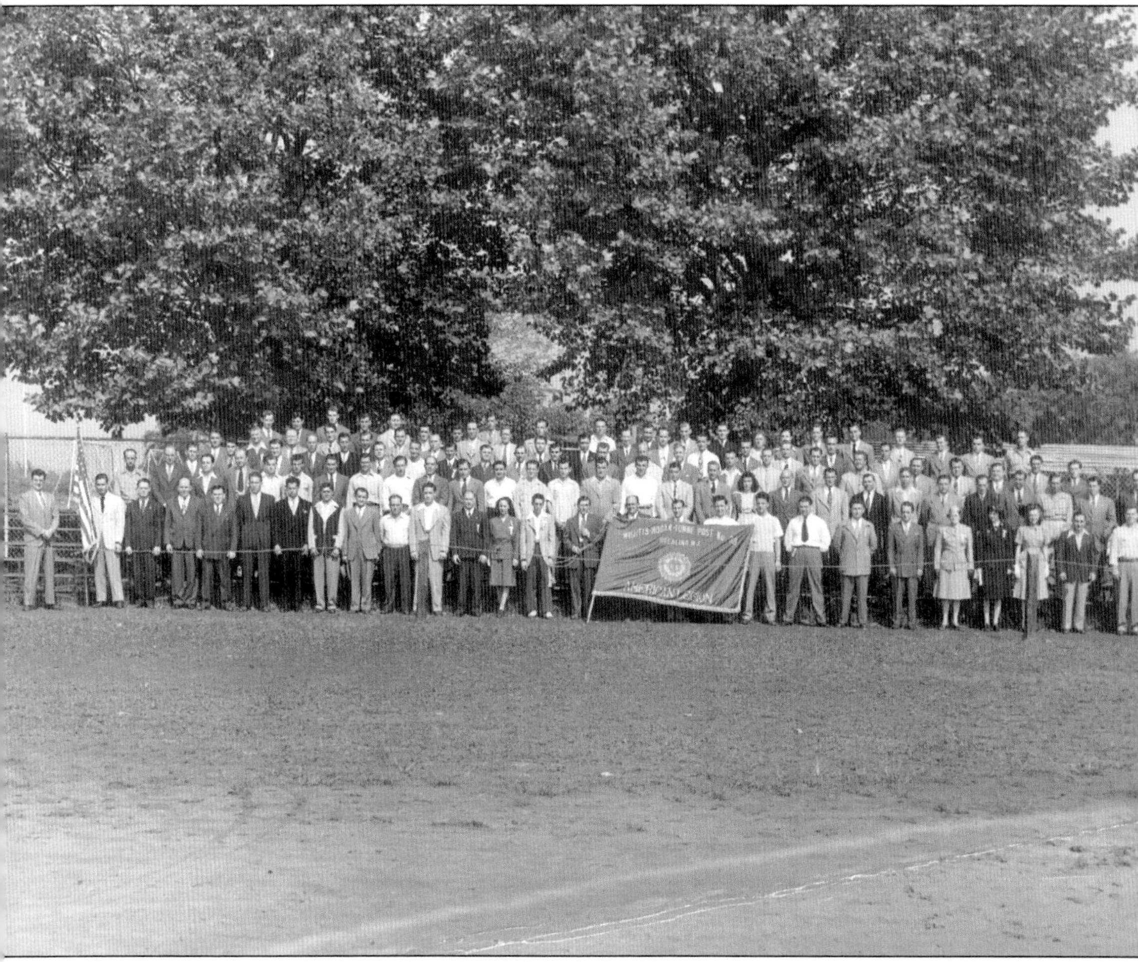

In 1946, the village of Roebling set aside a day to honor its sons and daughters who served in the armed forces. (Courtesy Shirley and Tom Pierson.)

Five

Religious Life

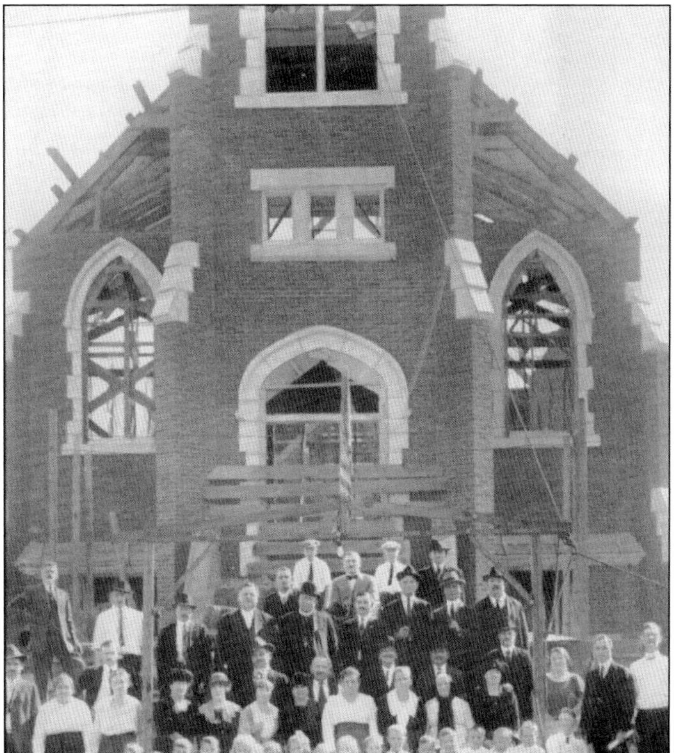

Parishioners are seen in front of Holy Assumption Church, which was under construction in 1922. (Courtesy Mary Arnold Montalto.)

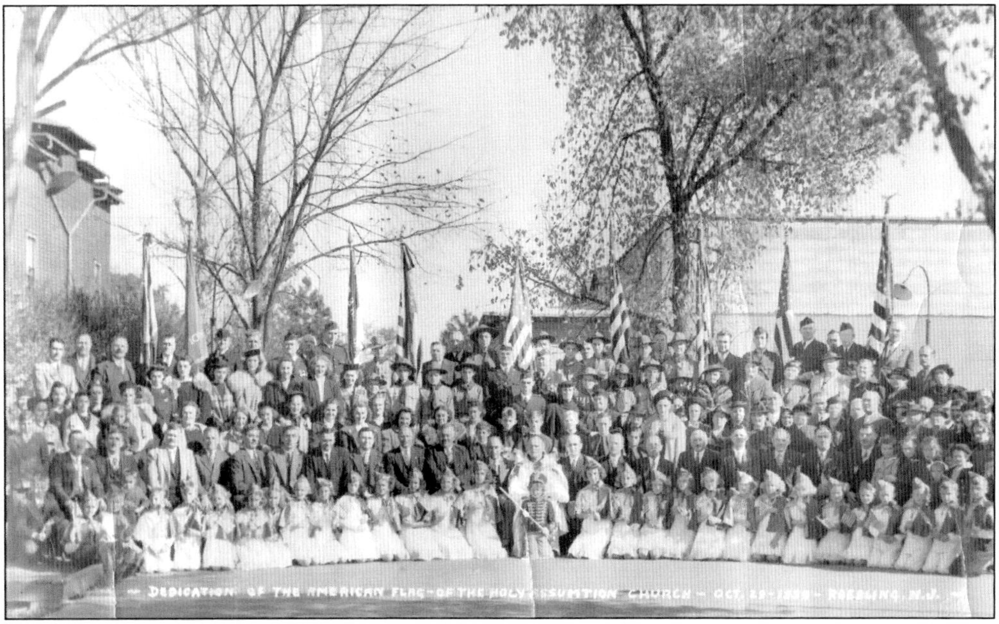

Members of the parish pose for a dedication of the American flag behind Holy Assumption Church on October 29, 1939. (Courtesy Louis Borbi.)

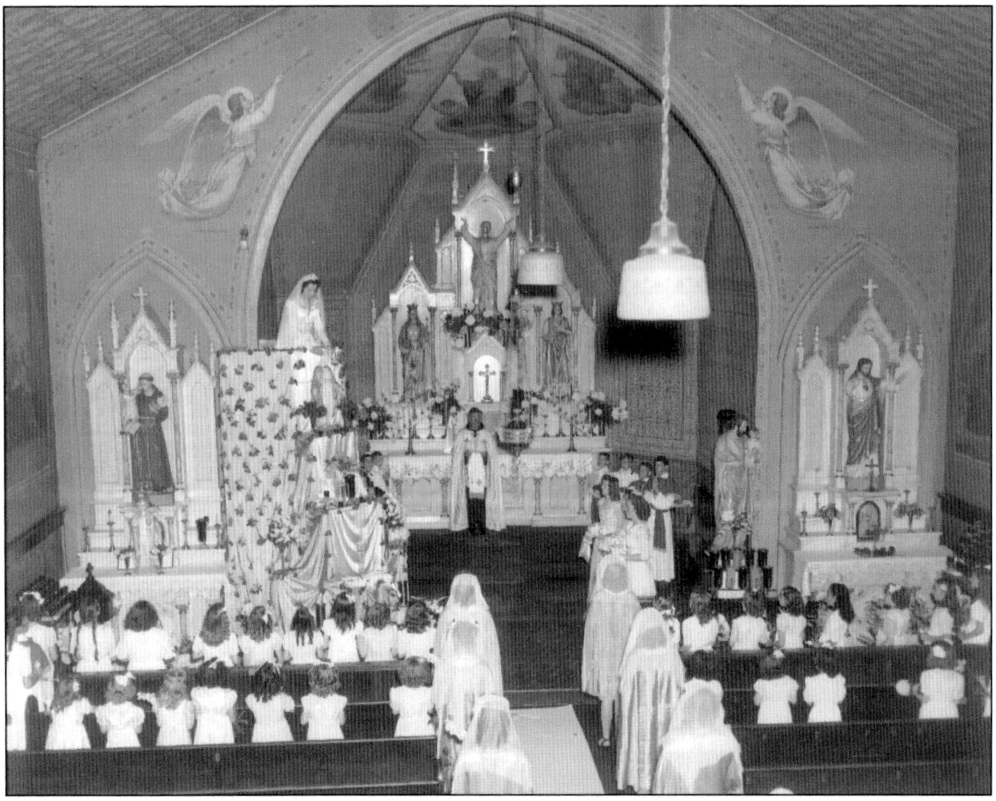

Parishioners participate in the May Crowning in 1946, as seen in this interior picture taken of Holy Assumption Church. (Courtesy Mary Arnold Montalto.)

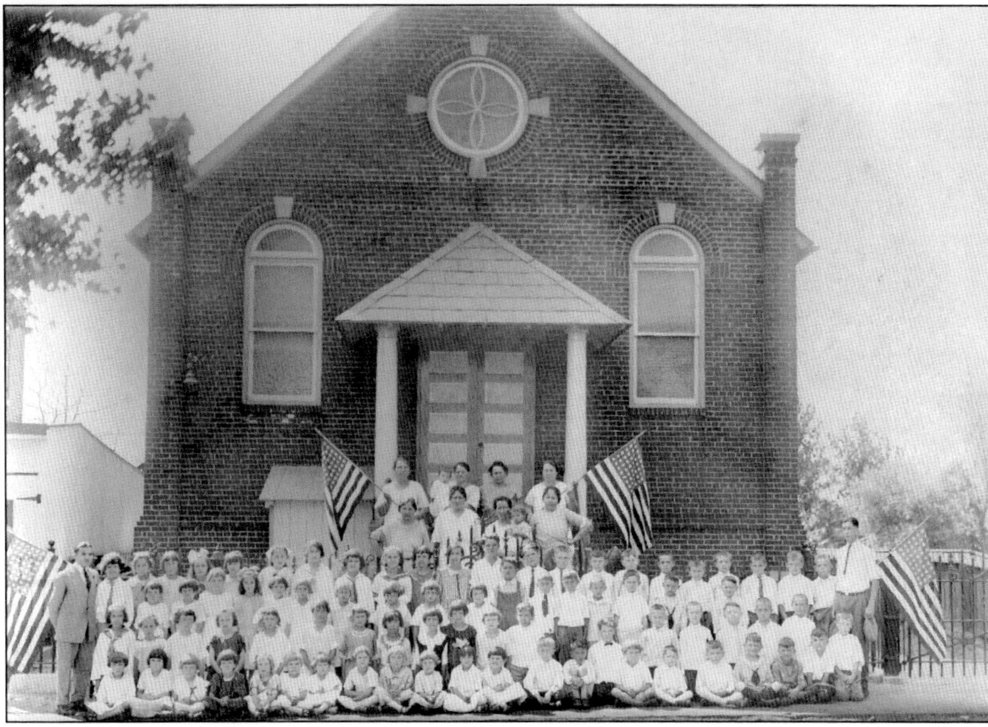

On July 26, 1924, young members of the Hungarian Reformed Church on Norman Avenue pose for a photograph. (Courtesy Hungarian Reformed Church.)

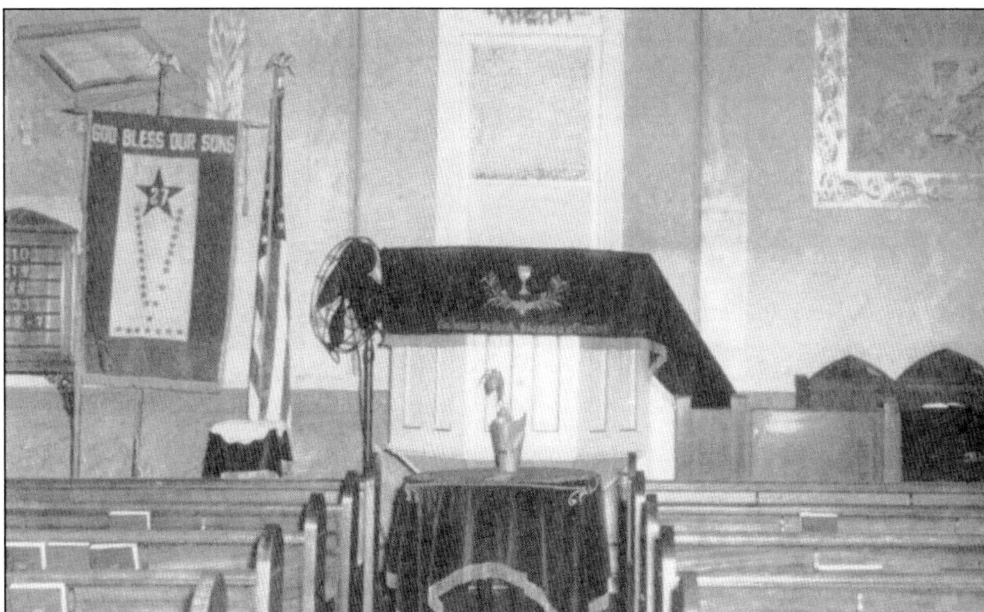

Pictured c. 1943 is the interior of the Hungarian Reformed Church, which was established in 1913 and was located on Norman Avenue. To the left is a banner with 27 stars, signifying the sons of members who served in the armed services during World War II. (Courtesy Mary Arnold Montalto.)

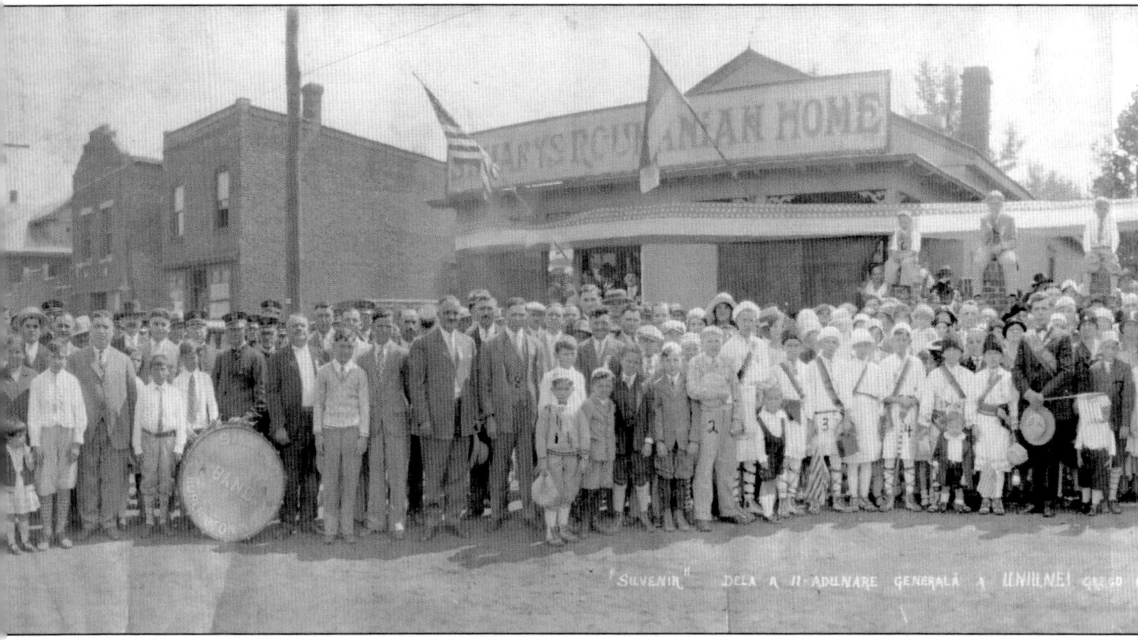

Members of St. Mary's Romanian Church are shown in this September 1928 photograph.

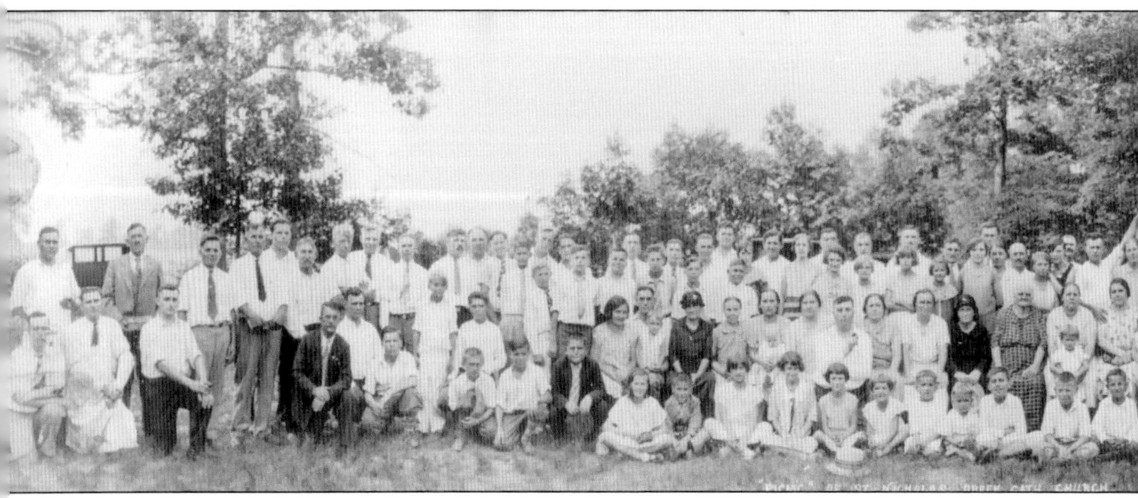

Members and friends of the St. Nicholas Greek Catholic Church pose at a picnic held for them at Hathazi's Farm on August 3, 1930. The man on the far left with the striped tie and pipe is

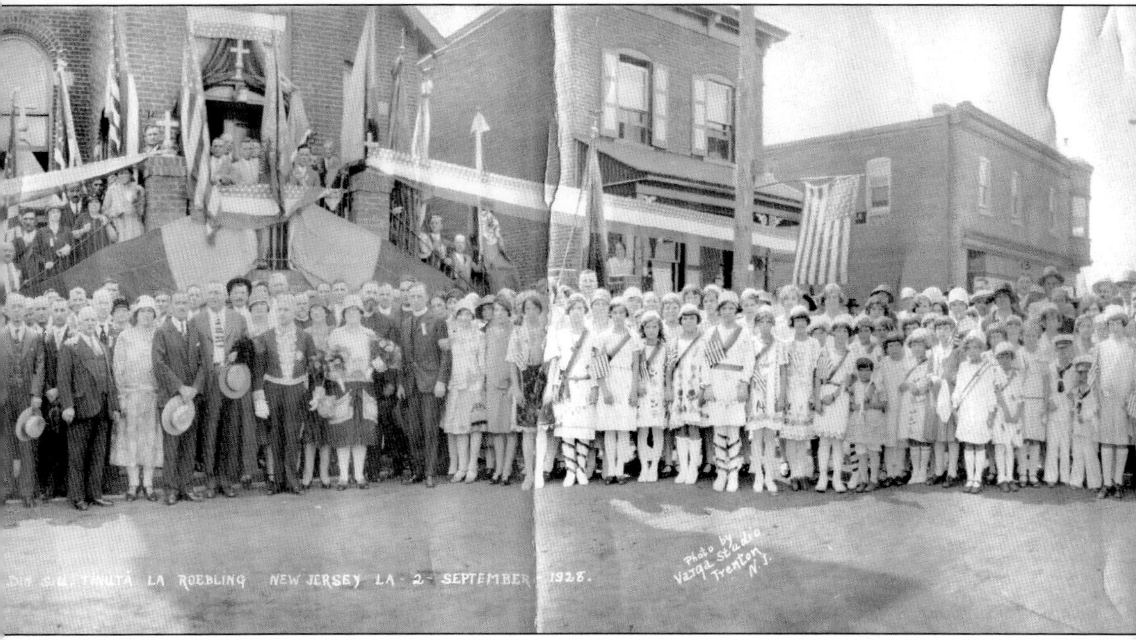

(Courtesy Maryann Bordas Bunnick.)

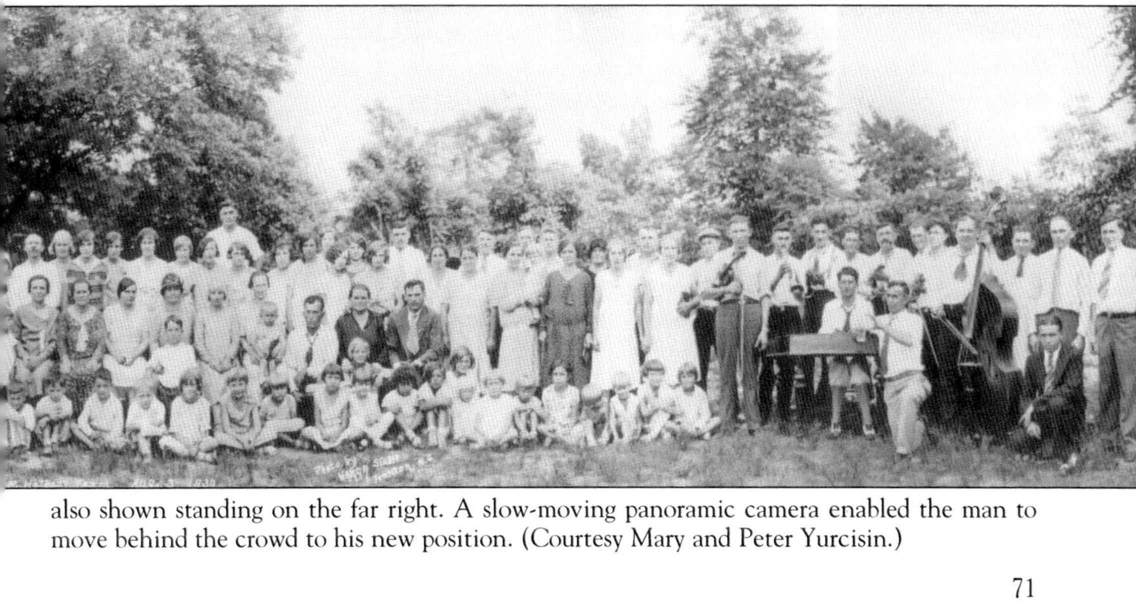

also shown standing on the far right. A slow-moving panoramic camera enabled the man to move behind the crowd to his new position. (Courtesy Mary and Peter Yurcisin.)

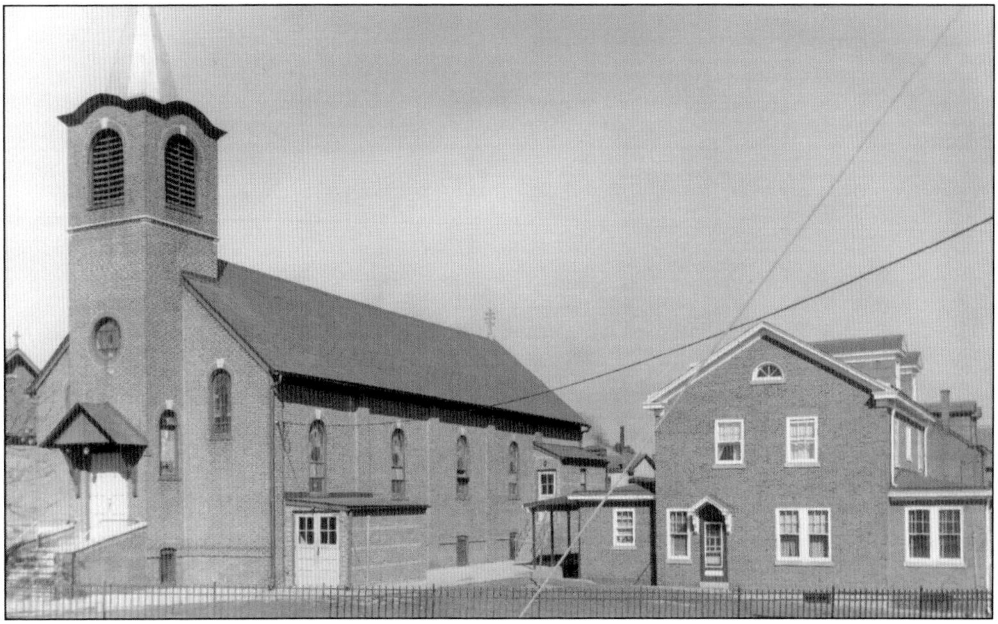

The St. Nicholas Greek Catholic Church of Roebling had its cornerstone blessed on May 30, 1914, and the building on Norman and Roland Avenues was completed in autumn of the same year. (Courtesy Joseph D. Zahorsky and Donna Orfe.)

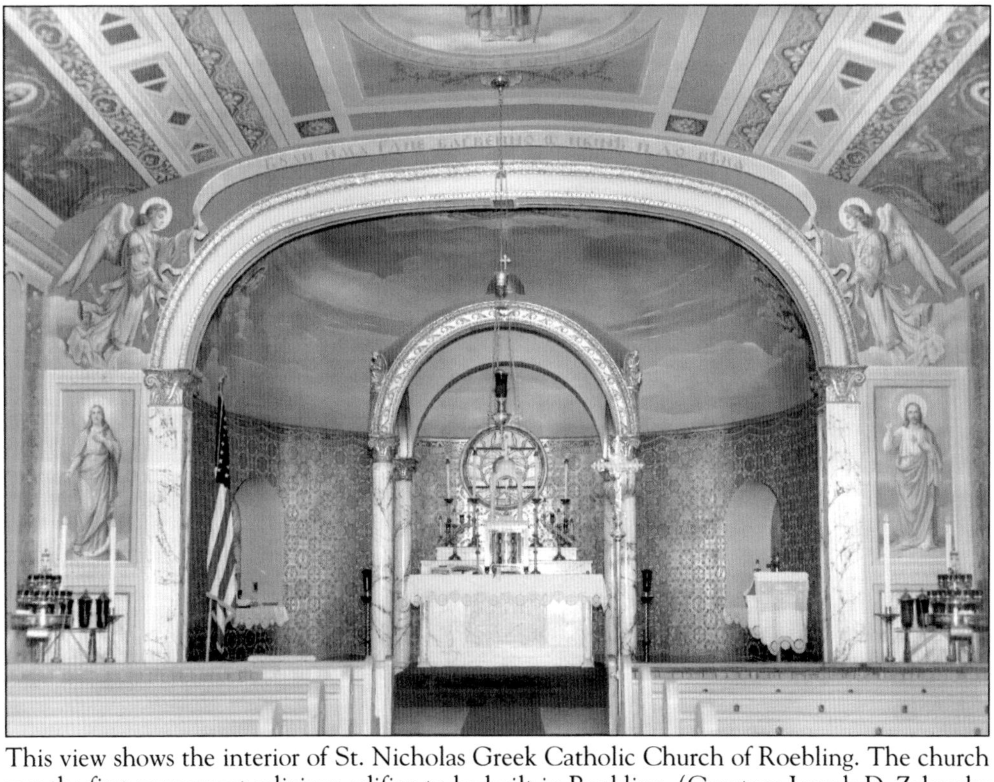

This view shows the interior of St. Nicholas Greek Catholic Church of Roebling. The church was the first permanent religious edifice to be built in Roebling. (Courtesy Joseph D. Zahorsky and Donna Orfe.)

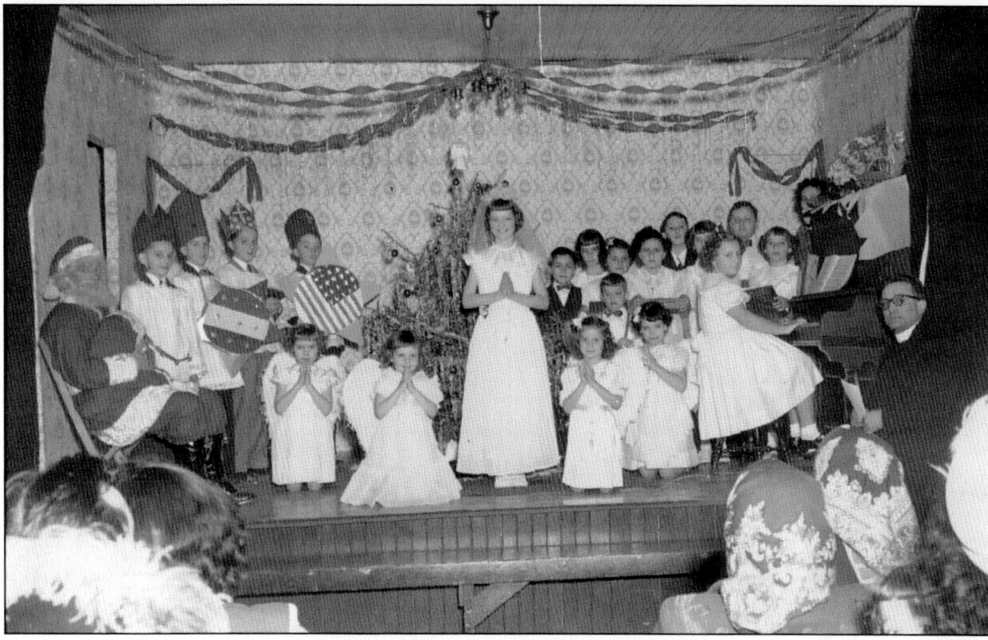

Parishioners at St. Mary's Romanian Church gather for a Christmas program in the church hall on Alden Avenue on December 12, 1951. Shown from left to right are the following: (front row) Louise Borbi Czartorski, Ruthann Marias, Mary Ann Borbi Rinaldi, Sandy Paglione, Ronald Oros, Valerie Bunnick Sweeney, Margaret Nyalka, and Fr. Gabriel Ivascu; (back row) Valentine Bunnick (dressed as Santa Claus), Louis Borbi, Michael Bunnick, Louis Cardis, Louis Bunnick, Robert Puccio, unidentified, Patricia Sandor, Rose Cardis, George Lengel, Eleanor Bonatz Travia, Jerry Sandor, Loretta Borbi Boyle, and unidentified. (Courtesy Maryann Bordas Bunnick.)

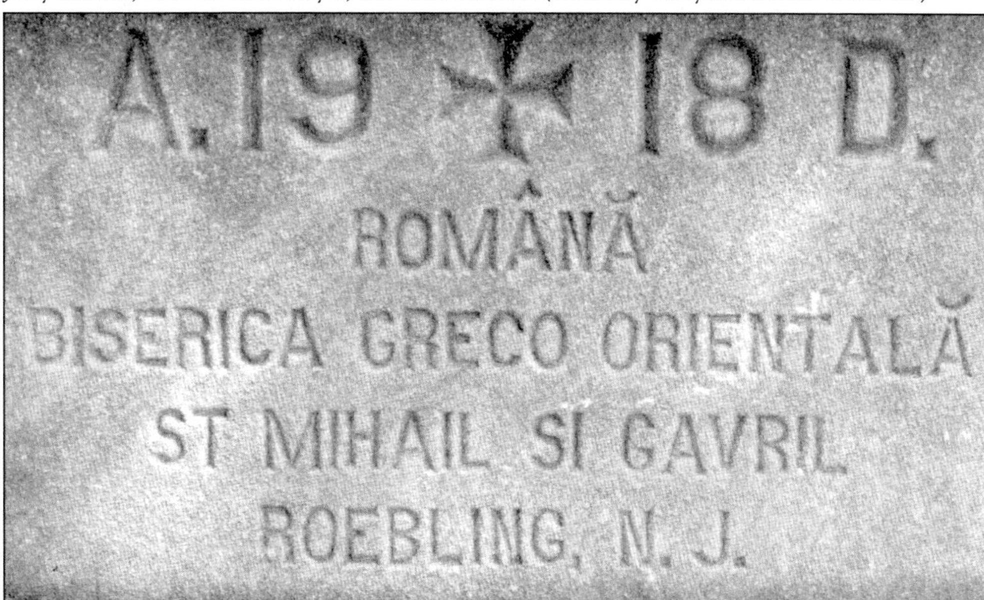

This photograph shows the cornerstone of St. Michael and St. Gabriel Romanian Orthodox Church. The reason for the inscription "Romanian Greek Oriental Church" is orthodoxy began in Greece and then spread throughout Europe. (Courtesy Pastor and Mrs. Iosif Chereches.)

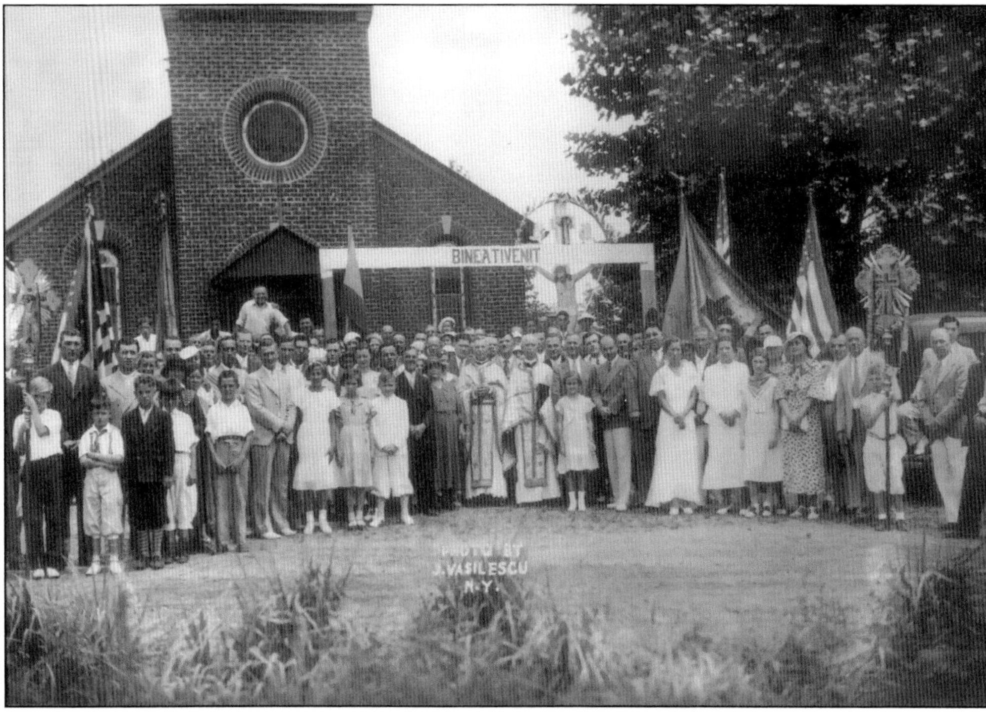

Members of the St. Michael and St. Gabriel Romanian Orthodox Church pose for a picture in front of their church in the mid-1940s. (Courtesy Pastor and Mrs. Iosif Chereches.)

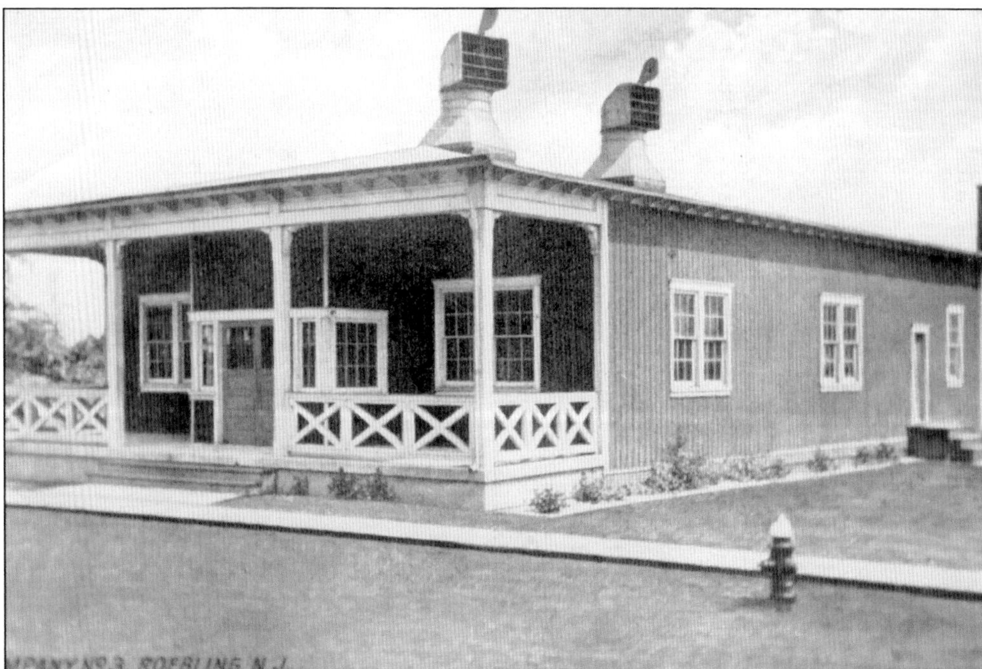

On Sundays this building on Railroad Avenue became the Tabernacle Baptist Church. Under the ministry of Rev. Edmund Alexander, this church served the spiritual needs for many of the black residents in Roebling from 1934 through 1941. (Courtesy Louis Borbi.)

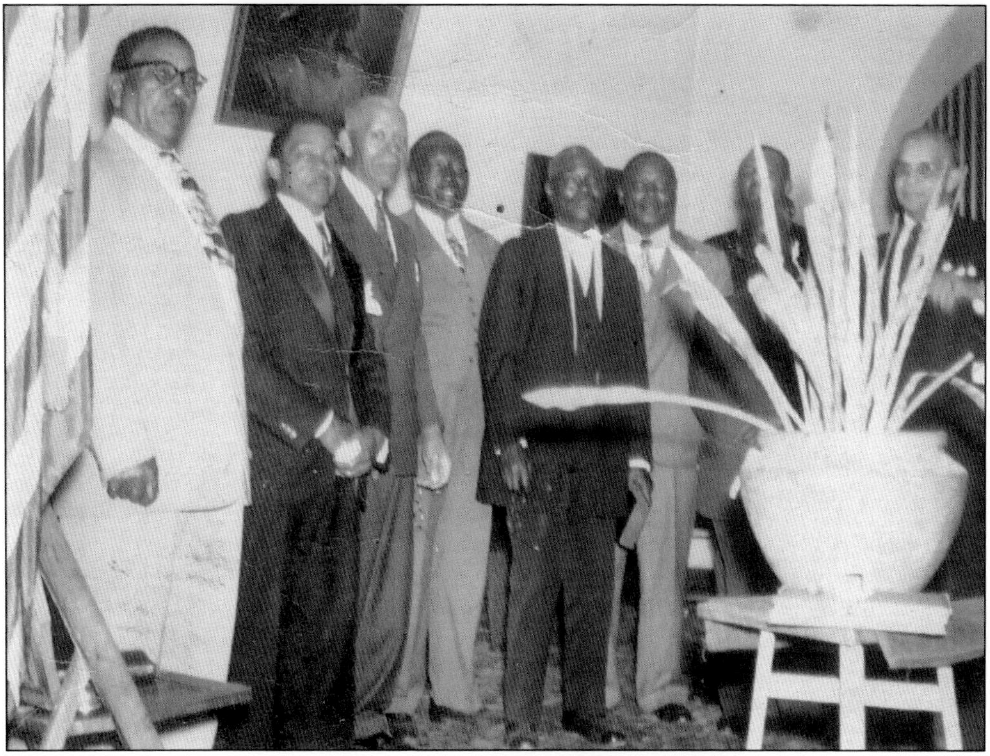

Rev. Edmund Alexander (second from left) is shown in the Tabernacle Baptist Church during a minister's union gathering. (Courtesy Shirley Alexander-Williams and Gus Alexander.)

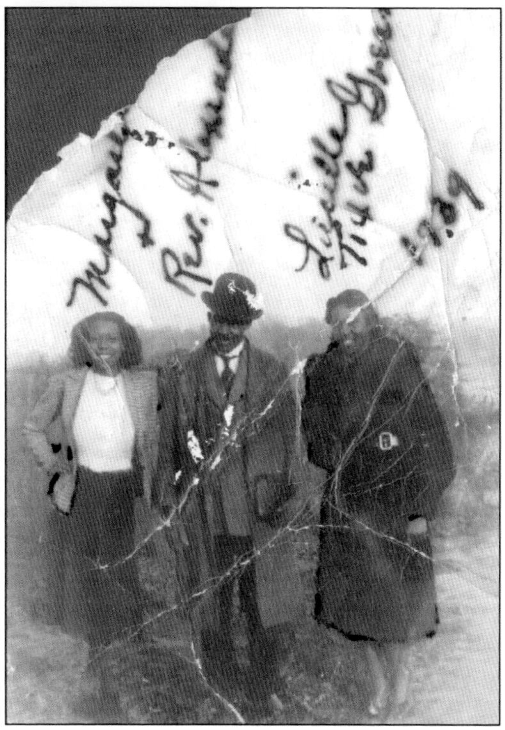

Rev. Edmund Alexander is flanked by his daughter-in-law Margaret Alexander (left) and his daughter Lucille Green. This Railroad Avenue photograph was taken in 1939. (Courtesy Shirley Alexander-Williams and Gus Alexander.)

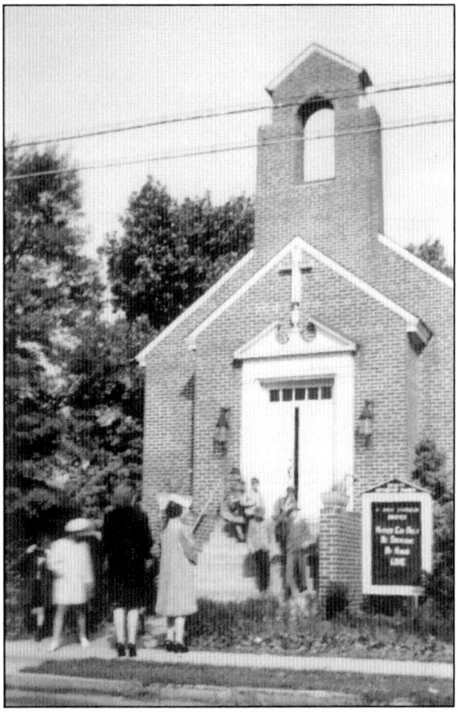

The Trinity Methodist Episcopal Church began on March 11, 1916, with the election of trustees. Worship services were held over the drugstore on Main Street. Plans were begun to build a church structure but were discontinued in 1924. The project was again taken up and the present church was dedicated in 1936. In 1968, the name Trinity United Methodist was adopted when all Methodist Episcopal Churches were merged with the Evangelical United Brethren Church. (Courtesy Marion and Alex McDowall.)

Trinity Methodist Church

Roebling, New Jersey

■

May 11, 1947 — 11:00 A. M.

REV. A. B. PARKER, *Minister* MRS. E. LORING, *Organist*

■

MORNING WORSHIP

Presiding — MRS. M. ECKERT, *President W. S. C. S.*

Organ Prelude, "Songs My Mother Taught Me" . . . . *Dvorak*
Introit . . . . Choir
Invocation . . . . Mrs. M. Eckert
Processional Hymn No. 1 . . . Congregation stand on second stanza
Apostles Creed
Baritone Solo—"Beautiful Isle of Somewhere" (*Fearis*) Mr. Russell Sheaffer
Morning Prayer—Mrs. Hodson . . . . Choral Response
Fellowship Choir—"Mother of Mine" . . . . *MacCarthy*
Psalter, No. 19—Page No. 584 . . . . Mrs. K. Ibach
Gloria Patri
Offertory, "Song of the Soul" . . . . *Nolte*
Presentation of Tithes and Offerings . . . . . . Choral Response
Anthem, "Mothers' Hymns"—*Jacobus* . . . . Senior Choir
Scripture Lesson—Proverbs 31:10-31 . . . . Mrs. Peet
Hymn No. 428
Message . . . . Mrs. Ira S. Pimm
Baritone Solo, "I Come to Thee"—*Roma* . . . Mr. Russell Sheaffer
Presentation and Acceptance of Window . . . Mrs. Carrie Mullen
Unveiling of Window . . . . Carol Sheaffer
Dedication of Window
Hymn No. 416
Benediction and Moment of Meditation
Postlude

Ushers—MRS. E. SWANBERG AND MRS. M. JOYCE

DEDICATION OF WINDOW

In Memory of

MORRIS W. AND MARY E. SHEAFFER

Presented by the Children

■

Minister—To the glory of God our heavenly Father, to the service of Jesus Christ and His Church, and to the quickening influence of the Holy Spirit.

People —We dedicate this Window.

Minister—To ever remind us of the friendliness and generosity that prompted the giving of this beautiful window to this our church; and with a prayer to God that we, the members of this church and congregation, may ever strive to equal this same spirit.

People —We dedicate this Window.

Minister—For the ministry of Christian Art; for the inspiration of the life and character represented by this window; and for the direction of the thoughts of the congregation in Christian meditation.

People —We dedicate this Window.

Minister—For the continual invitation suggested by this picture to accept the challenge of leaving all to follow the vital teaching of Jesus; and for the suggestion that we ever seek to know the truth; to practice faith, hope, charity, prayer, joy, love and peace in our daily lives.

People —We dedicate this Window.

Minister—With Honor and Loving Memory of
MORRIS W. AND MARY E. SHEAFFER
to the spirit of their devoted Christian life, and the prepetuation of their devotion and sacrificial service to this church.

People —We dedicate this Window.

Let us Pray.

This is the program of the Trinity Methodist Church, dated May 11, 1947, which was Mother's Day that year. The Window Dedication was in honor of Morris and Mary Sheaffer. (Courtesy Carol M. Sheaffer, M.D.)

Six

Sports and Entertainment

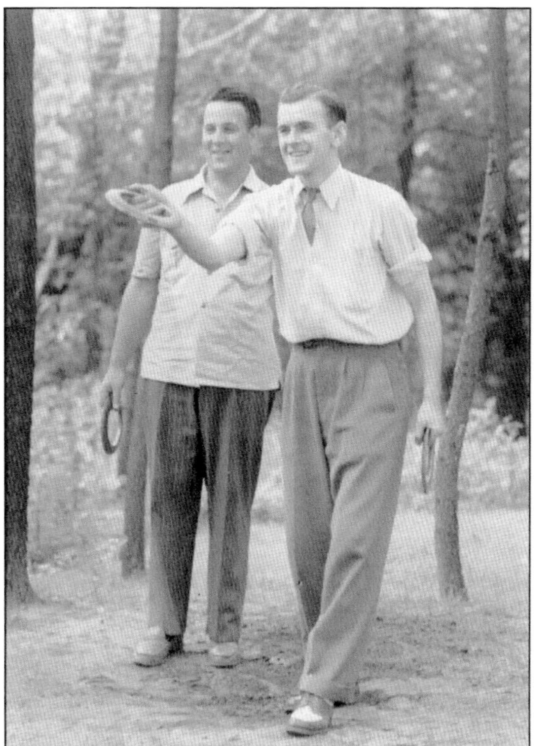

Joseph Zahorsky is ready to throw a quoit in the 1940s. (Courtesy Joseph D. Zahorsky and Donna Orfe.)

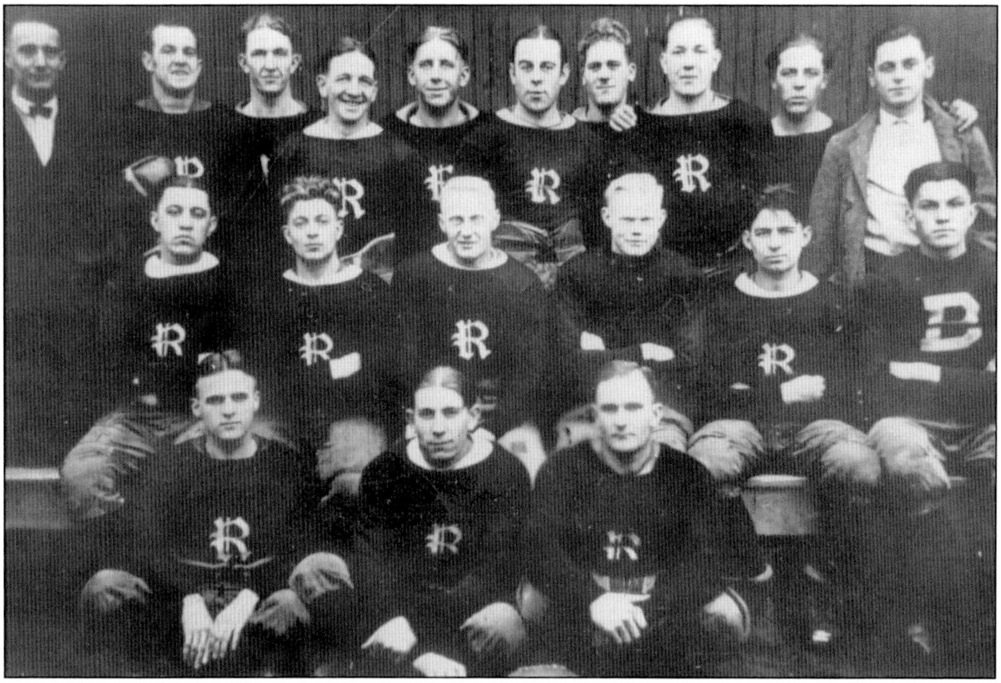

This photograph shows the Roebling Blue Centers football team. The players are, from left to right, as follows: (front row) Frank Bogdin, John Kostrub, and Toby Houseworth; (middle row) Bruce Hubley, Jack Thomas, Bruno Quistberg, Hilgo Quistberg, Andrew Drangula, and Charles Wall; (back row) Maw Pickett, Weast F. Gren, "Hecker" Miller, Ray Carter, Joe Carter, Stan Vechesky, Henry Englund, Arnold Wall, unidentified, and Jack Madden. (Courtesy Louis Borbi.)

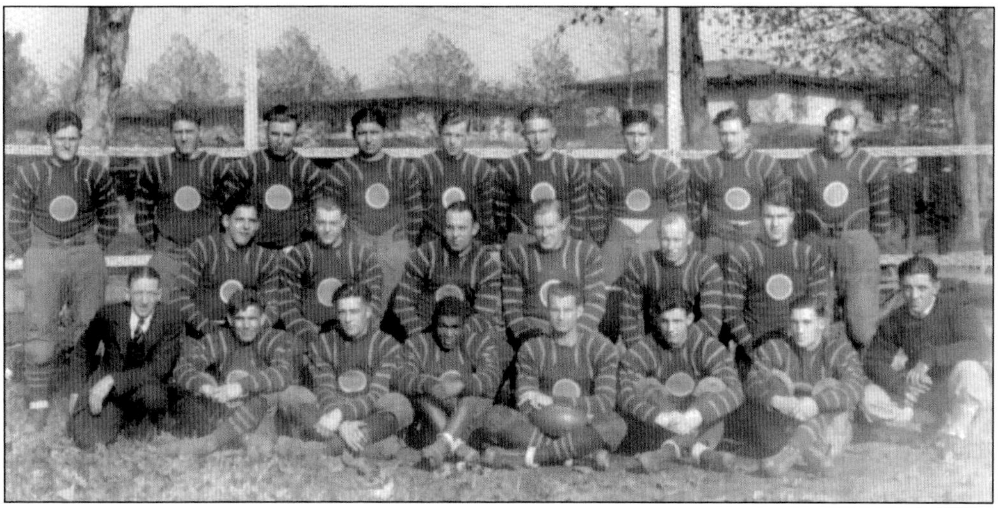

This picture shows the Roebling Blue Centers of 1930. They are, from left to right, as follows: (front row) Ray Carter, Lee Carr, Jack Pitman, Eddie Hutton, Charles Crilley, Murphy, Bob Applegate, and Bruce Hubley; (middle row) George Olah, Phil Sheridan, Stan "Gotch" Vechesky, ? Richardson, Bud Jeanette, and Alge Parker; (back row) Jack Gardener, Henry Englund, R. Fenton, Andrew "Bung" Drangula, Ted Hague, Bill "Hecker" Miller, Charles Ledger, Clarence Ledger, and Bulligan Bogdany. This team played the first indoor professional football game in Atlantic City's Convention Hall on November 9, 1930. (Courtesy Louis Borbi.)

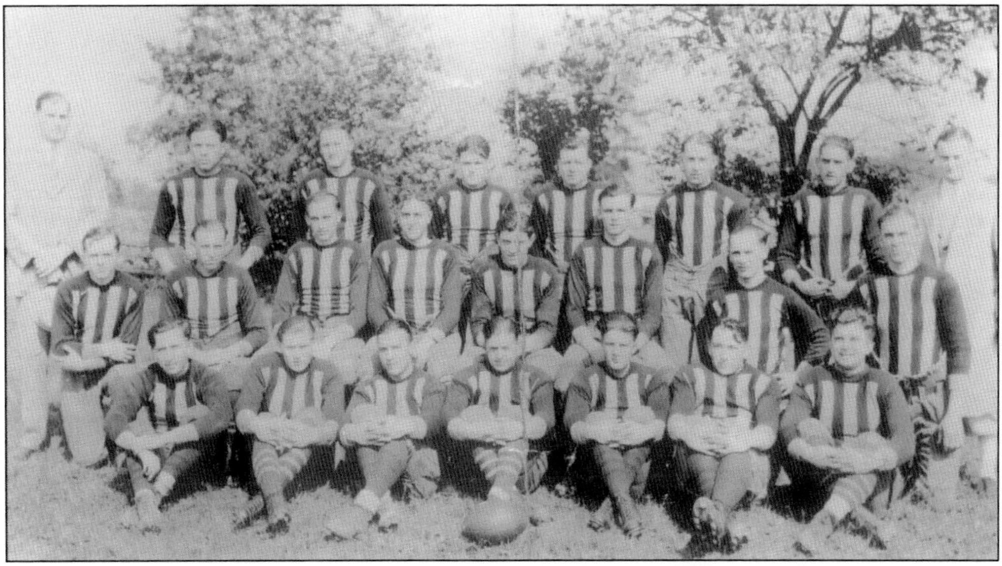

Pictured at Hathazi's Farm are the 1929 Roebling Bulldogs football team. The players are, from left to right, as follows: (front row) Joe Garbley, George Lengel, Mike Lastishen, John Kotch, Bud Marshall, Martin Bucs, and Joe Breza; (middle row) George Tiffenback, Mike Kostrub, Andy Sahol, "Legs" Wargo, Bundy Papp, John Ligos, John Wargo, and Ted Ivins; (back row) Manager Charley Keiley, Andy Rusnak, John Alter, Nick Kleiner, Mr. Anch, John Kostrub, Ziggy Garbley, and George Alter. (Courtesy Louis Borbi.)

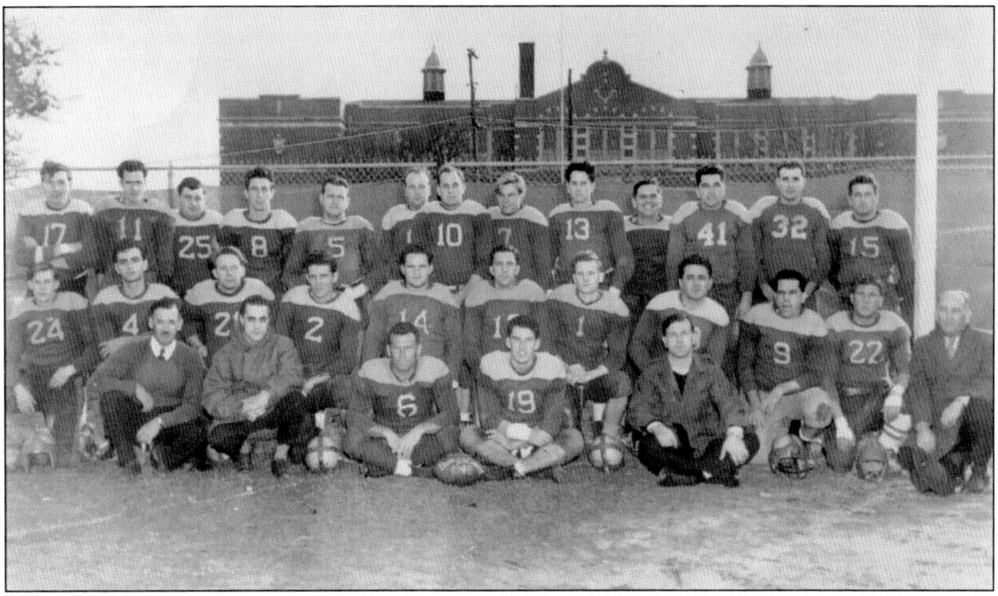

Shown are the members of the Roebling Holy Name football team, the 1946 Burlington County Champions. They are, from left to right, as follows: (front row) Martin Vrgoyti, assistant manager; Ben Bell, trainer; Sam Dudik, co-captain; Jack Lichvarcik, co-captain; and J. "Sep" Csercsevits, coach; (middle row) Dinky Tonne; John Mazar; G. Tymash; Bill Schaum; Chubby Cronin; R. Bintliff; A. Joyce; F. Savuly; G. Schaum; J. Nagy; and R. Bintliff, assistant manager; (back row) L. Varga; J. Quig; J. Horvath; J. Papp; P. Shoriak; J. Bodrog; M. Miyo; J. Miyo; P. Stone; M. Kovacs; J. Buhan; G. Magyar; and Pete Litus. (Courtesy Louis Borbi.)

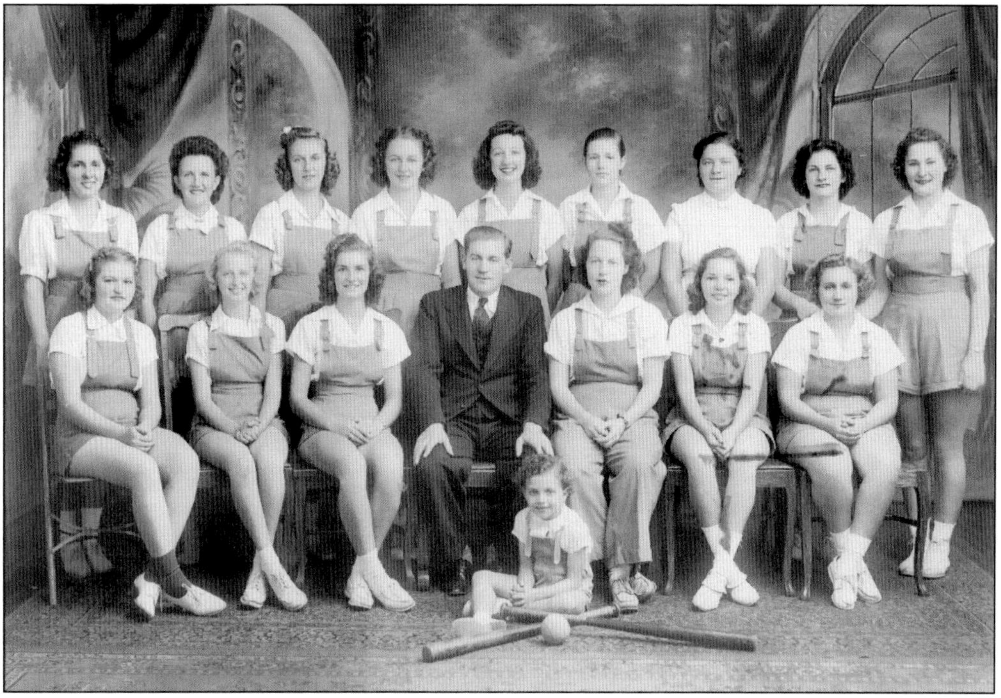

The members the 1938 Burlington County Softball League Championship team are, from left to right, as follows: (front row) Catherine Zotta; (middle row) Julia Csik, Isabel Cspreghy, Flossie Sabo, "Unk" Lengel, Norma Stone, Mags Boldizar, and Julie Varga; (back row) Esther Boldizar, Eleanor Ledger, Eleanor Echgelmeier, Emma Orban, Helen Litus, Iva Giehl, Helen Wide, Julie Mocan, and Thelma Pannick. (Courtesy Louis Borbi.)

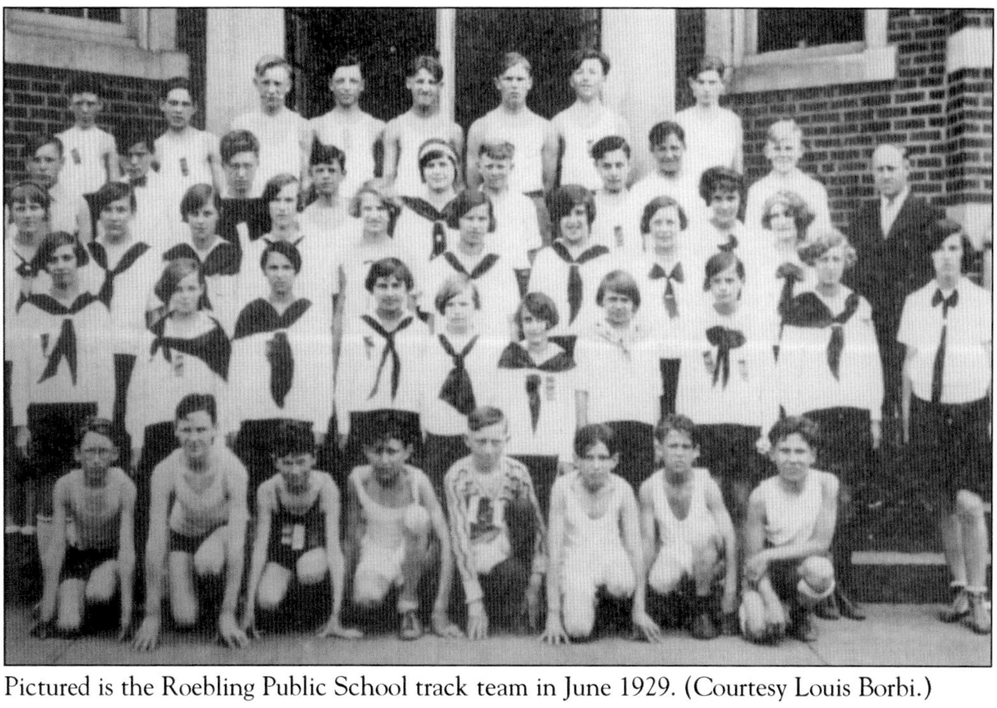

Pictured is the Roebling Public School track team in June 1929. (Courtesy Louis Borbi.)

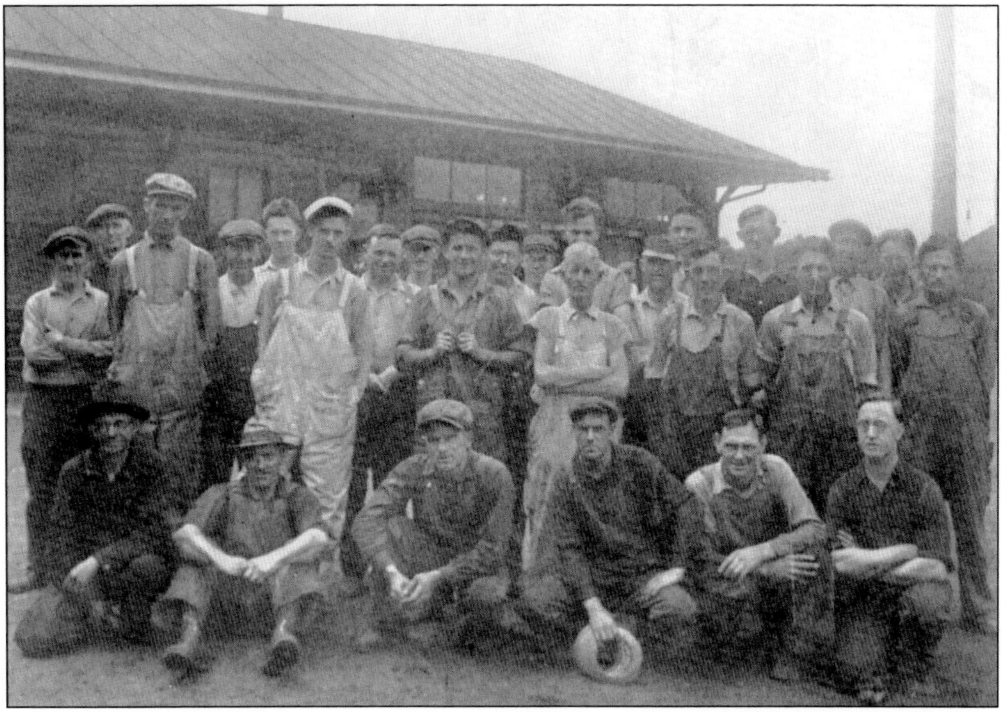

The workers played quoits, a game similar to horseshoes. The various departments of the mill would compete against each other. The members of the Pipefitters team are, from left to right, as follows: (front row, kneeling) S. Hull, C. Platt, J. Kish, W.H. Scott, J. Madden, and J. James; (back row, standing) J. Taylor, R. Robbins, L. Reed, C. Mason, A. Fergerstrom, J. Baker, J. Clayton, H. Wainwright, A. Heep, George Kline, J. Obinger, E.R. Reeves, A. Matthews, R. Flynn, W. Zelly, H, Sudfole, J. Bogden, E. Horner, S. French, T. Fewkes, L. and ? Wargo. (Courtesy Mary Arnold Montalto.)

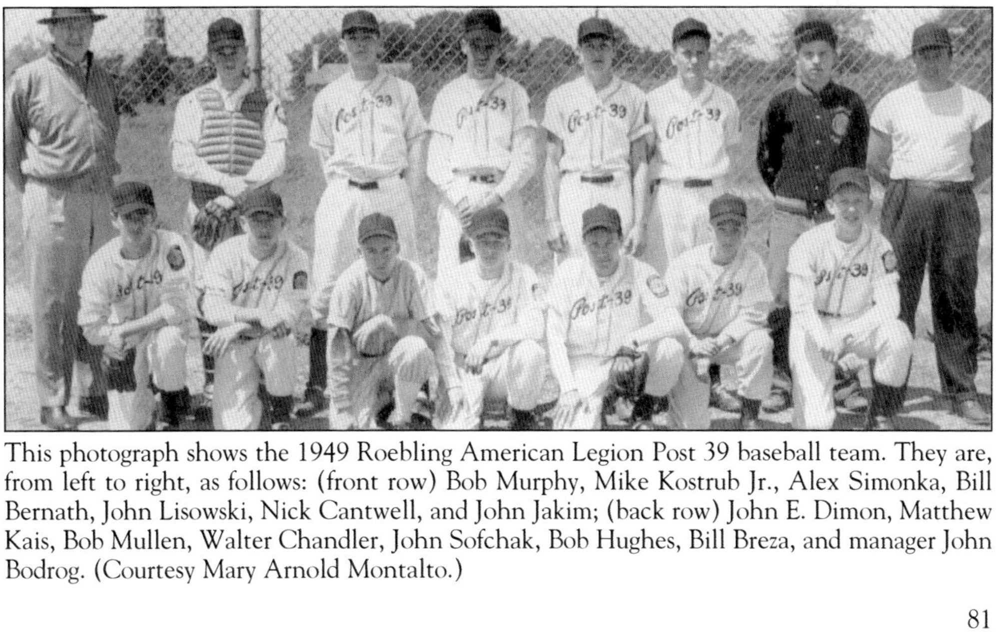

This photograph shows the 1949 Roebling American Legion Post 39 baseball team. They are, from left to right, as follows: (front row) Bob Murphy, Mike Kostrub Jr., Alex Simonka, Bill Bernath, John Lisowski, Nick Cantwell, and John Jakim; (back row) John E. Dimon, Matthew Kais, Bob Mullen, Walter Chandler, John Sofchak, Bob Hughes, Bill Breza, and manager John Bodrog. (Courtesy Mary Arnold Montalto.)

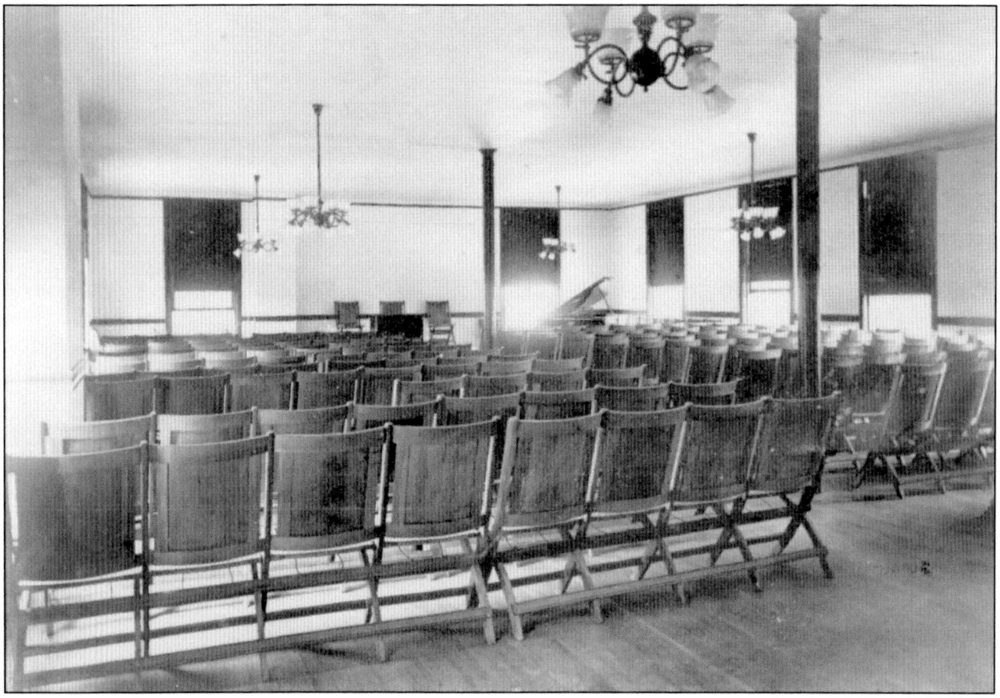

This view shows the meeting room on the upper floor of the Roebling Drugstore. The room had a variety of uses, including the showing of silent films and holding services for members of the Trinity Methodist Church until the church was built. (Courtesy Louis Borbi.)

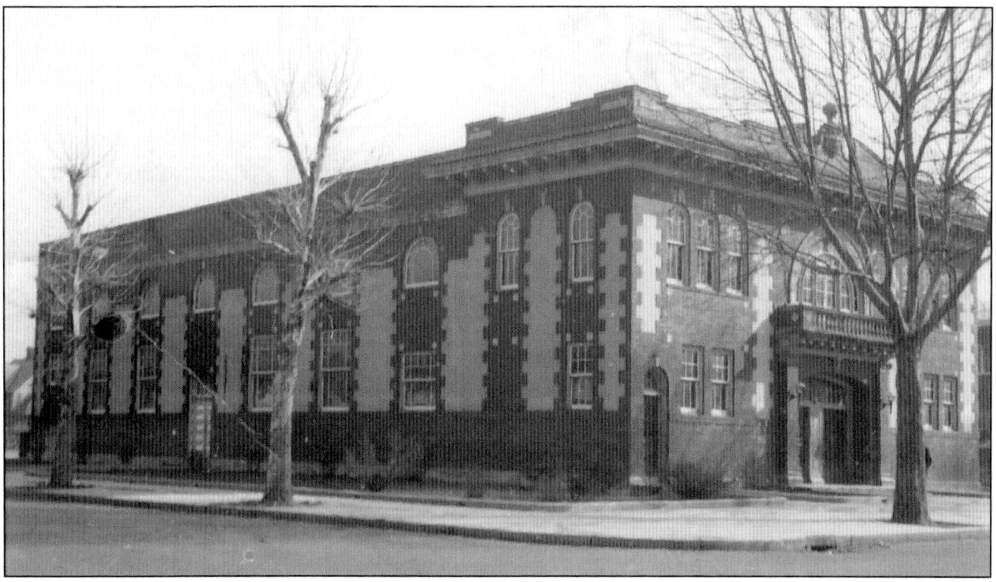

The air-conditioned auditorium was built in 1915 to provide a place for entertainment. The seats were removable, thus opening up the room into a large ballroom. It was the site for vaudeville shows, minstrels, boxing matches, silent movies, and later, sound movies. In the 1940s, its use was predominantly as a movie theater, showing films all week. On Saturdays, they had a matinee for children at 2:00 P.M. Sunday movies began at 2:00 P.M., continuing nonstop until 11:00 P.M. (Courtesy Joseph Varga.)

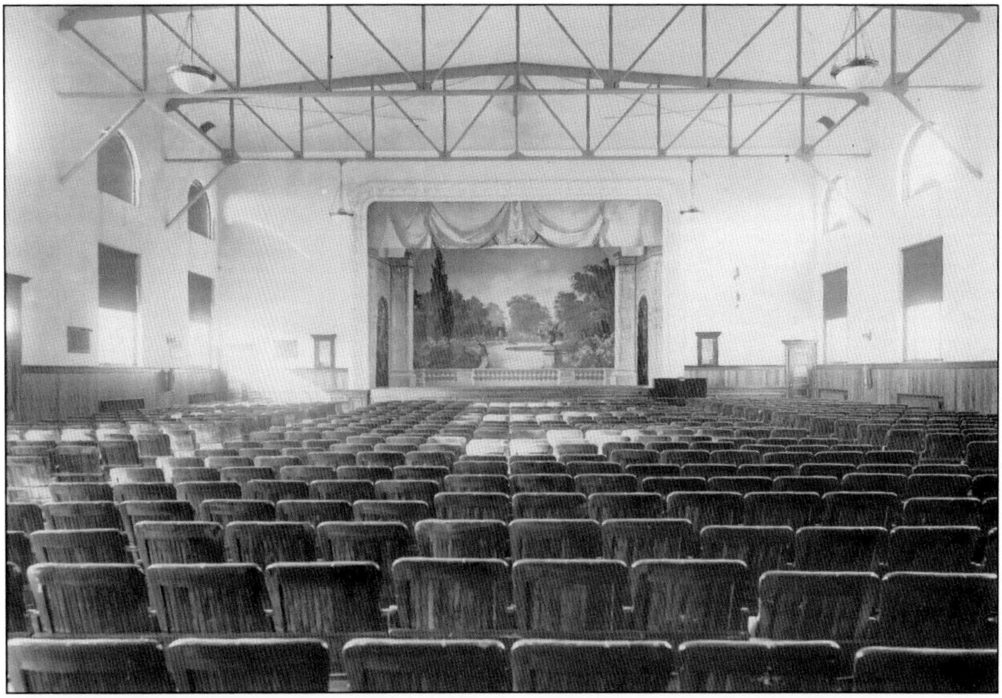

This is an interior view of the Roebling Auditorium from the back of the auditorium. (Courtesy Carol M. Schaeffer, M.D.)

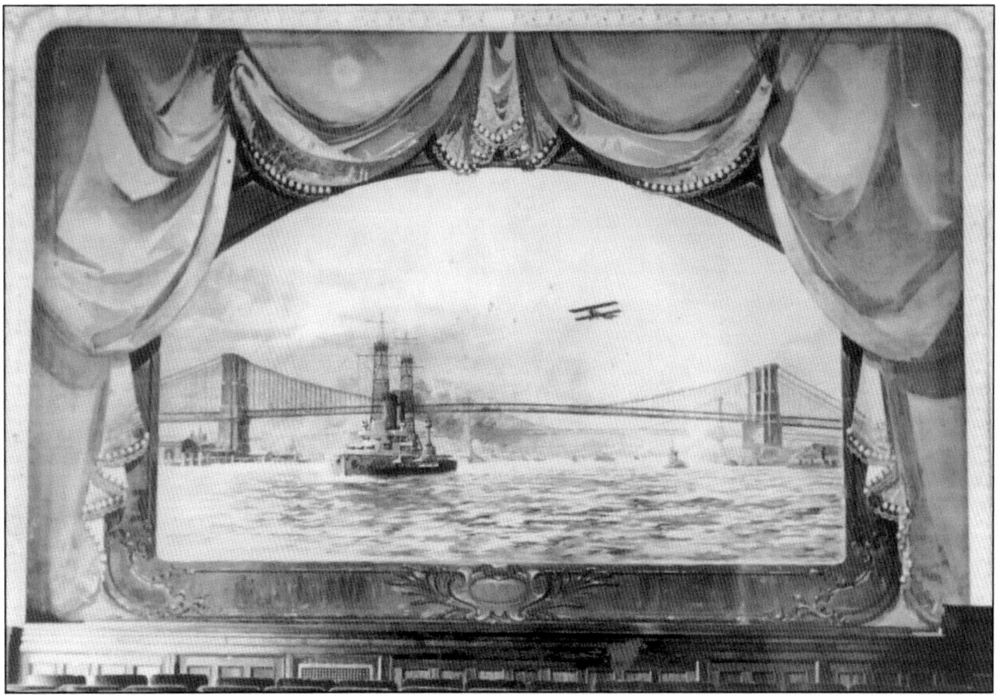

Pictured is the original stage curtain of the Roebling Auditorium. It was made of heavy cloth and featured a hand-painted picture of the John A. Roebling–designed Brooklyn Bridge. (Courtesy Louis Borbi.)

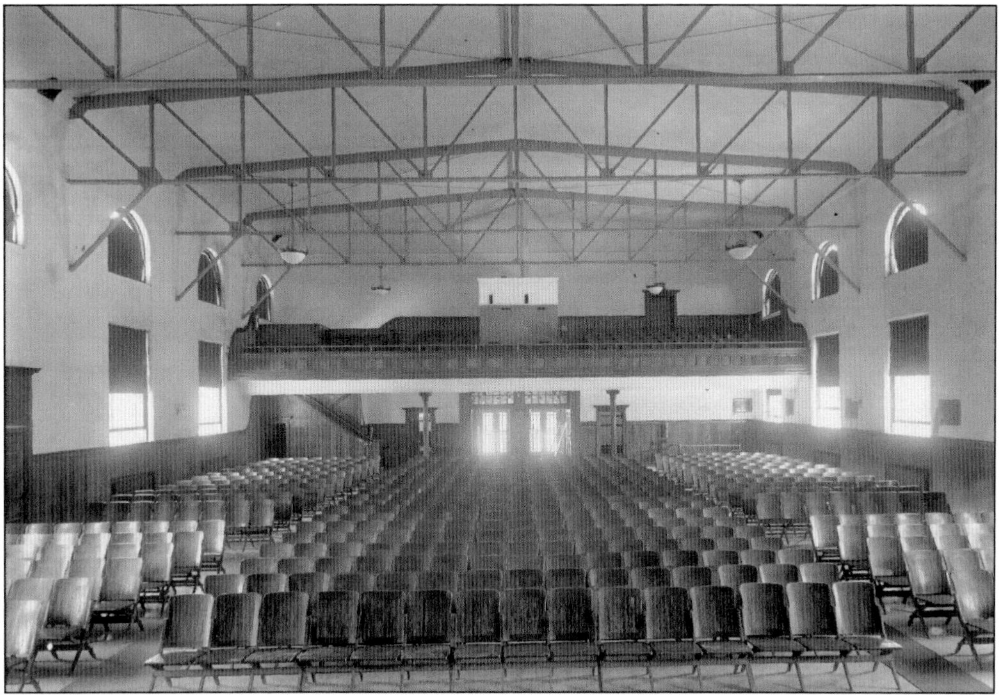

This is an interior view of the Roebling Auditorium as viewed from the stage. (Courtesy Carol M. Shaeffer, M.D.)

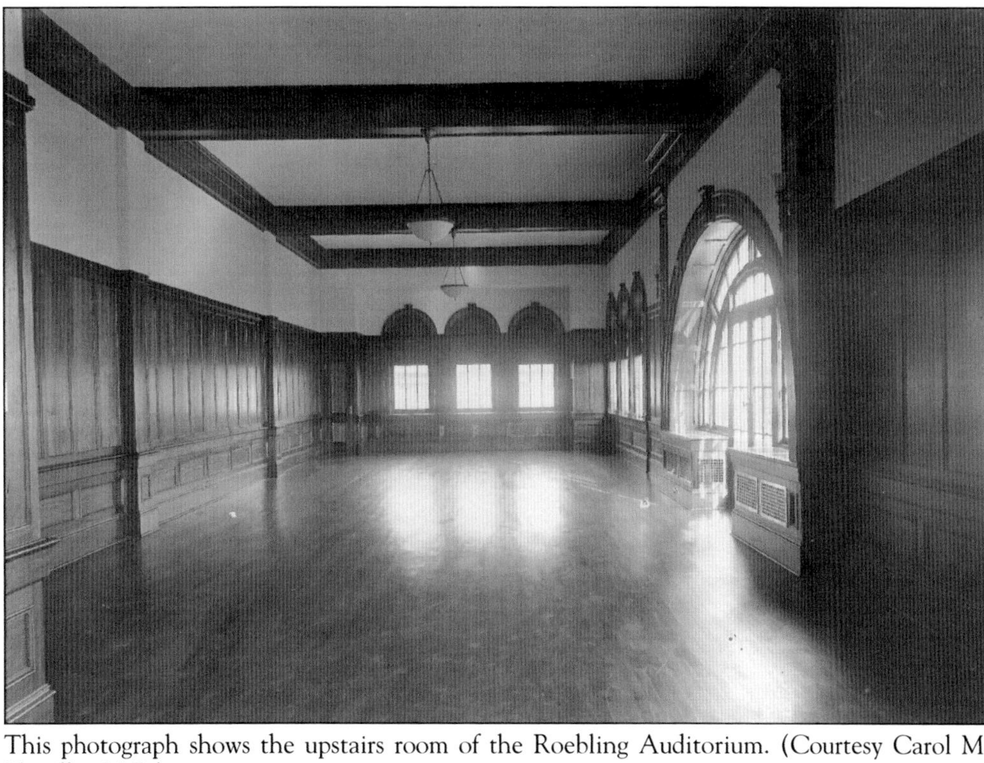

This photograph shows the upstairs room of the Roebling Auditorium. (Courtesy Carol M. Shaeffer, M.D.)

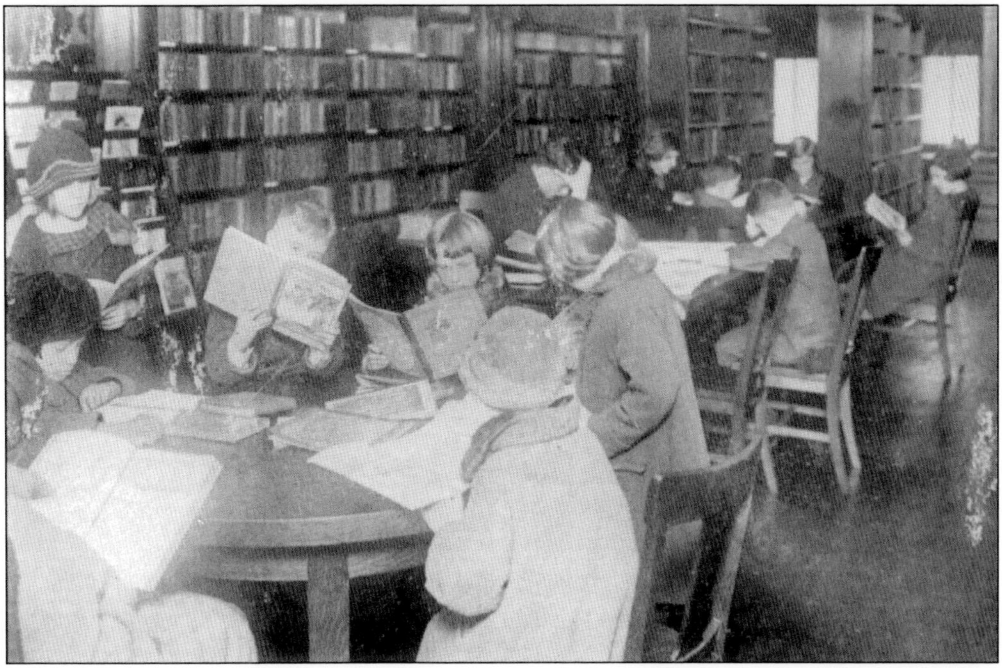

In 1920, the Roebling Library opened in the upstairs of the Roebling Auditorium. It was opened six days a week, including everyday but Saturday. On weekdays, the hours were 3:00 P.M. to 9 P.M. and, on Sundays, 3:00 P.M. to 8:00 P.M. (Courtesy Louis Borbi.)

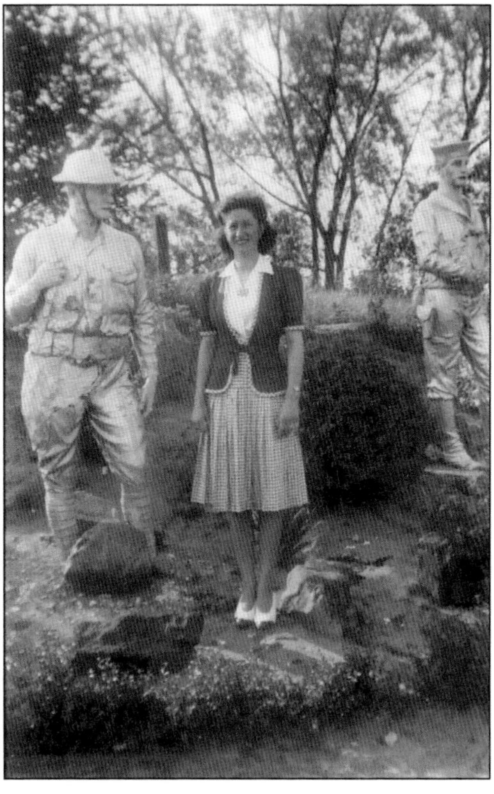

On May 26, 1942, Katherine Borbi is standing by the two statues of a World War I army soldier and navy seaman, near the entrance of the Boy Scout Hut on Ninth Avenue. (Courtesy Louis Borbi.)

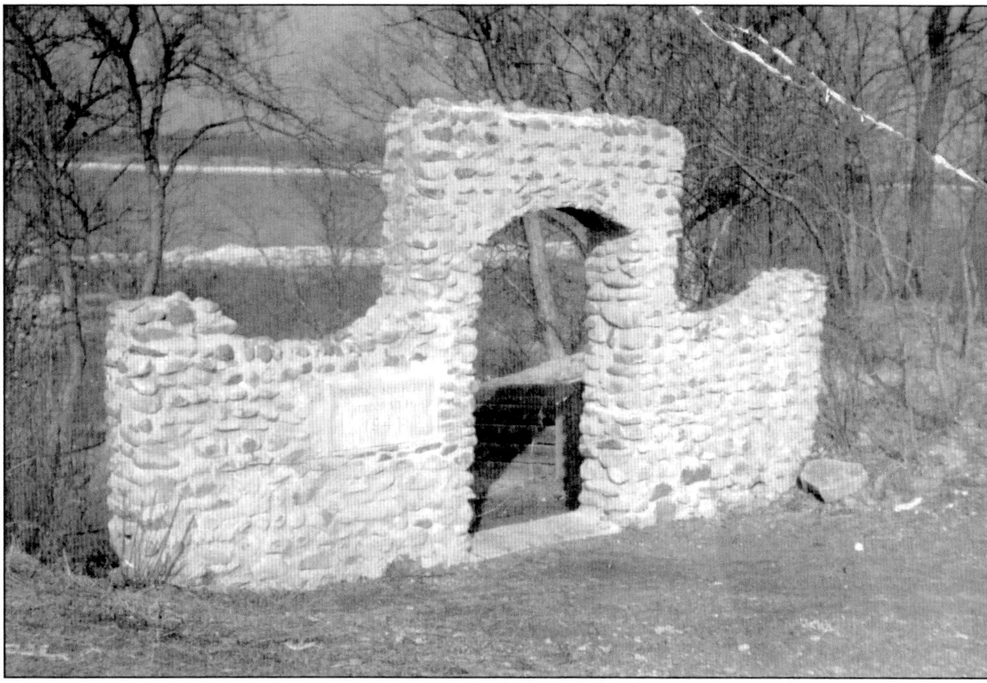

This view shows the stone entrance gate to the Boy Scout Hut in 1922. (Courtesy Louis Borbi.)

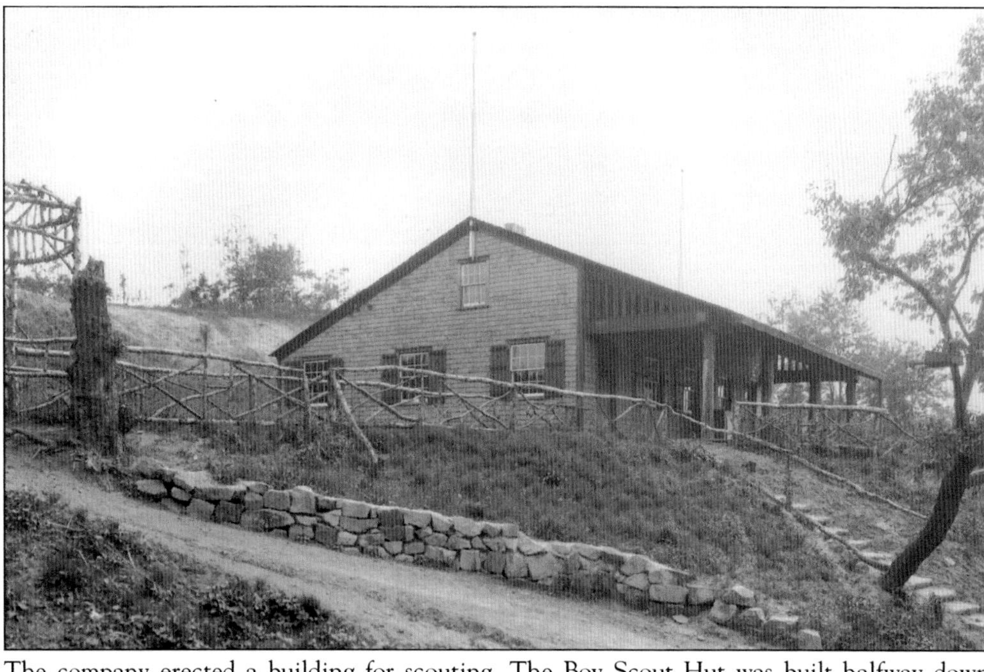

The company erected a building for scouting. The Boy Scout Hut was built halfway down an embankment on the Delaware River at the end of Ninth and Tenth Avenues. The rustic building housed a large meeting room, office, workroom, rest room with showers, and a storage room. It had a boiler room and a coal room. The company provided for all the utilities and maintenance. A trapeze, rope rings, floor mats, and sports equipment were also provided by the company. (Courtesy Louis Borbi.)

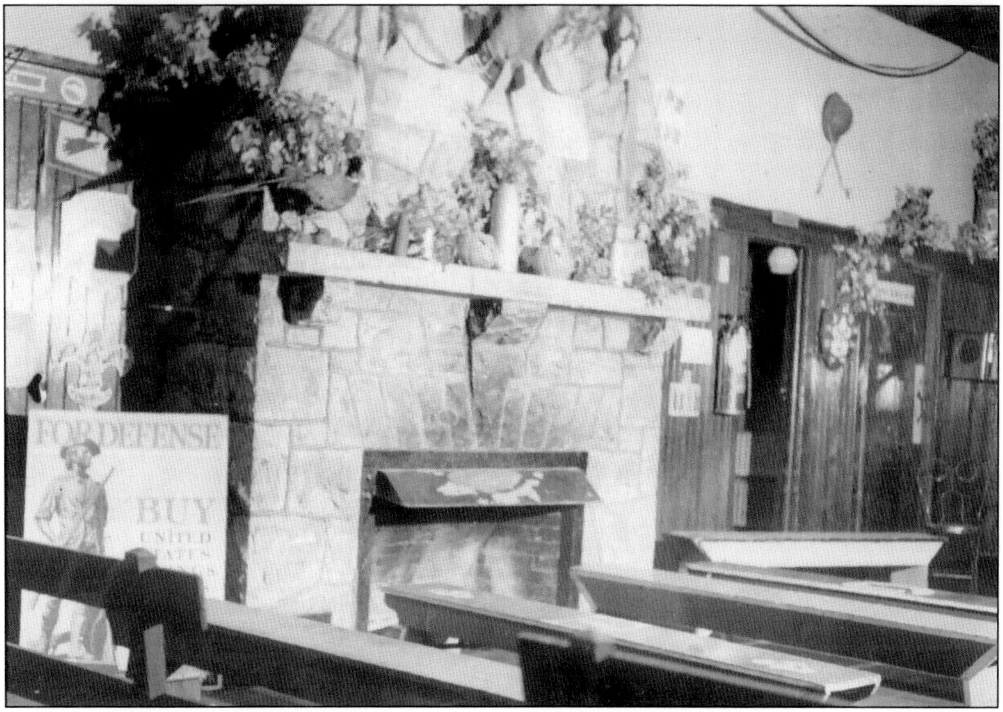

The meeting room of the Boy Scout Hut was spacious, with a large fireplace. A deer head was mounted in the center of the chimney, and the walls were decorated with scouting paraphernalia. William Thomas served as the first scoutmaster. (Courtesy Louis Borbi.)

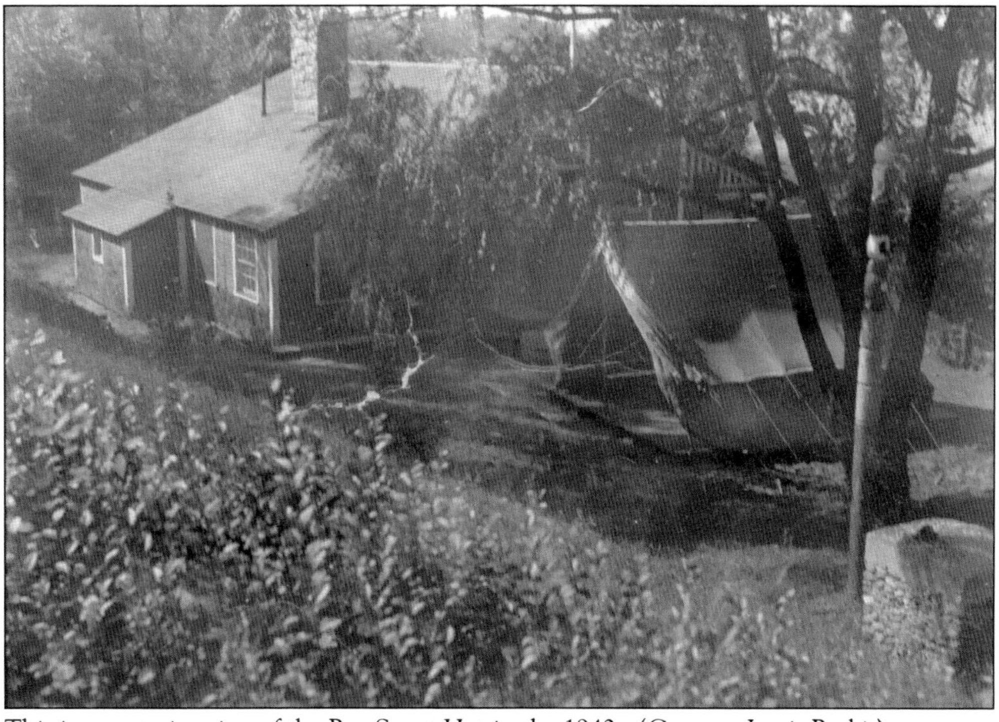

This is an exterior view of the Boy Scout Hut in the 1940s. (Courtesy Louis Borbi.)

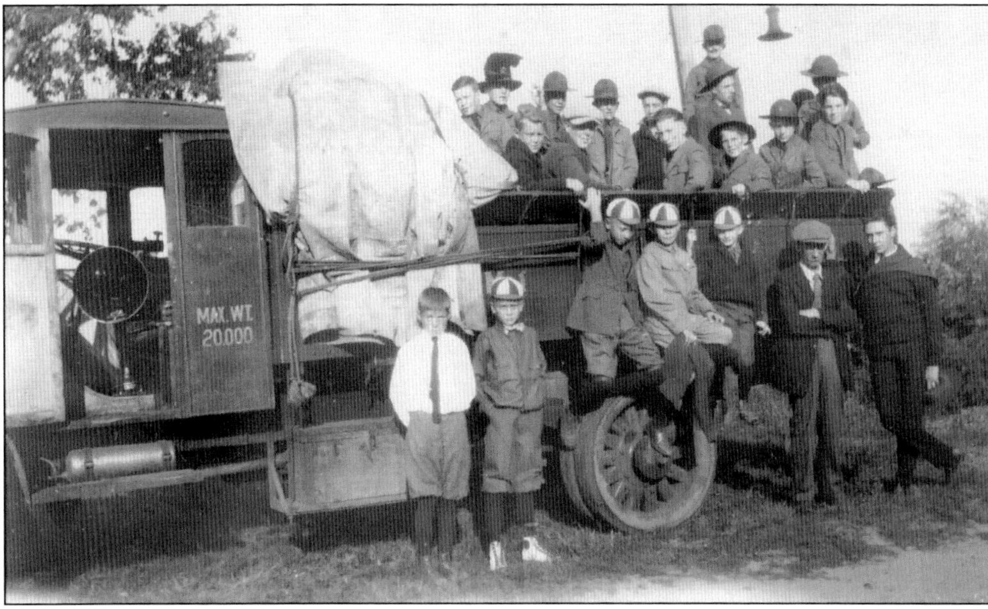

Here are some Roebling Boy Scouts ready to hit the road for camp *c.* 1926–1927. Shown from left to right are the following: (front row) Carl Morgan and William Fuhrman; (middle row) Mario Vacenta, Yebby Anderson, ? Stout, Ted Thorn, and Earl Kerr; (back row) William McGough, Harry Pierson, Earl Allen, William Milburn, Paul Allen, ? Stout, Sam Cesaretti, unidentified, unidentified, Fred Stout, Joe Saybe, Harry McClosky, and unidentified. (Courtesy Carl G. Friday.)

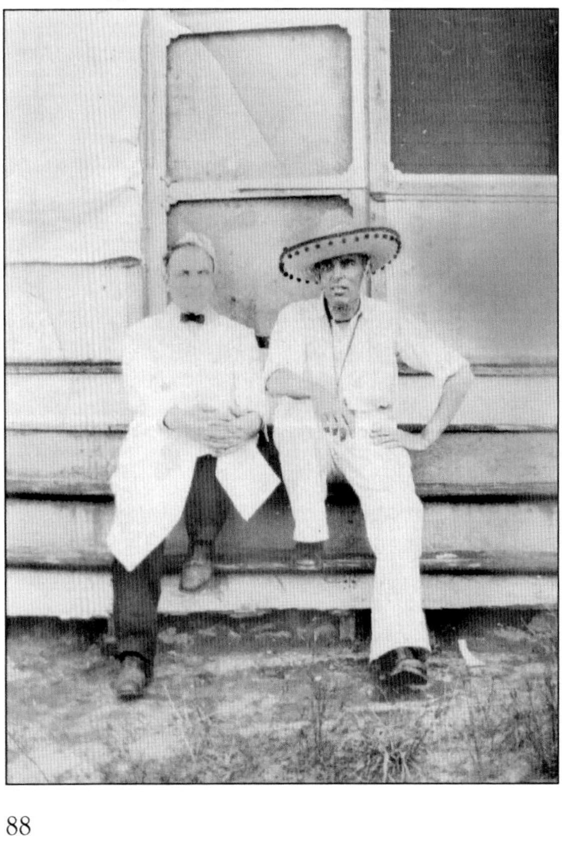

Pictured in 1926 is cook Mark Whitfield with gate guard and scoutmaster William Thomas, who was the foreman of the four-by-four billet yard. (Courtesy Carl G. Friday.)

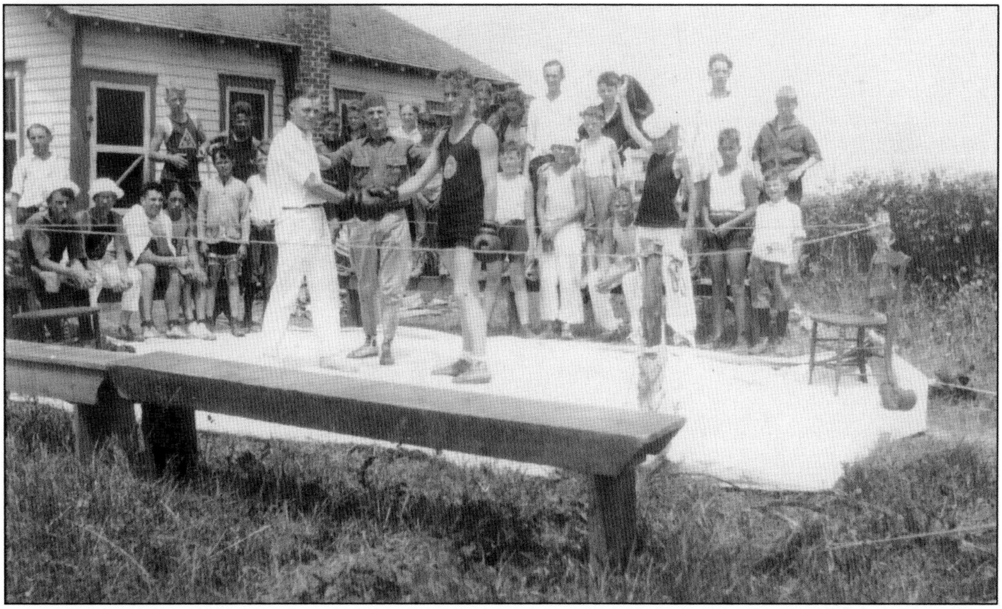

This photograph shows a 1927 boxing match between Danny Cooney and Henry Englund. Mr. Stout, the scoutmaster, was the referee. This match occurred on the Boy Scout camping trip. (Courtesy Carl G. Friday.)

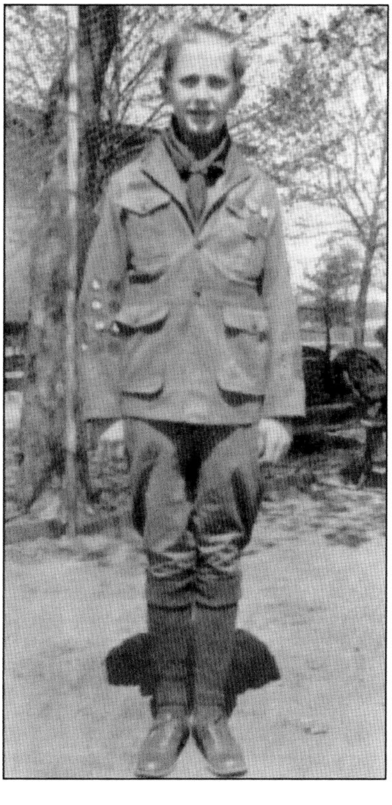

Pictured is 15-year-old Francis Ehaze, who was the honor scout in 1926. The ceremony was held at the Roebling Boy Scout Hut. Francis received the Star Scout Badge in recognition of passing 10 tests in one court of honor. Ehaze was the first scout in Troop No. 3 to receive the honor. He passed First Aid, Safety First, Civics, Pioneering, Music, Craftsmanship, Personal Health, Public Health, First Aid to Animals, Art, and Physical Development. (Courtesy Ray Thompson.)

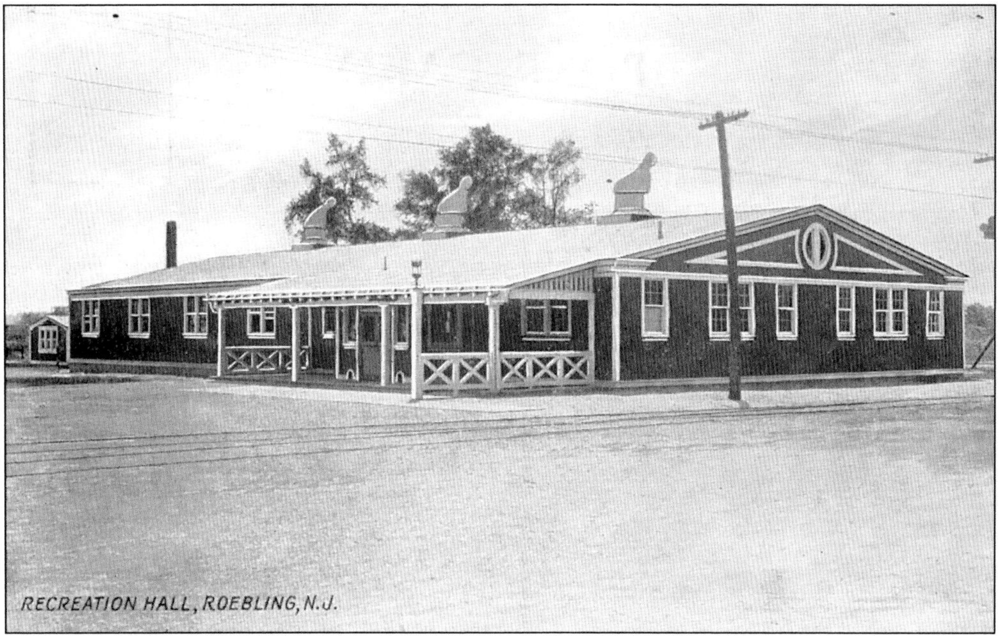

The Roebling Recreation Center was built in the early 1920s. This building contained four bowling lanes, six pool tables, and two shuffleboard tables. Young boys were paid 2¢ a game to set up the duckpins, and a game cost 15¢. There was a bar inside that served only soda and candy. The Township Library now sits on the site of the recreation center. (Courtesy Louis Borbi.)

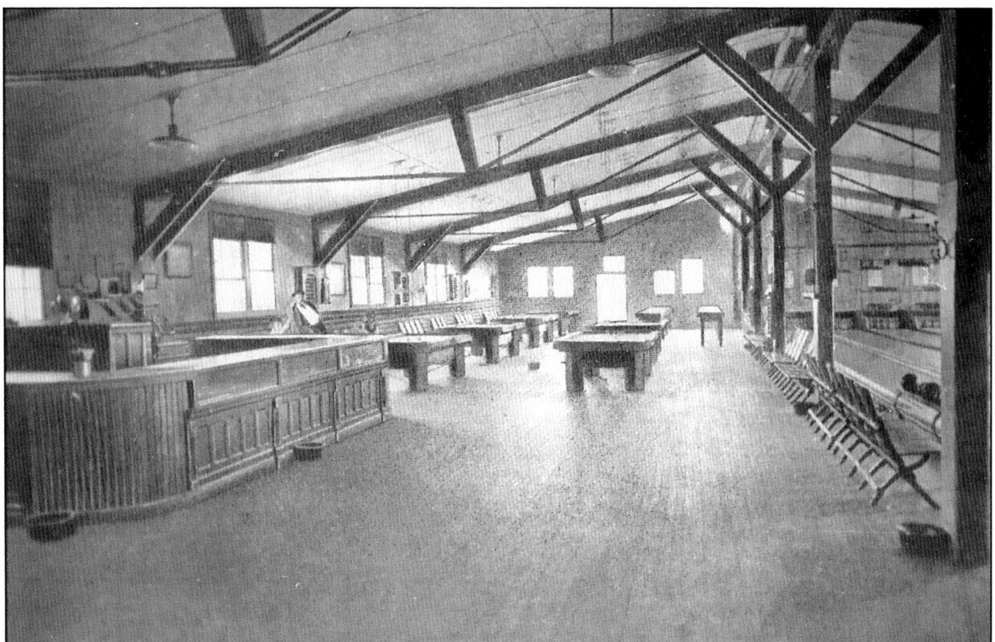

This view shows the interior of the Roebling Recreation Center. Patrons could enjoy bowling for 15¢ a game. The company built the bowling alley. Mr. Meyers was the last manager. The bar sold candy and soda. The recreation center was torn down in 1929. (Courtesy Louis Borbi.)

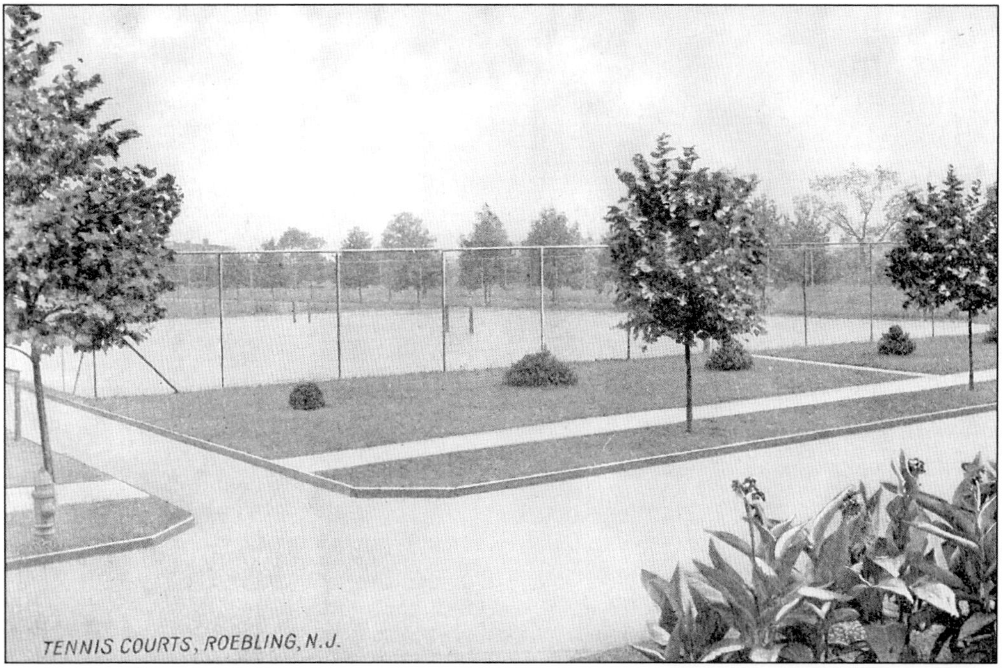

Three tennis courts were located in the village for Roebling residents. (Courtesy Louis Borbi.)

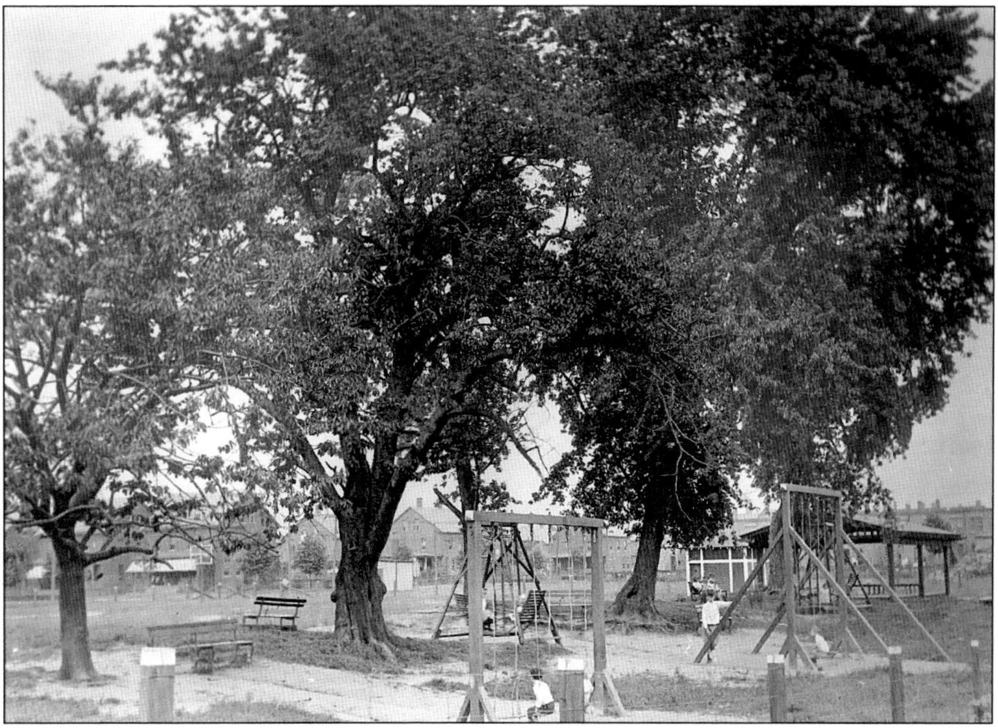
This photograph shows the playground behind the Roebling Recreation Center at Sixth and Knickerbocker Avenues before the Fifth and Sixth Avenue homes were built. This area was known as "Gypsy Town." (Courtesy Louis Borbi.)

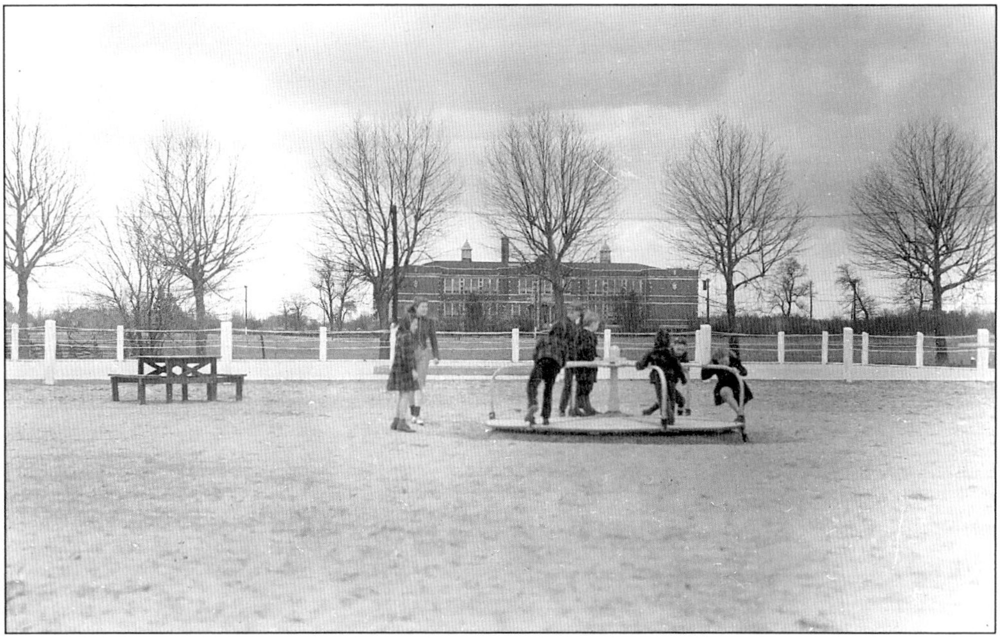

Children are at play in this *c.* 1940 photograph. In the background is the Roebling Public School. The white fence surrounded the roller-skating rink. In the winter, the rink was flooded for outdoor ice-skating. (Courtesy Louis Borbi.)

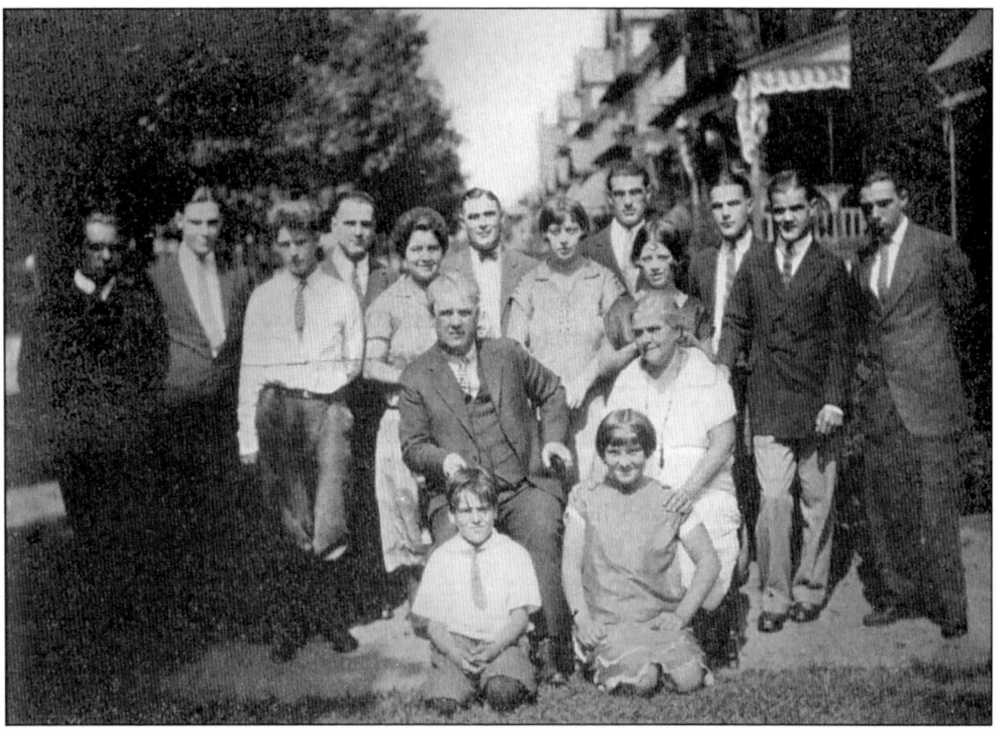

John T. Marshall, a lover of music as well as a foreman with the labor department at the mill, led the Marshall Band. The band entertained the villagers and workers from 1917 to 1988. Pictured here are Marshall, his wife, and their children. (Courtesy Carl G. Friday.)

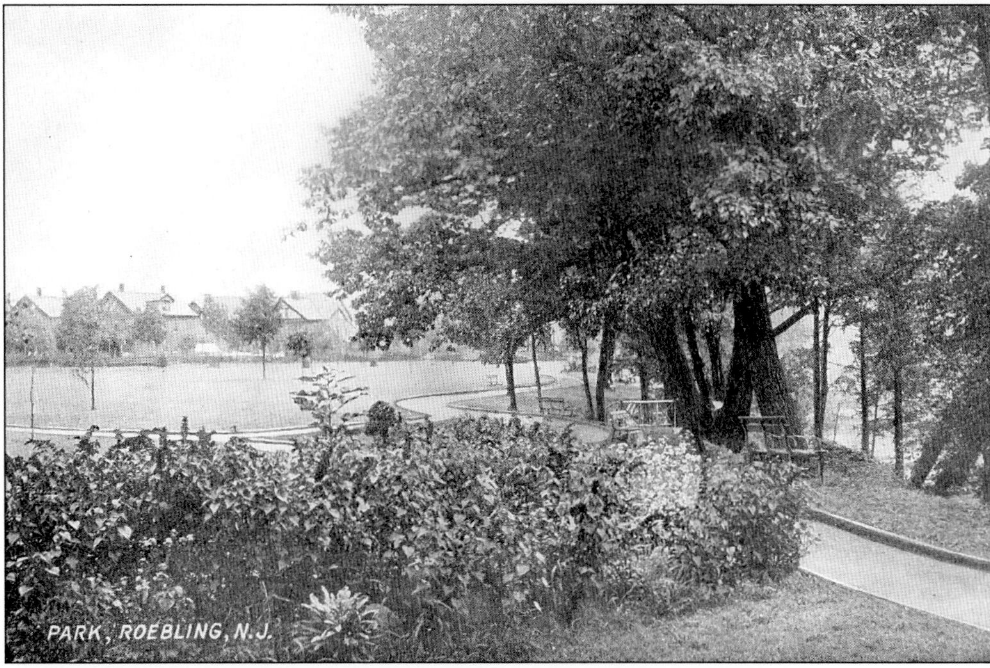

A beautiful park was located along the river in the village. It had walking paths, colorful flowers, and shade trees. The well-groomed park also had a bandstand between Fourth and Fifth Avenues. Families would come on Sundays during the summer to listen to the Marshall Band and picnic. Villagers could rest on the park benches placed along the paths, as viewed in this picture. The homes can be seen in the background. (Courtesy Louis Borbi.)

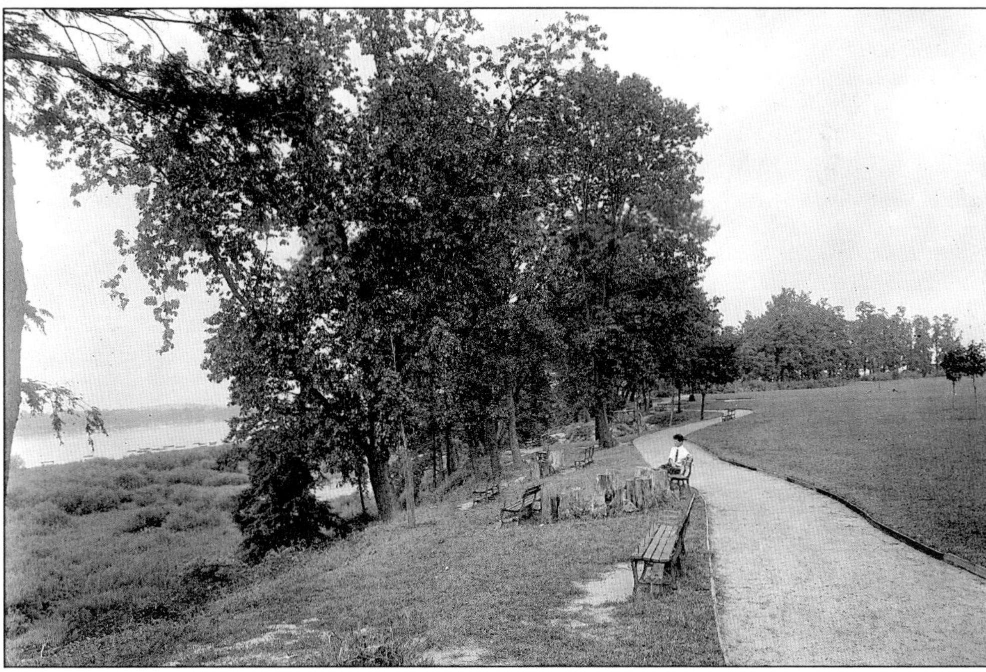

A visitor gazes at the Delaware River while relaxing on a bench in Roebling Park. (Courtesy Carol M. Shaeffer, M.D.)

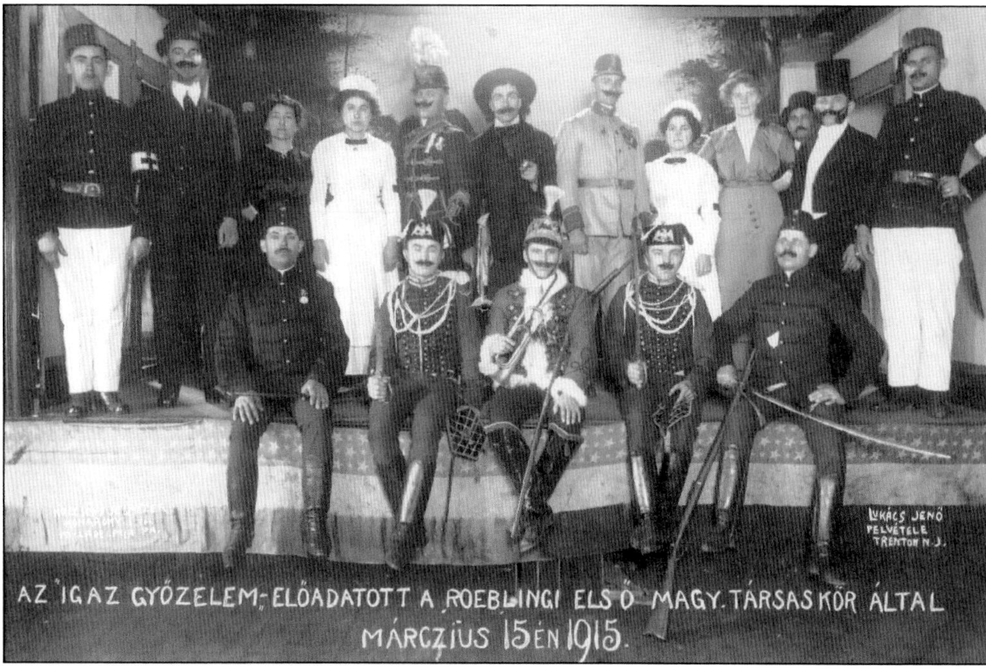

The "True Victory Performance of the March Fifteenth 1848 Independence of Hungary" was presented by the First Hungarian Players of Roebling in 1915. Some of the players are, from left to right, as follows: (front row) Andrew Furjesz (second to the left) and Joseph Halasz (fourth to the left); (back row) Mary Paykos (fourth from the left) and Paul Paykos (sixth from the left). (Courtesy Janet Paykos Griffith and Irene Paykos Maher.)

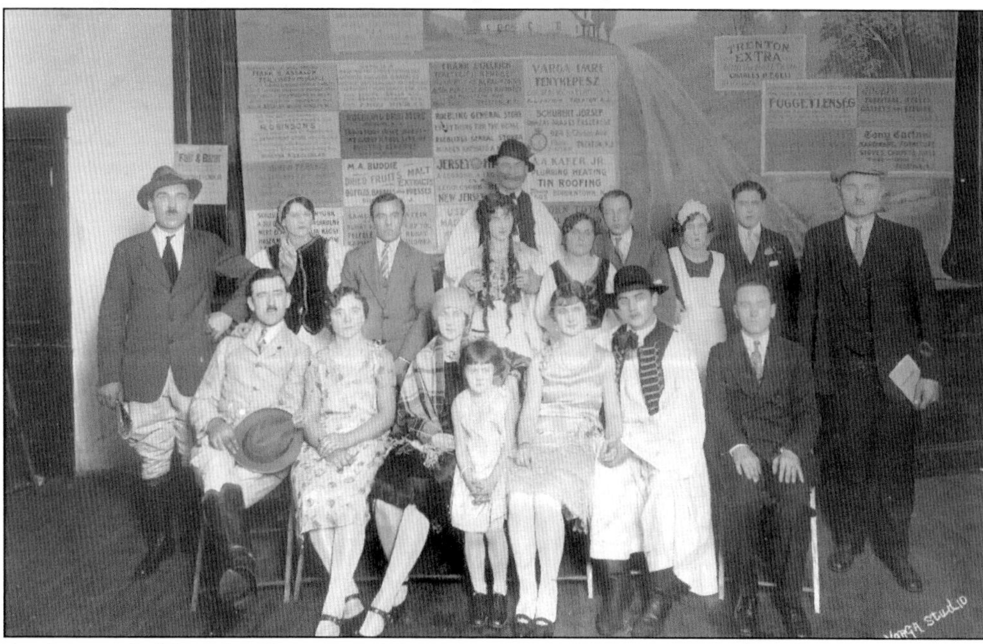

A play was held at the Hungarian Home on November 29, 1928. The play was entitled *A Paraszt Kisazony* or the *Little Peasant Women*. Local business advertisements are pictured on the backdrop. (Courtesy Hungarian Reformed Church.)

Seven

Life in Roebling

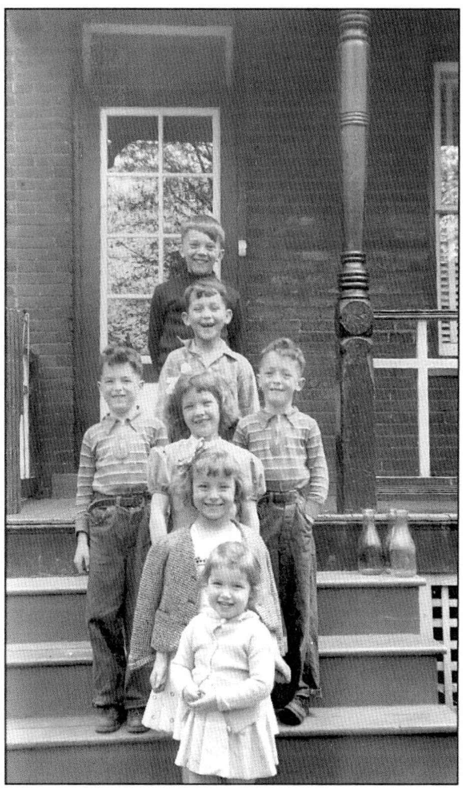

This 1948 photograph shows children in Roebling on the steps of a Third Avenue home. They are, from front to back, as follows: Louise Borbi, Loretta Borbi, MaryAnn Borbi, twins Michael and Louis Bunnick, George Lengel, and John L. Borbi. (Courtesy Louis Borbi.)

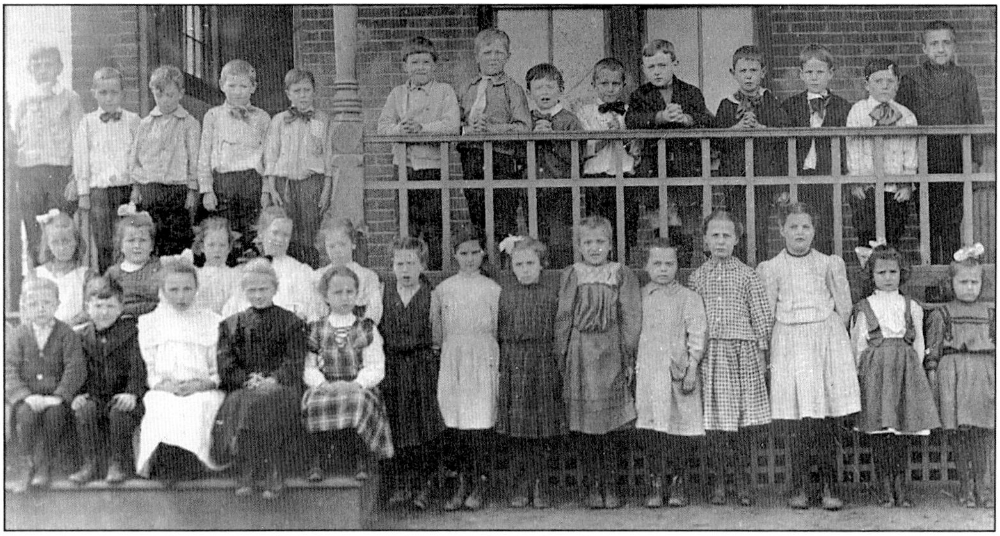

This photograph shows the first- and second-grade classes in 1908. They are, from left to right, as follows: (front row) Francis Cunningham, Jimmy Yeager, Bill Major, unidentified, ? Abele, and Mabel Daline; (middle row) unidentified, Theresa Koberg, Anna Errickson, Kathy Errickson, unidentified, Eva English, Madeline Lucas, Mabel Griffin, unidentified, Idamay Hull, ? Kovacs, Elsie Lucas, Ida Jones, and Viola Claus; (back row) James Sackly, Bill Craft, unidentified, Charles Finlayson, Paul Anderson, unidentified, Mike Kovacs, Russell Schaeffer, Austin Craft, unidentified, unidentified, Helmer Borgston, ? Kelly, and unidentified. This school was located at 159 Third Avenue. (Courtesy Louis Borbi.)

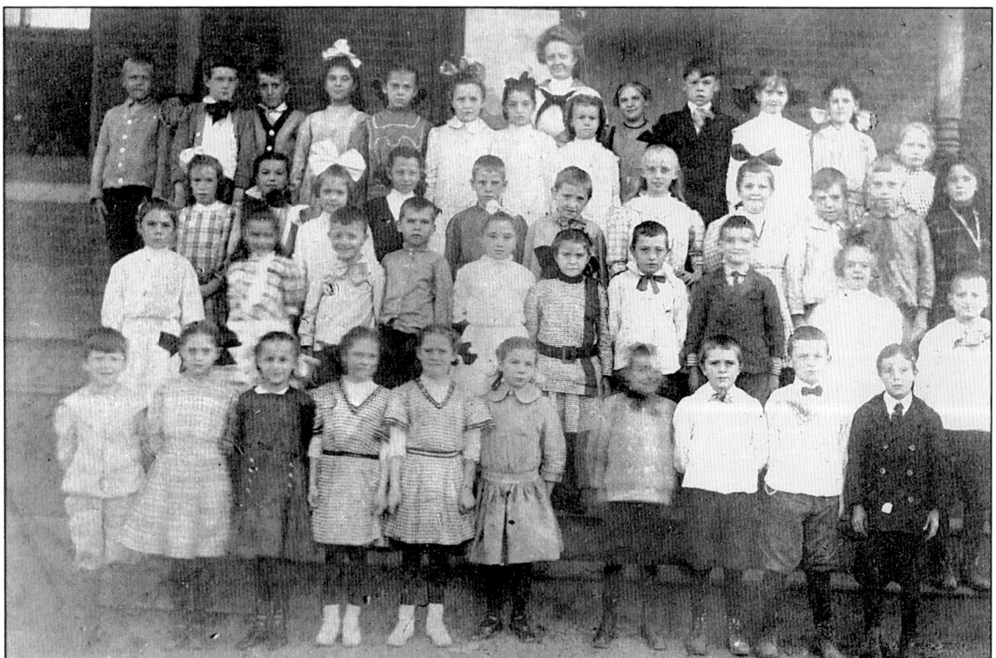

This 1911 picture of Miss McKenzie's third-grade class was taken at the Roebling Public School, located on Fourth Avenue. McKenzie came from Trenton, New Jersey, each day by train to teach the children. (Courtesy Louis Borbi.)

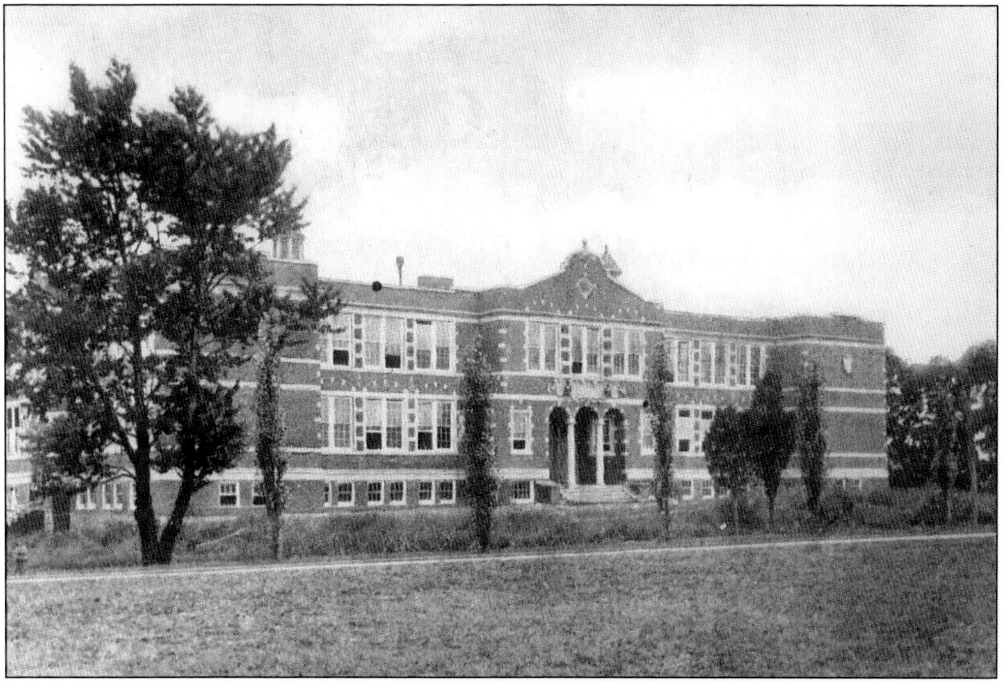

Prior to the construction of a public school, the John A. Roebling's Sons Company conducted a private school for the children in the Fourth Avenue Boarding House. This school was taken over by the Florence Board of Education in 1913 and later moved to the new Roebling School. This school was constructed in 1914 and had its addition put on in 1924. It was considered the largest school building in Burlington County at that time. (Courtesy Louis Borbi, Joseph D. Zahorsky, and Donna Orfe.)

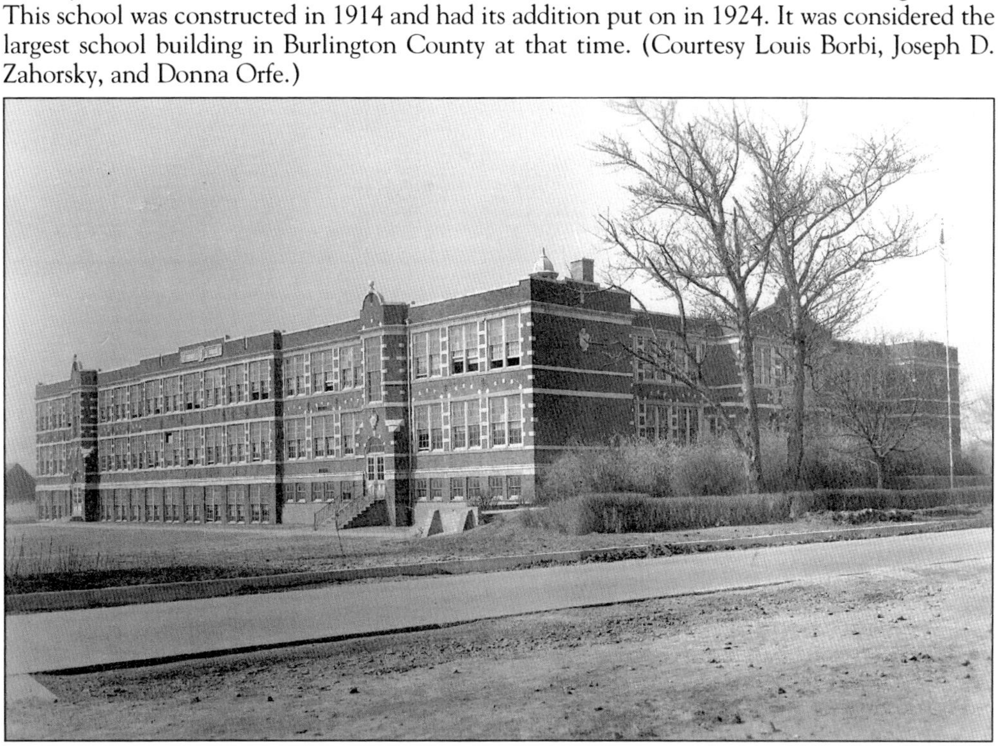

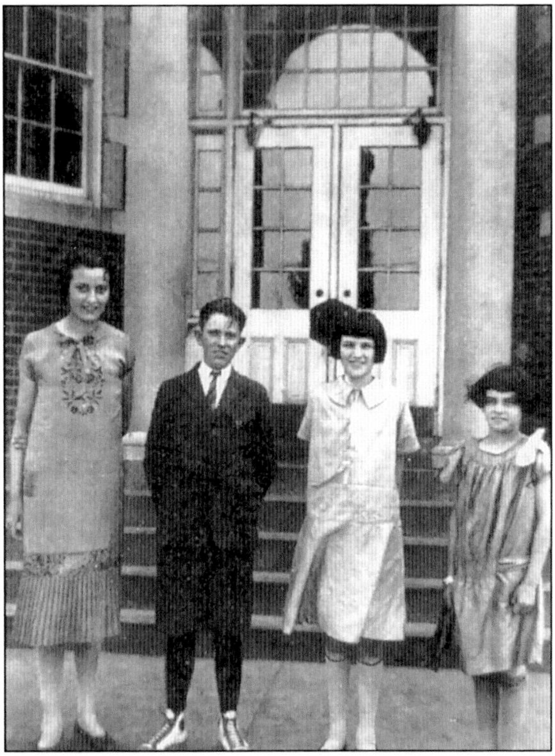

A "Better Teeth Contest" was held in 1926 at the Roebling Public School, with 900 children participating. Helen Sunavecz, on the left, possesses the best teeth. The others are, from left to right, Eugene Dorr, Alice Piggot, and Virginia Wharton. Each of the winners, together with principal Ada L. Daniels, received a Schaeffer fountain pen—gifts from Dr. Dickinson and Dr. Reisinger. (Courtesy Louis Borbi.)

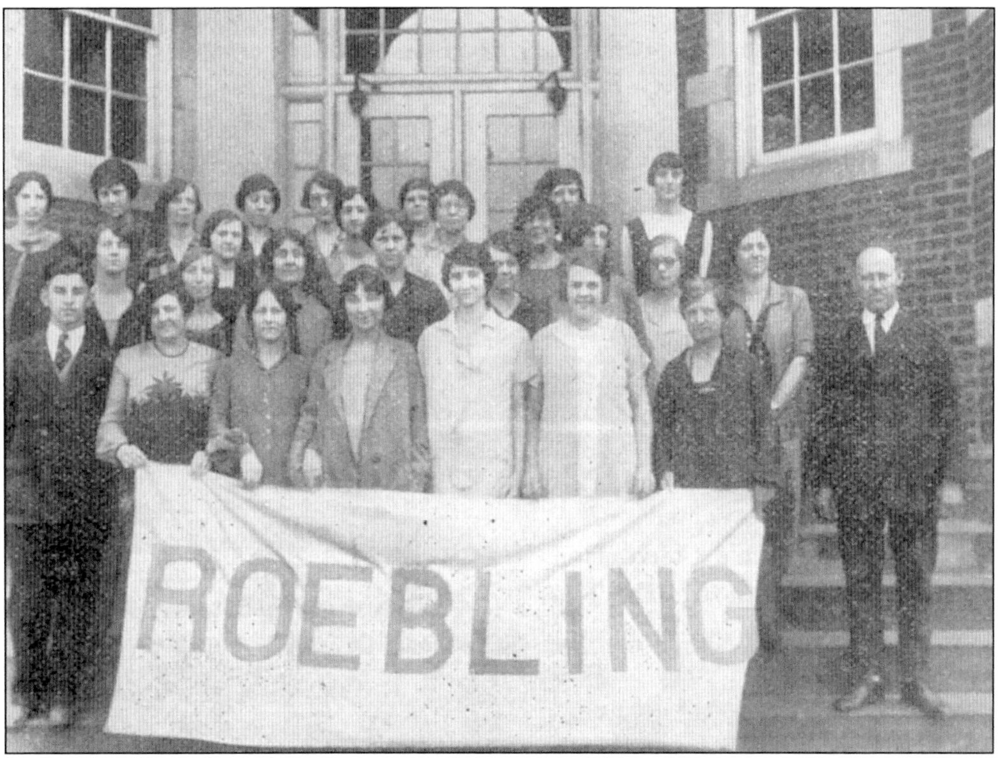

Pictured in 1926 is the faculty of the Roebling Public School. (Courtesy Ray Thompson.)

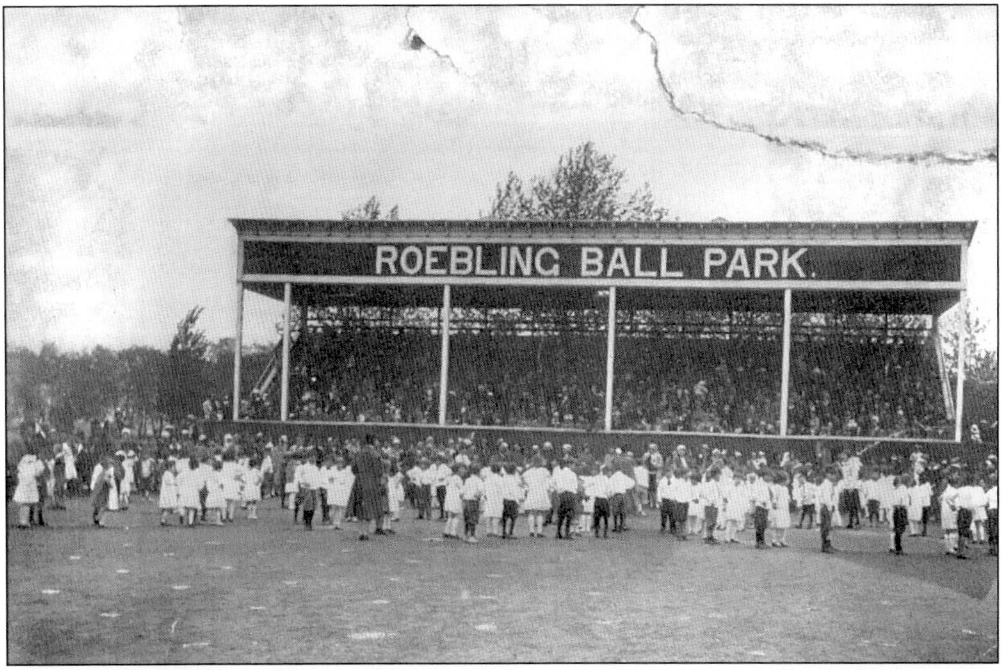

The "Sandal Polka" was given by the second-graders of Florence Township Public Schools at the annual field day exercises held in the Roebling Ball Park in 1927. (Courtesy Louis Borbi.)

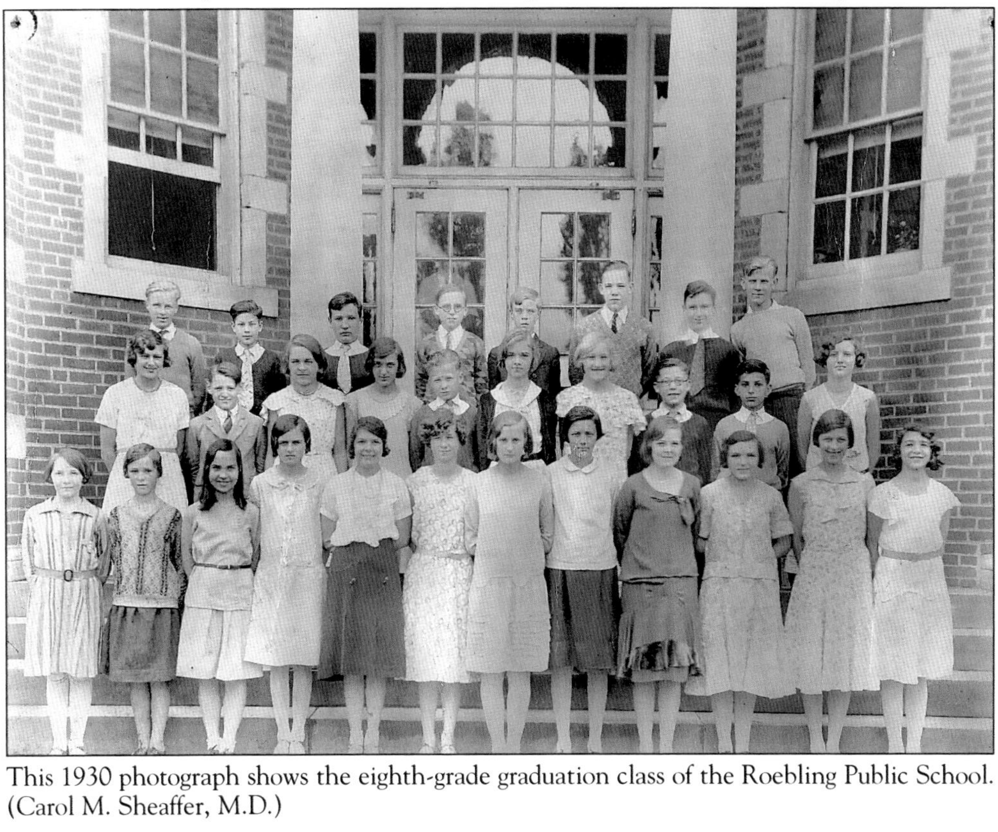

This 1930 photograph shows the eighth-grade graduation class of the Roebling Public School. (Carol M. Sheaffer, M.D.)

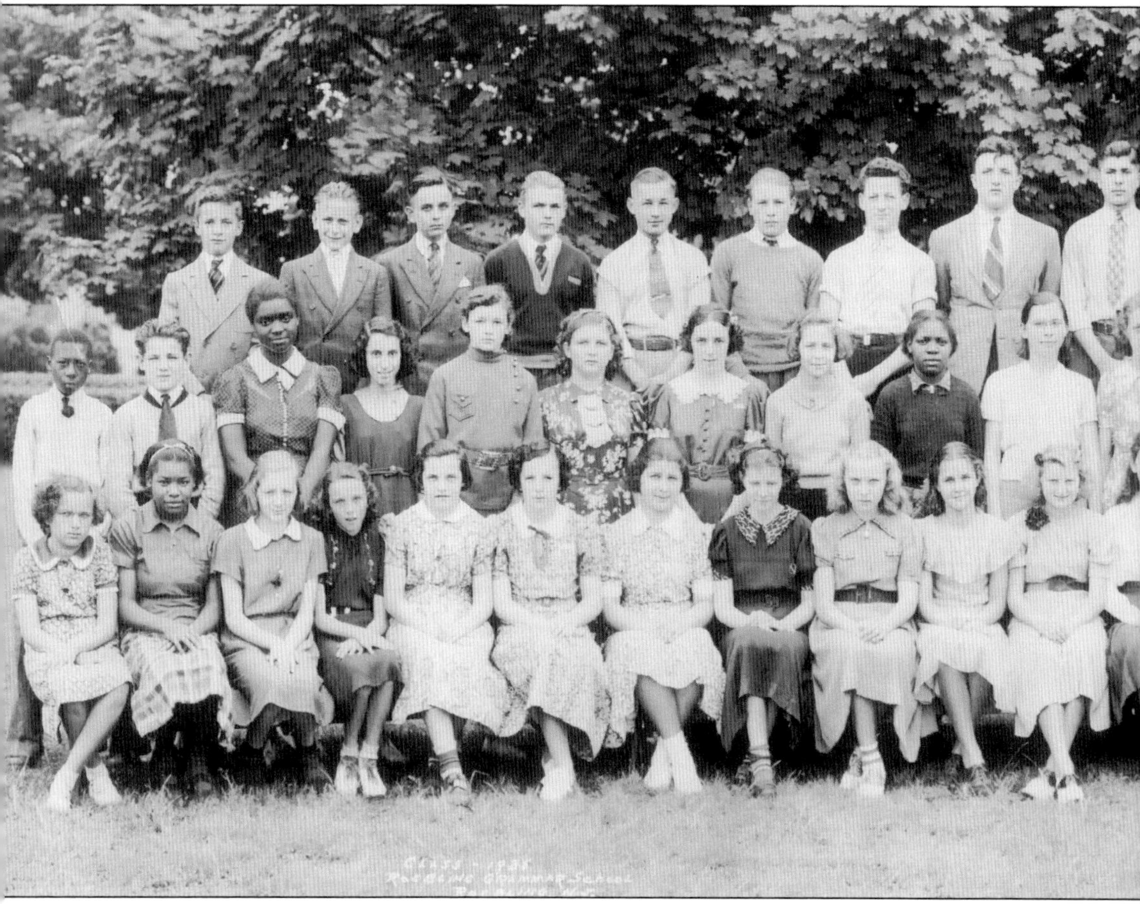

The 1938 eighth-grade class is shown at the Roebling Public School. They are, from left to right, as follows: (front row) Agnes Fererci, Louise O'Neil, Lillian Matlack, Dorothy Thomas, Emma Mocan, Clara Shinn, Helen Zitnick, Eleanor Carlson, Pauline Kitson, Edna Kern, Grace Nagy, Mary Finch, Betty Bago, Margaret Hathazi, Ana Shoriak, Anna Masiko, Doris Dobbins, Irene Simonka, Julia Chorba, Margaret Andrako, Dorothy Dzwryachk, Mildred Austin, Catherine Martin, and Clare Cantwell; (middle row)Edward Scott, William Schaum, Rosaline Taylor, Shirley Bintliff, Stephanie Waing, Jean Wilson, Eileen Cantwell, Dorothy Birgl, Louis

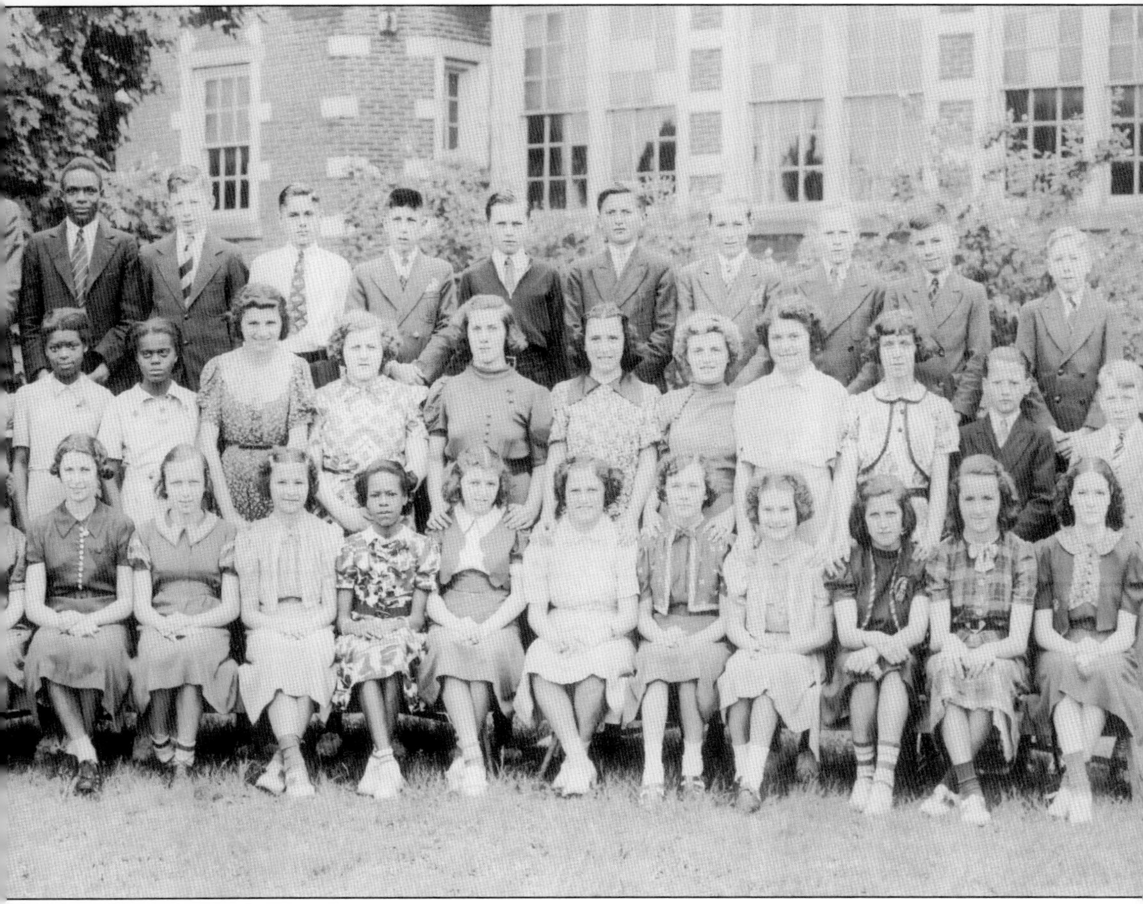

Richerson, Margaret Szathmary, Betty Ford, Lu Lu Boone, Ethel Taylor, Marita Perkins, Viola Blake, Isabel Orban, Alice Archibald, Betty Bintliff, Sylvia Morisi, Martha Malmas, Jenney Anikowski, Emeric Karpac, and George Swanberg; (back row) Lawrence Kern, Michael Buddie, Michael Pustie, John Halasz, Louis Hadaric, John Moller, Edward Cesaretti, George Lang, Julius Nemeth, Winfield Scott, William Alexander, Arthur Hartzell, John Timko, Joseph Cuicla, George Zaharchuk, Michael Pustay, Raymond Danley, Walter Jones Jr., Louis Kocsis, and Ralph Shuler. (Courtesy Ellen Suydam Scott.)

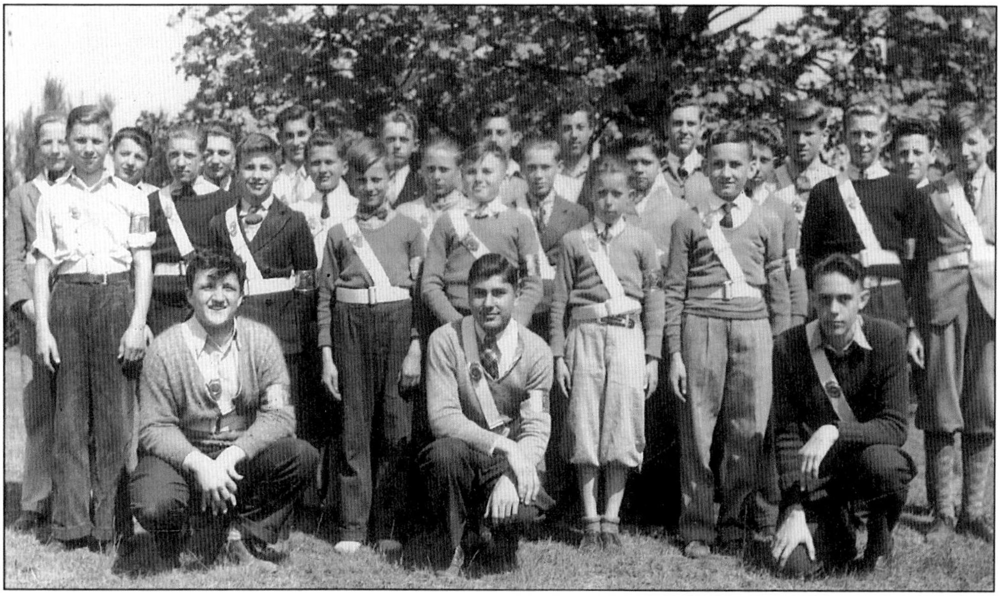

The patrol boys of the Roebling Public School are seen here on May 8, 1938. The boys were assigned to each street crossing to insure the safety of the Roebling schoolchildren on their way to and from school. (Courtesy Mary Arnold Montalto.)

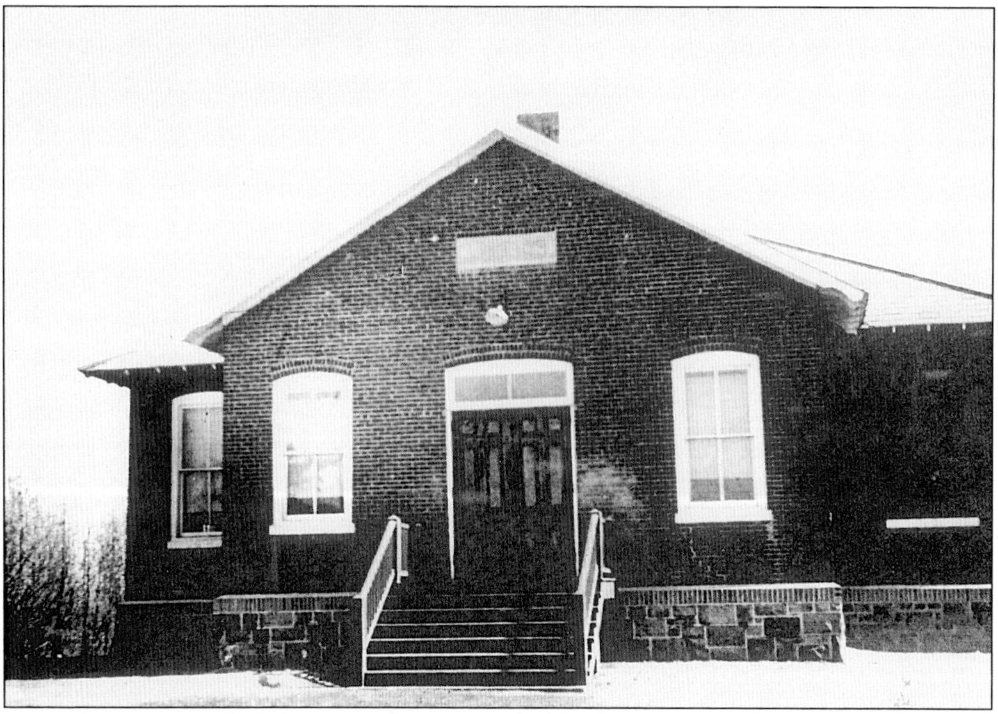

Located on Route 25 (now Route 130), just outside the village of Roebling in a region known as Florence Station, was this school for black students. During the 1920s and 1930s, black students from Roebling and surrounding areas attended this two-room brick building from grades one through six. Teachers at this school included Mary V. Mason, Marion E. Morris, and Wilbur L. Henry. (Courtesy William Alexander.)

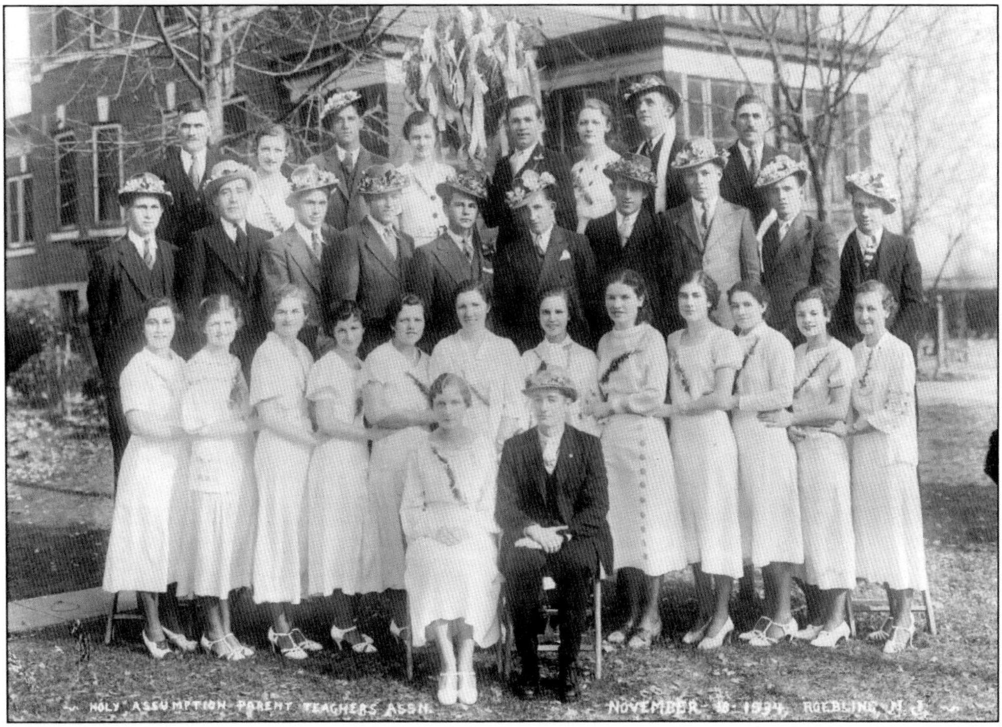

This photograph shows members of the Holy Assumption Parent-Teacher Association (PTA) celebrating on November 18, 1934. (Courtesy Louis Borbi.)

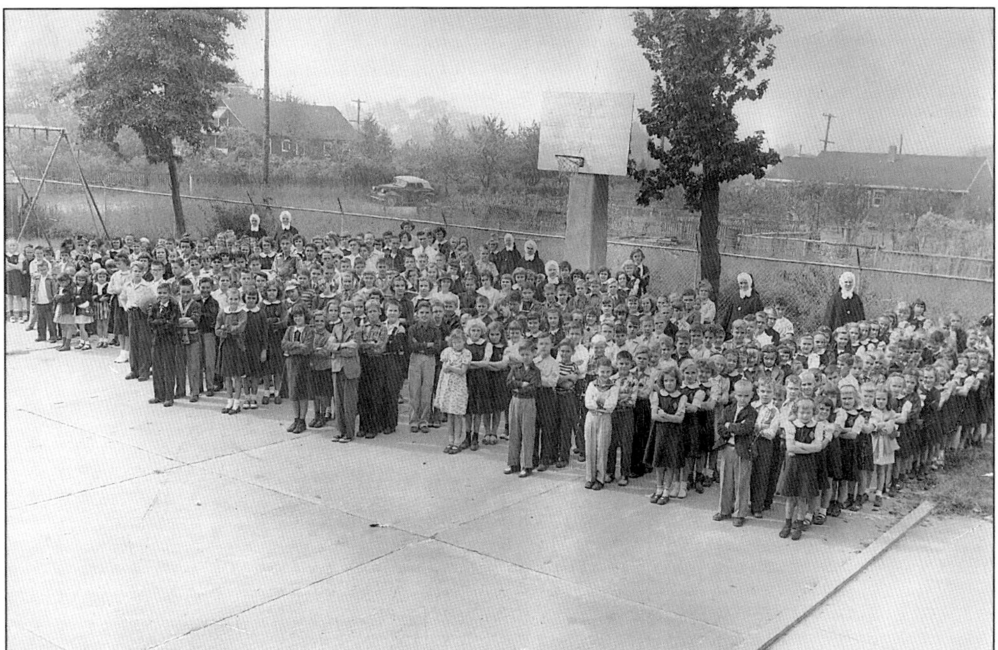

The Holy Assumption School opened in September 1923 with four classrooms in the basement of the church. When this photograph was taken in 1952, there were 320 students enrolled in the school. (Courtesy Joseph D. Zahorsky and Donna Orfe.)

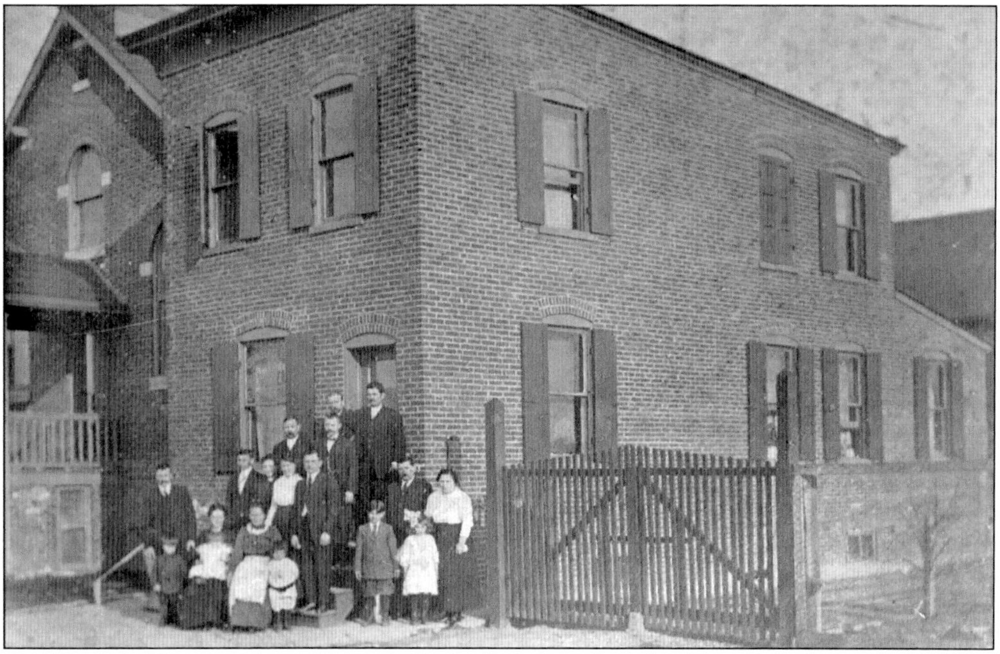

Charles Paul Egeli came to Roebling in 1905. He worked for the John A. Roebling's Sons Company until 1919. He started his own milk business in the house he built at 188 Alden Avenue. He received his raw milk from Hedding in 40-quart cans and placed them in his cellar, where they were kept cool with ice purchased from Mr. Carty of Fieldsboro. The villagers could come to his house with pitchers to be filled or have milk delivered by Mr. Egeli and his horse named Harry. (Courtesy Louis Borbi.)

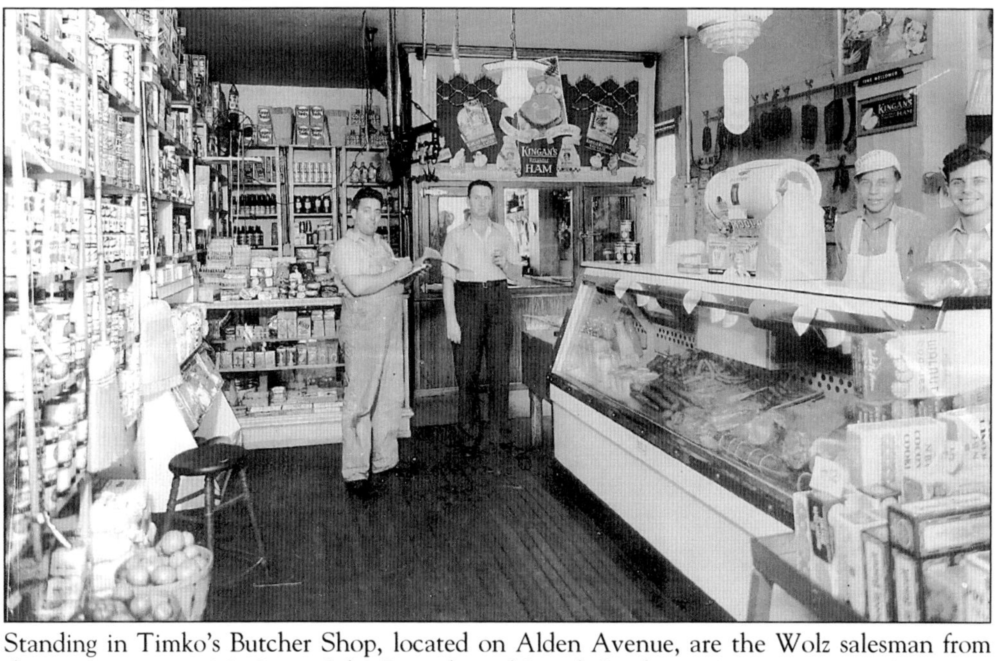

Standing in Timko's Butcher Shop, located on Alden Avenue, are the Wolz salesman from the meat company, Mr. Petro, John Rusnak, and Joseph Bordas on August 9, 1939. (Courtesy MaryAnn Bordas Bunnick.)

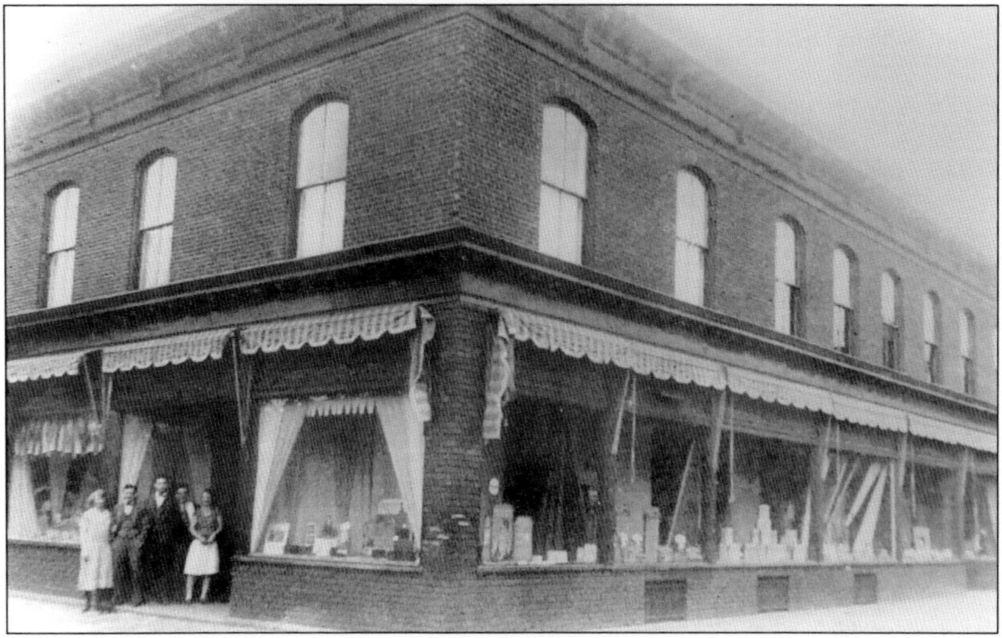

The Roebling Drugstore is shown in 1927. Mr. E. Mount was in charge. Pictured from left to right are Pearl Dobbs, Charles R. Grammer, Samuel Deszy, Peter Butchon, and Violet O'Donnell. (Courtesy Louis Borbi.)

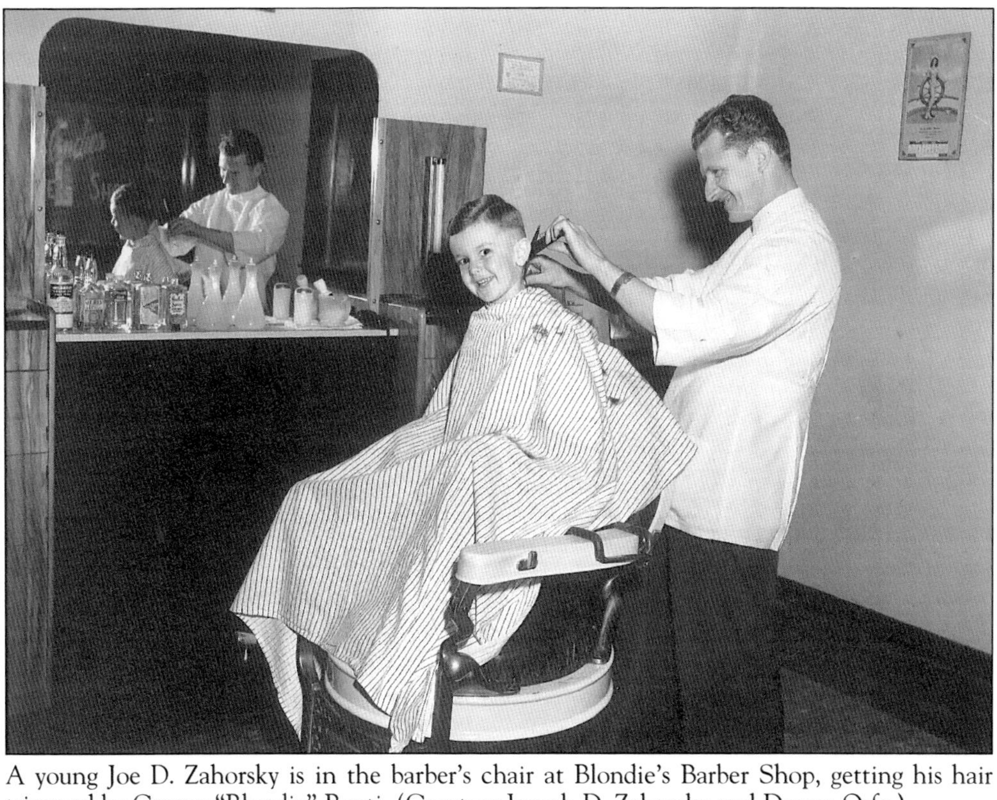

A young Joe D. Zahorsky is in the barber's chair at Blondie's Barber Shop, getting his hair trimmed by George "Blondie" Benti. (Courtesy Joseph D. Zahorsky and Donna Orfe.)

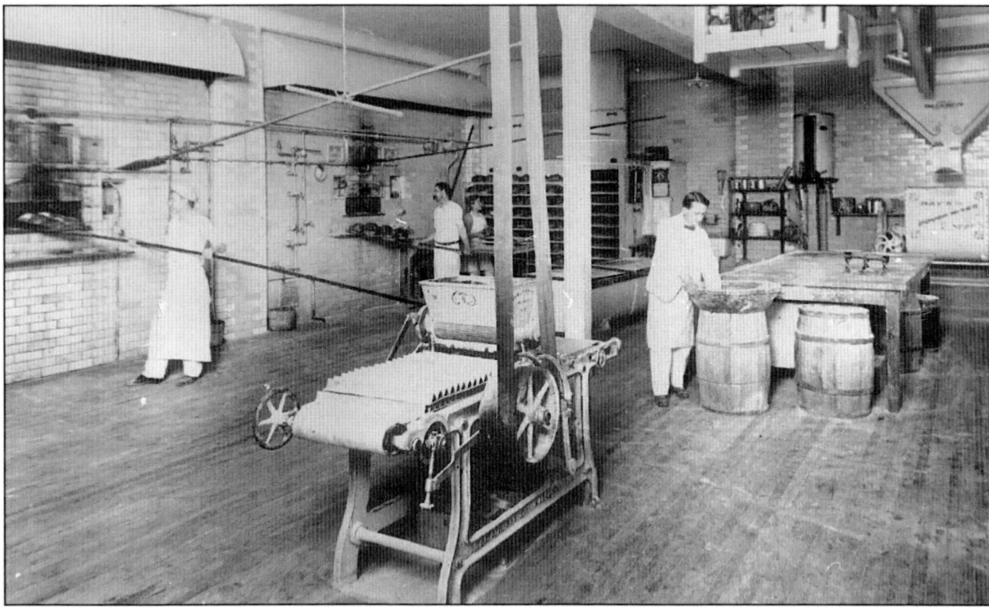

This view shows the interior of bakery in the Roebling General Store. The baking department was run by Charles Moser of 40 Fourth Avenue and was therefore known in the village as "Moser's Bakery." Moser had orders from the Roebling family to "bake the best bread you can, with the least profit for the company." They always used the best flour and butter. The bakery closed in the general store on August 6, 1926. (Courtesy Louis Borbi.)

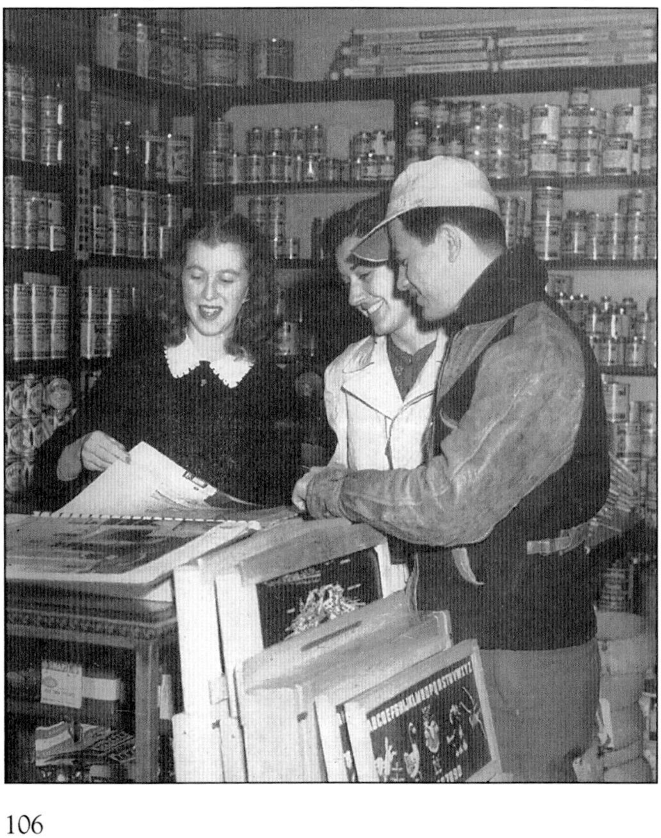

On January 2, 1930, the Roeblings turned the grocery and meat departments over to the Great Atlantic & Pacific Tea Company (A & P). On February 28, 1947, the Roeblings sold the Roebling General Store to a local corporation headed by H. Russel Brown, Theodore Zotta, and Herbert D. Rathburn. Pictured here is salesclerk Mary Arnold assisting newlyweds Harold and Jean Miller in selecting paint for their recently purchased home in Roebling. The store continued to operate until 1959. (Courtesy Mary Arnold Montalto; *Roebling* magazine, January 1948.)

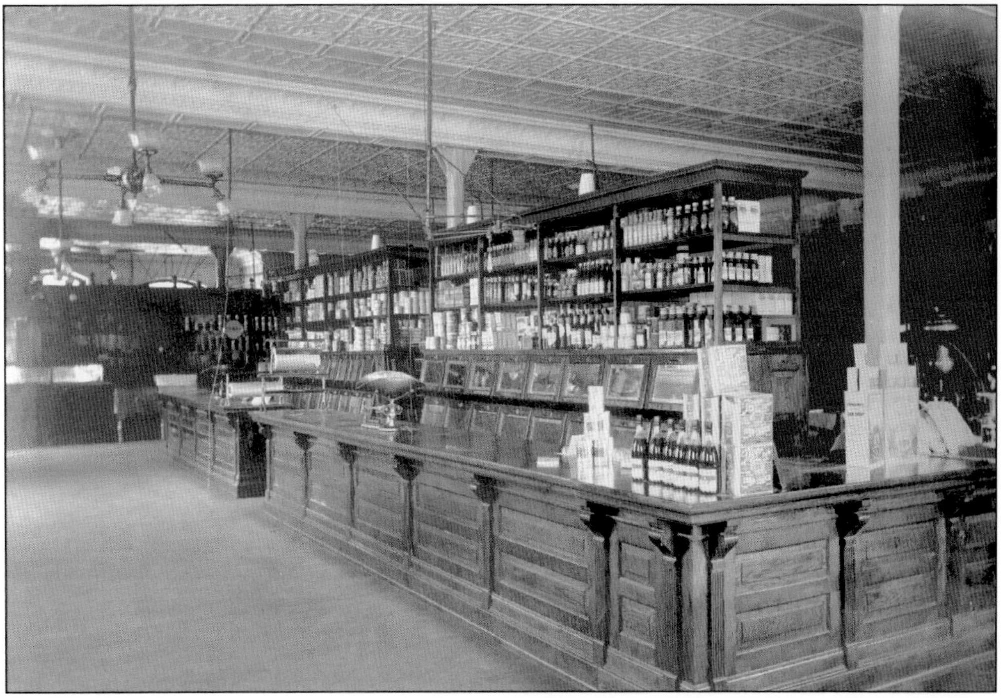

This is an interior view of the Roebling General Store. The store boasted of a complete line of goods. The first floor, pictured here, consisted of a large grocery store with butcher and bakery department. The second floor displayed kitchen supplies, dry goods, and furniture. The general store's motto was "We got It—We Will Get It—Or It's Not To Be Had." The store utilized one of the first Otis elevators using Blue Center cable. The elevator is still in use today. (Courtesy Carol M. Sheaffer, M.D.)

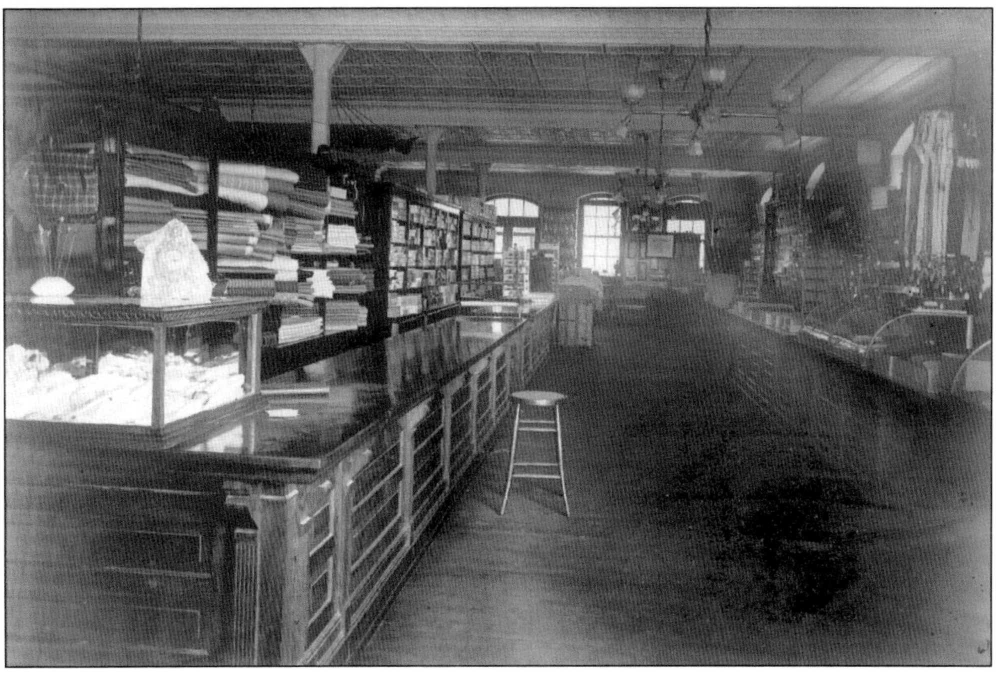

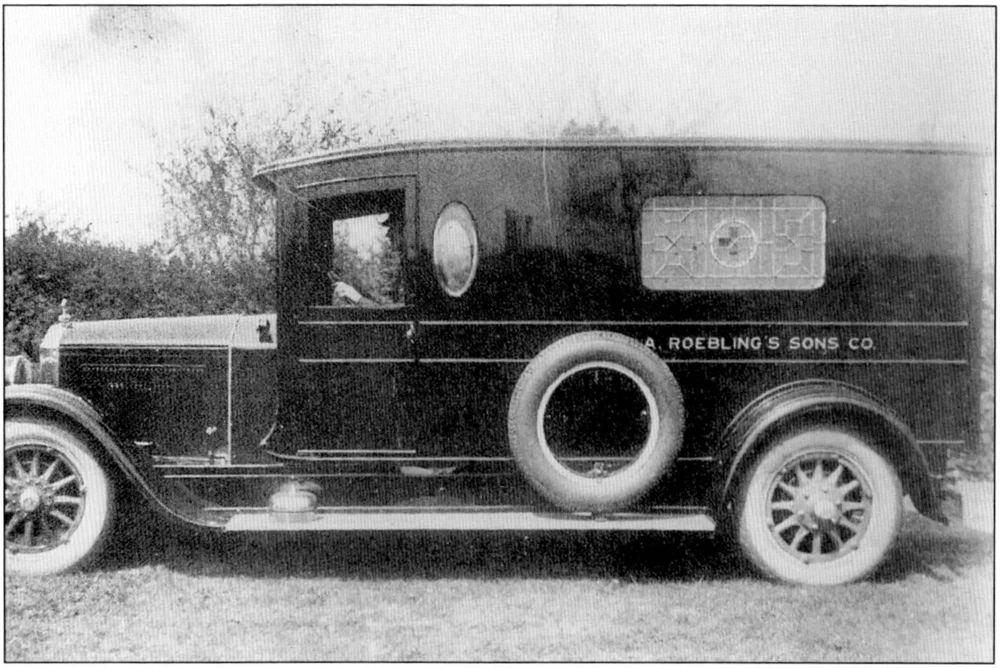

This ambulance was purchased by the John A. Roebling's Sons Company. It was stated that "although it is hoped that there will not be any occasion for using same in connection with accidents occurring in the mills, however, in case of serious accident or emergency cases it affords a safe and comfortable means of transportation." (Courtesy Louis Borbi.)

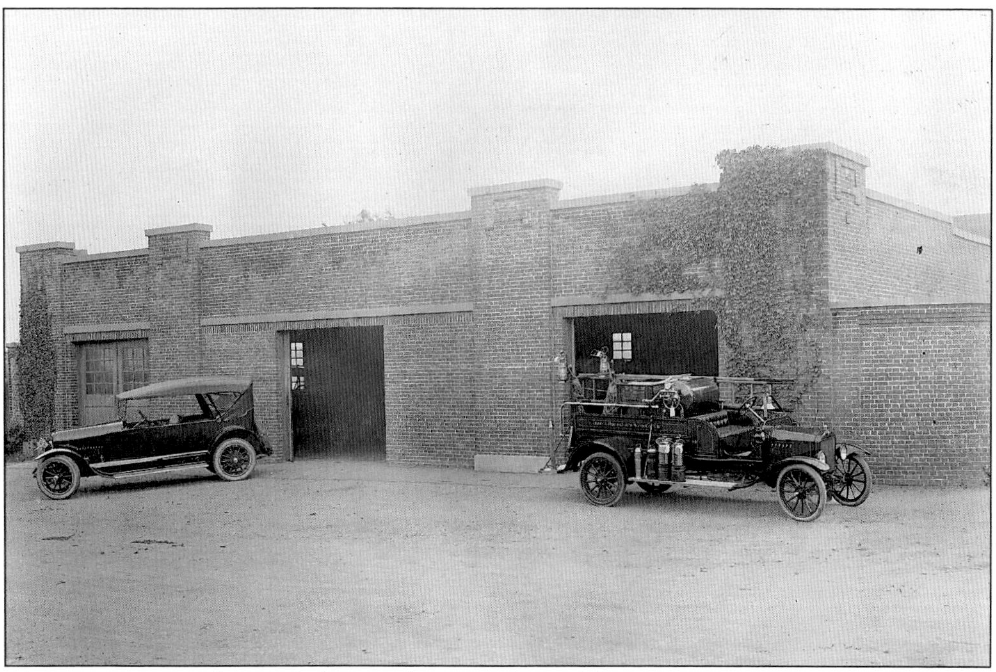

This garage, pictured in 1923, became home to the Roebling Rescue Squad in 1949. (Courtesy Carol M. Scheaffer, M.D.)

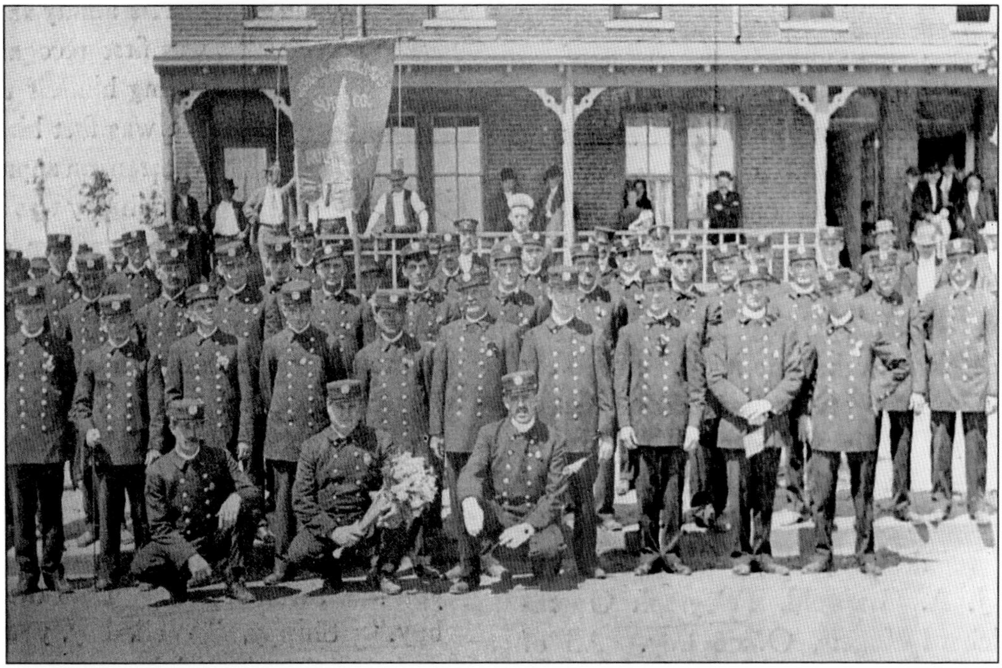

This photograph shows the Roebling Volunteer Fire Company No. 1 in front of 159 Third Avenue. Members are, from left to right, as follows: (front row, stooping) H. Ranier, Chief M. Madden and Assistant Chief E. Divine; (middle row) G. Holm, C. Moser, C. Snyder, W. Morris, W. Murphy, J.D. Hoffner, G. Ledger, J. McGrath, F. Smeltzeisen, and M. McGrath; (back row, on sidewalk) B. Connoly, M. Schaffer, H. Price, G. Mirick, J.J. Frazier, C. Strick, T. Callery, T. Lucas, A. Wharton, J. Czak, J. Fisher, W. Mirick, L. Murphy, C. Dennis, C. Gallagher, O. Swanson, W. Hoffner, G. Jones, F. Earley, T. McGrillis, T.J. Barrett, P. Murray, D. Frazier, W. Miller, W. Williams, M. Woodward, and G. Carr. (Courtesy Louis Borbi.)

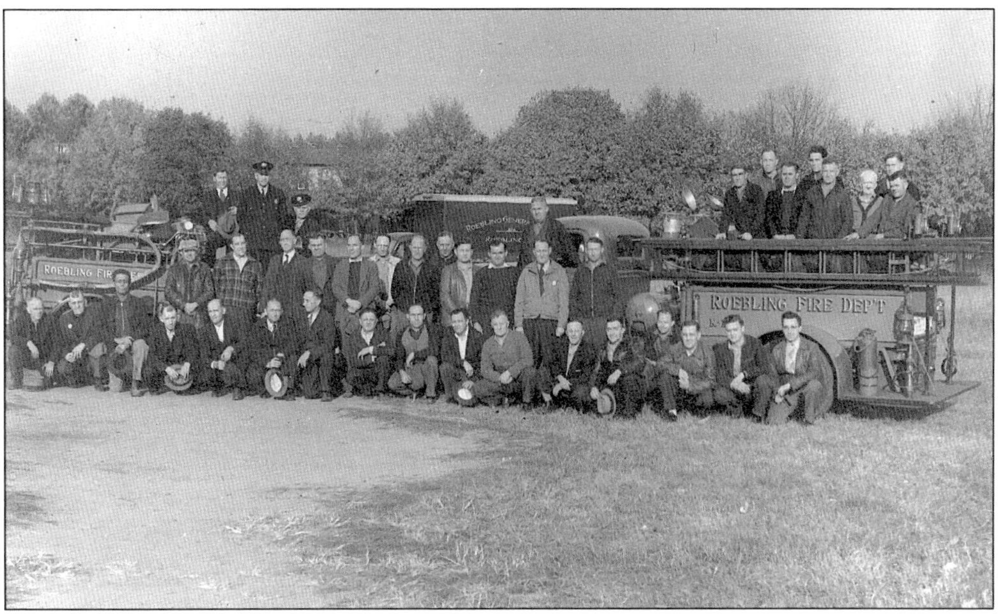

Seen here are the members of the Roebling Fire Department in 1946. (Courtesy Louis Borbi.)

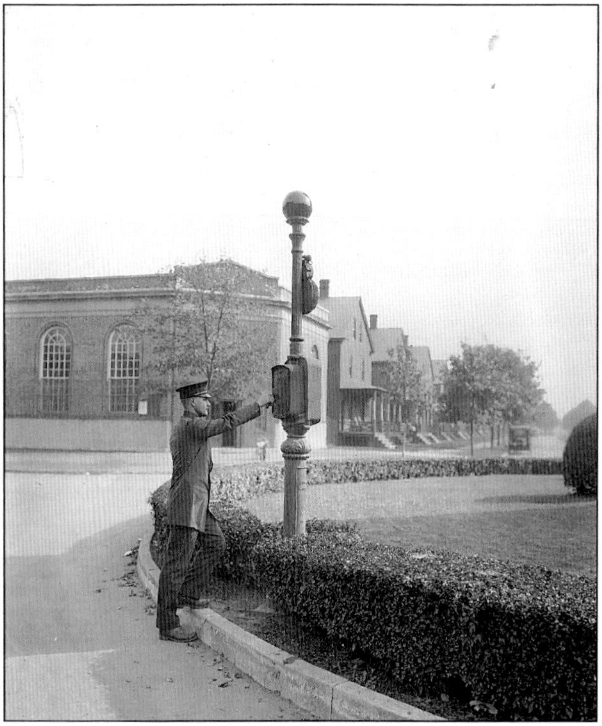

A Roebling police officer makes his rounds in the village in 1926. He is checking one of 44 call boxes in the village. Three policemen patrolled the streets in the village, each working one shift. The mill had its own security force. (Courtesy Carol M. Sheaffer, M.D.)

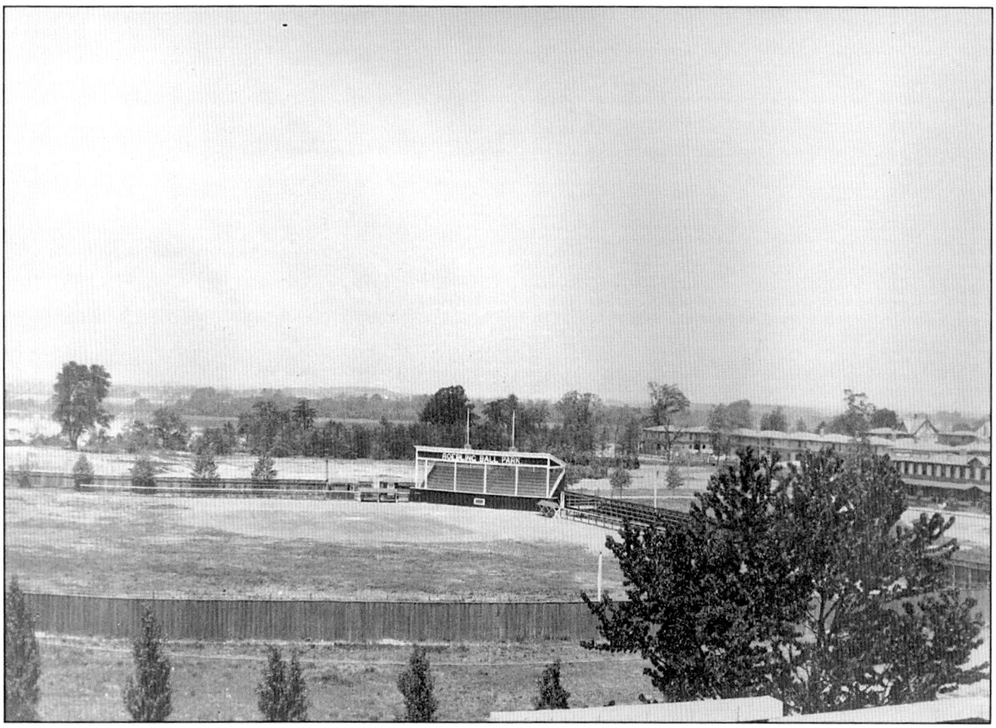

Villagers enjoyed many sporting activities at the Roebling Ball Park. A fence surrounded the field. This c. 1930 picture was taken from the roof of the Roebling Public School. (Courtesy Louis Borbi.)

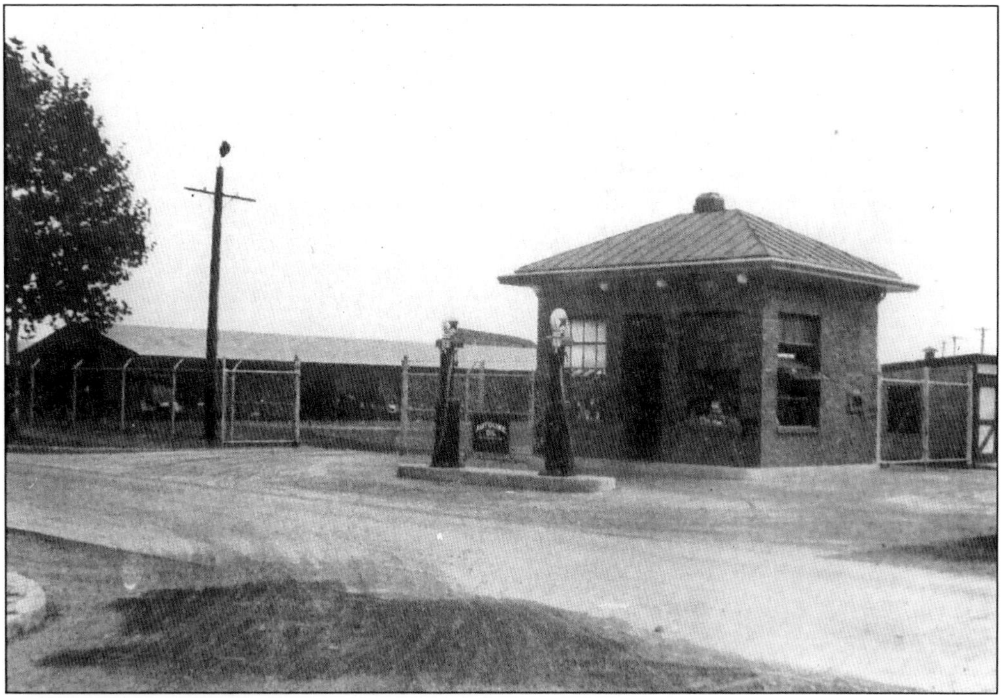

The parking yard and gasoline station, shown c. 1927, was located on Knickerbocker and Fourth Avenues. The plot was graded and cindered. The management constructed three double rows of shelters to accommodate the automobiles and the site was enclosed with wire fence. For each stall, a fee of 50¢ per month was charged. The service attendant at the gasoline station was also the watchman. The effort by the John A. Roebling's Sons Company to provide satisfactory parking was appreciated by the automobile owners. (Courtesy Louis Borbi.)

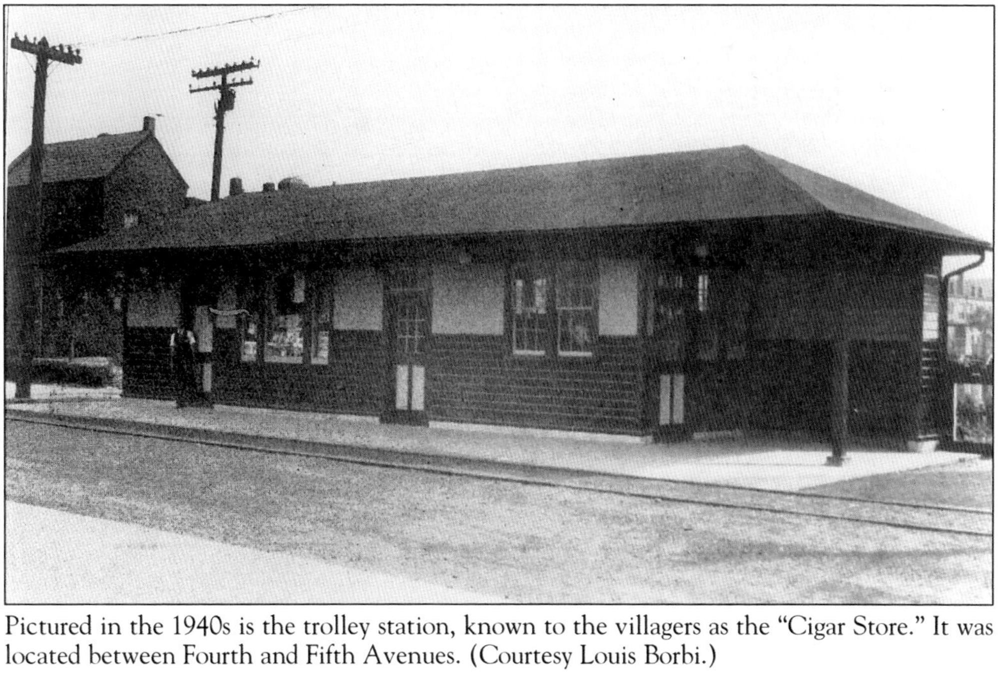

Pictured in the 1940s is the trolley station, known to the villagers as the "Cigar Store." It was located between Fourth and Fifth Avenues. (Courtesy Louis Borbi.)

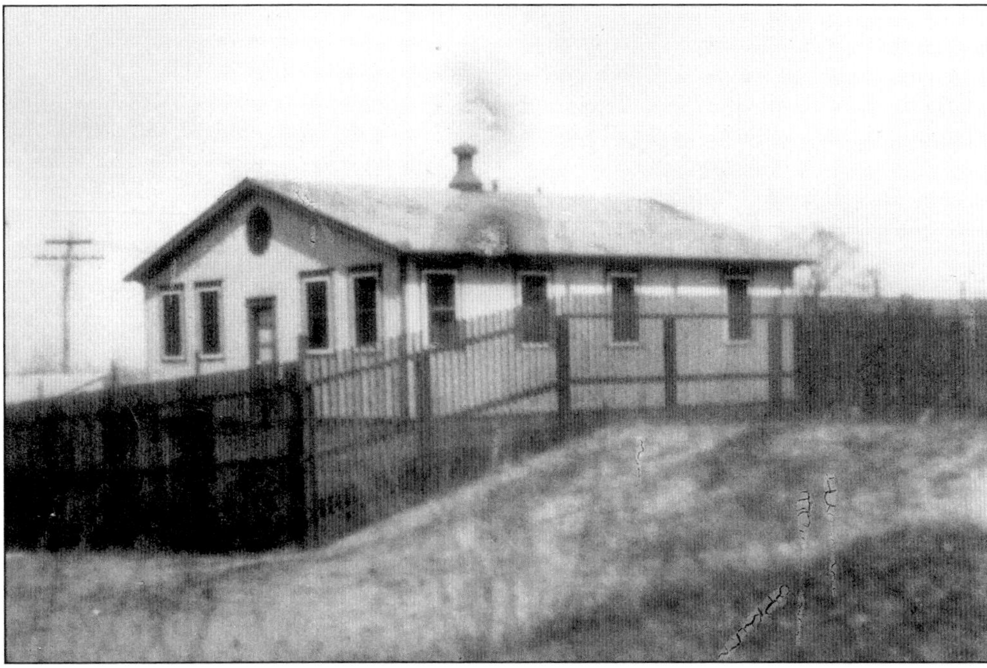

Pictured is the "Pest House" *c.* 1935–1941. People who contracted communicable diseases were sent to live in this building, under quarantine, until they were well again. Later on, the building was used as a gym, primarily for the boxers in the village. The Veterans of Foreign Wars (VFW) Hall now stands on this site. (Courtesy Louis Borbi.)

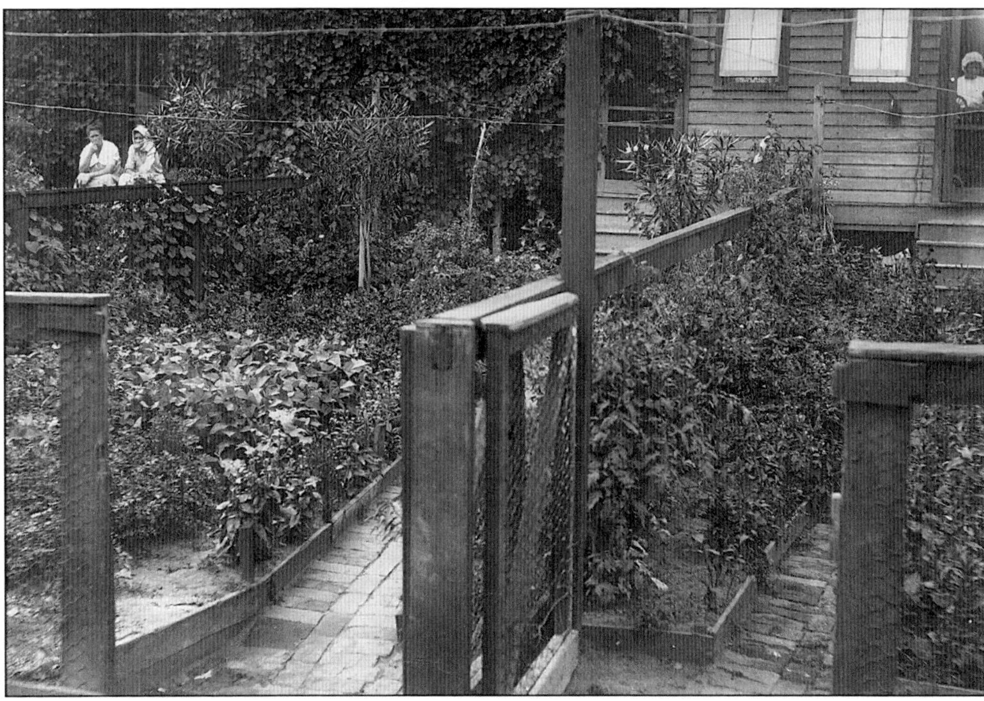

This view of row homes shows the backyard gardens where the villagers grew flowers and vegetables. (Courtesy Carol M. Sheaffer, M.D.)

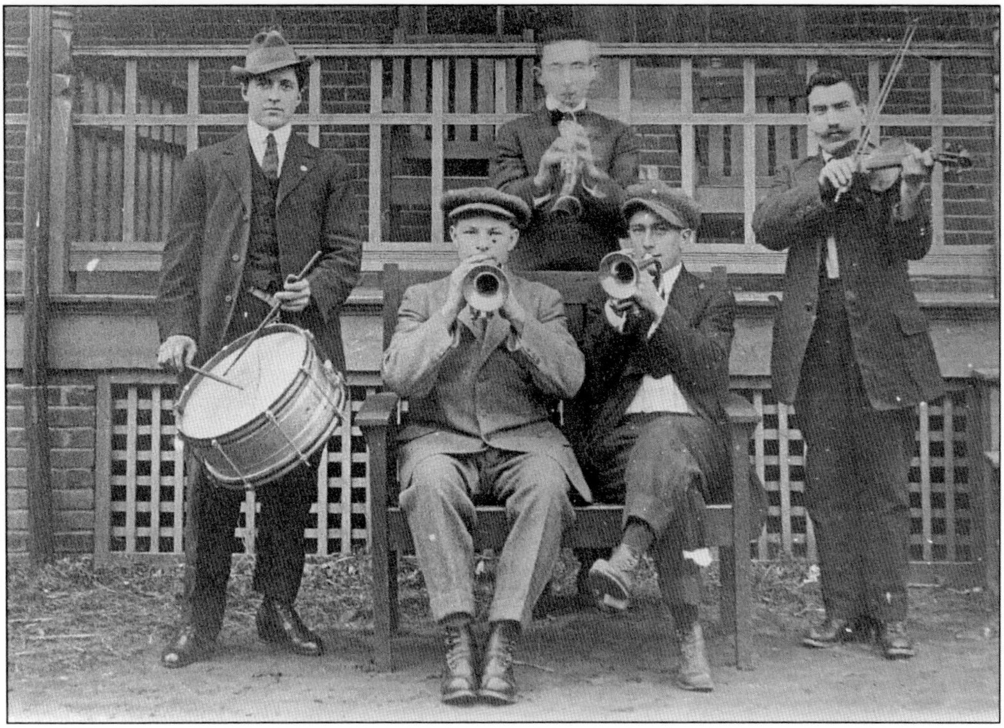

A quintet performs on Third Avenue in 1912. From left to right are John Kirka (drum), George Rusnak (trumpet), Sam Salaga (clarinet), Mike Salaga (trumpet), and John Mihalchik (fiddle). (Courtesy Louis Borbi.)

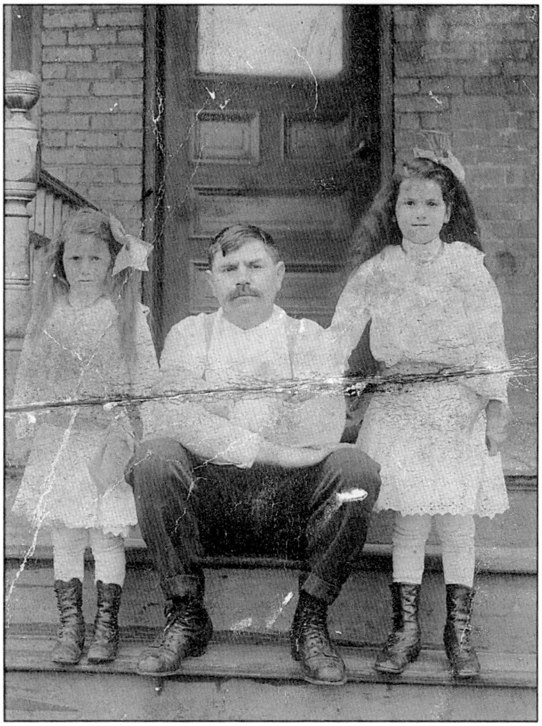

George Varga, an employee of the John A. Roebling's Sons Company, sits on the steps of a Third Avenue boardinghouse in 1925. (Courtesy Joseph Varga.)

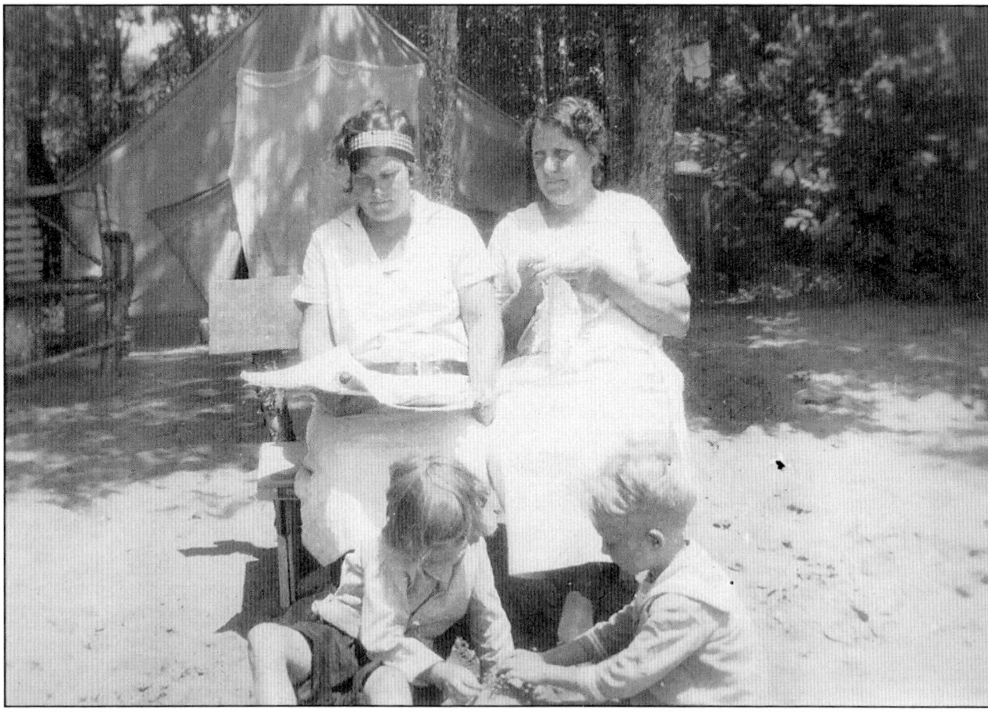

Pictured on Warner's Island in the 1920s are the following: (front row) Dorothy Pierson and Tom Pierson; (back row) Margaret Robbins-Pierson and Anna Pierson. The family would leave their Roebling home to vacation the entire summer on the island, located just across the Delaware River from Roebling. (Courtesy Shirley and Tom Pierson.)

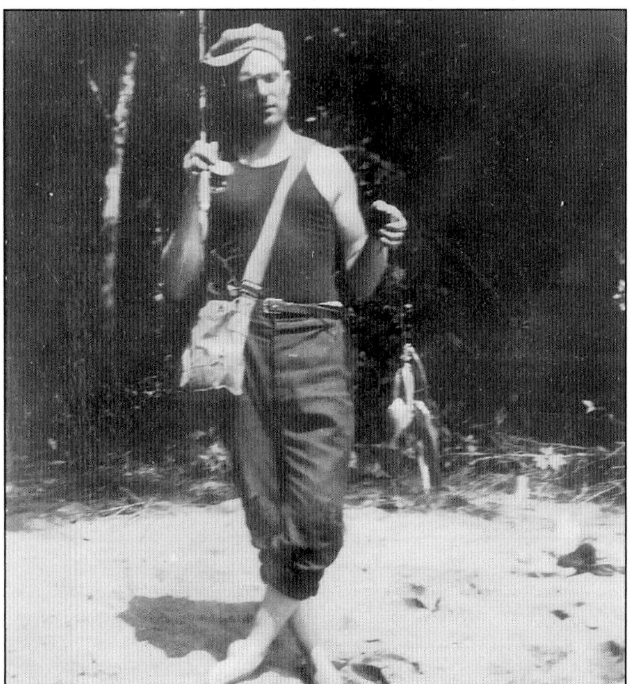

Mill worker Leon Pierson, shown here with the catch of the day, would canoe from the family's camp on Warner's Island to the John A. Roebling's Sons Company plant every day to work. (Courtesy Shirley and Tom Pierson.)

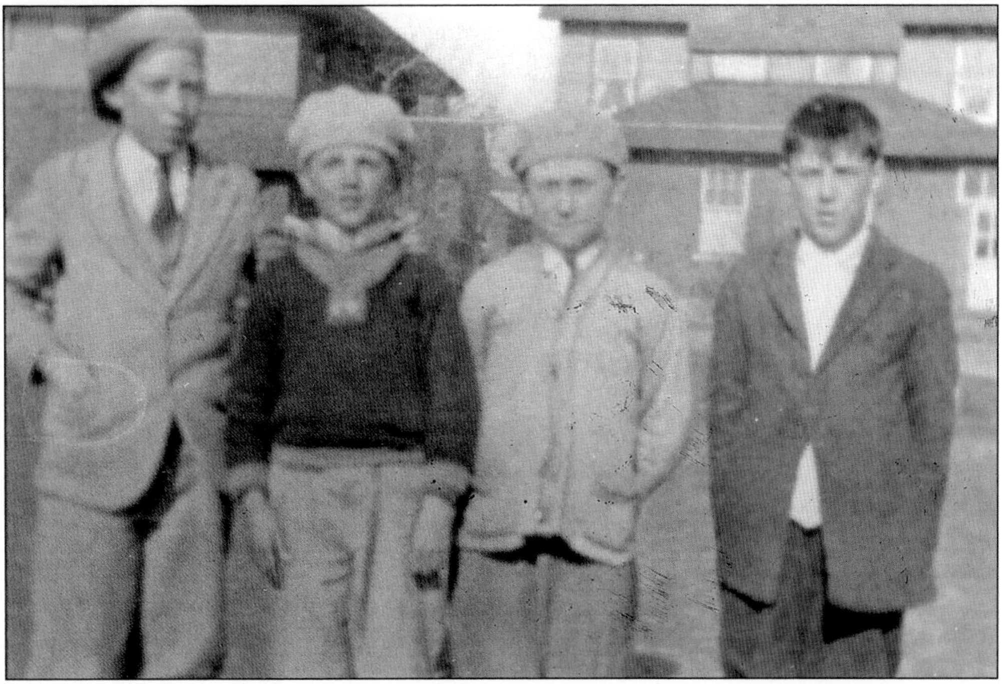

Photographed at the Marble Championship Elimination Contest in May 1928 are, from left to right, William Van Ness, John Buzash, George Desmond, and Paul Seaman. (Courtesy Louis Borbi.)

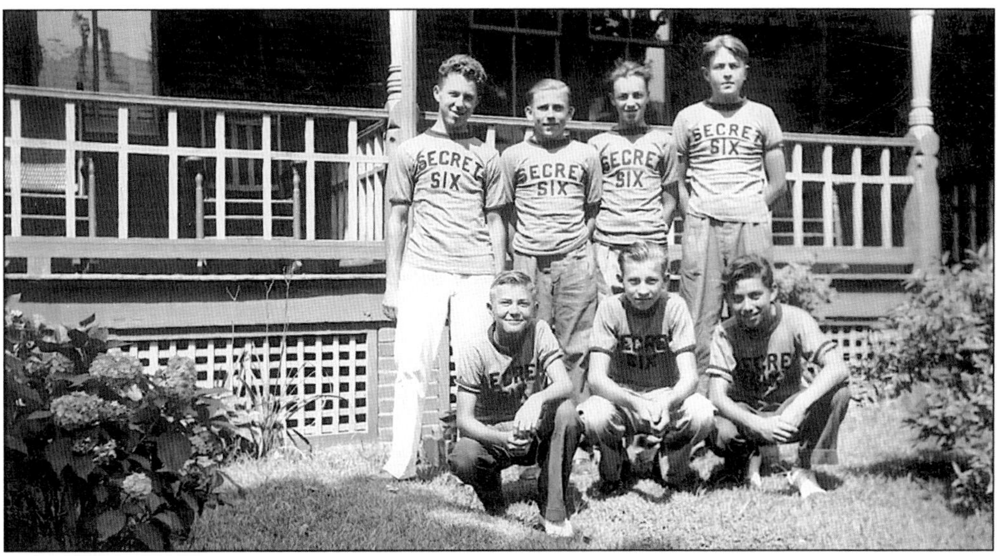

Pictured in July 1940 are the members of the Secret Six. They are, from left to right, as follows: (front row) John Tinnick, Joe Talpas, and Alex Marion; (back row) Steve Tinnick, George Nykita, Johnny Szucs, and Charlie Urban. (Courtesy Louis Borbi.)

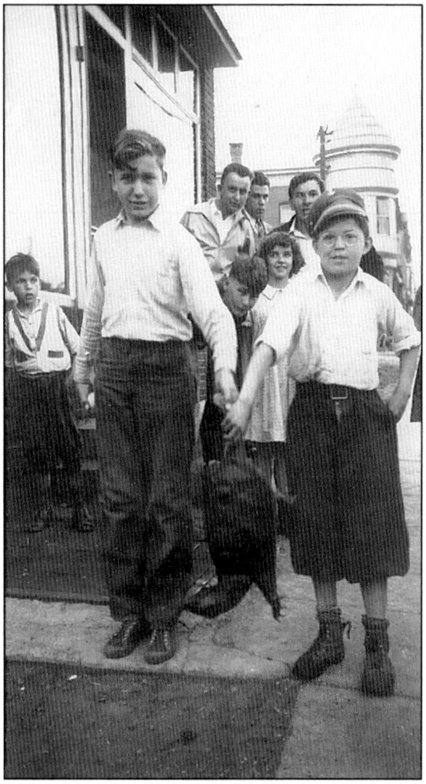

Friends congregate on Knickerbocker Avenue, near Norman Avenue, in 1941. (Courtesy Louis Borbi.)

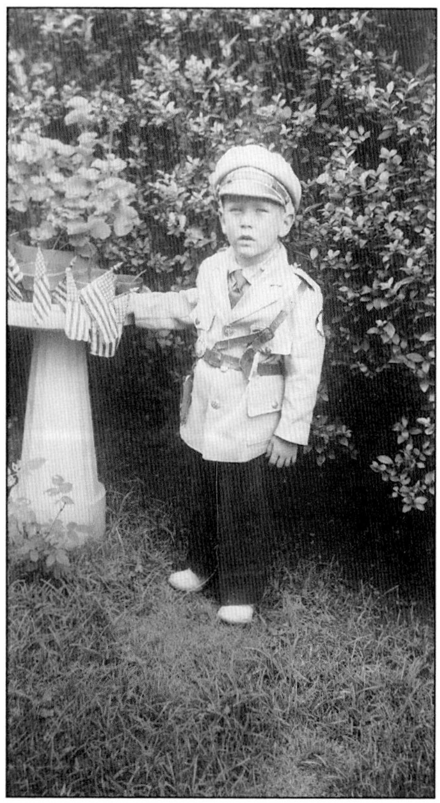

Harold Smith of Amboy Avenue celebrates the Fourth of July in 1943. (Courtesy Louis Borbi.)

A young musician stands with his bugle in his backyard in 1943. (Courtesy Louis Borbi.)

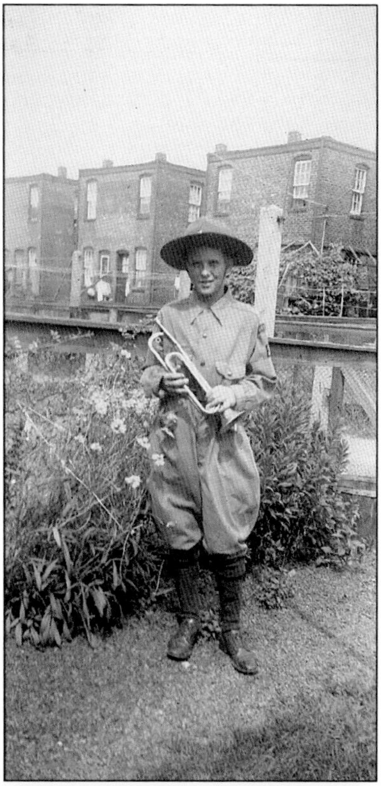

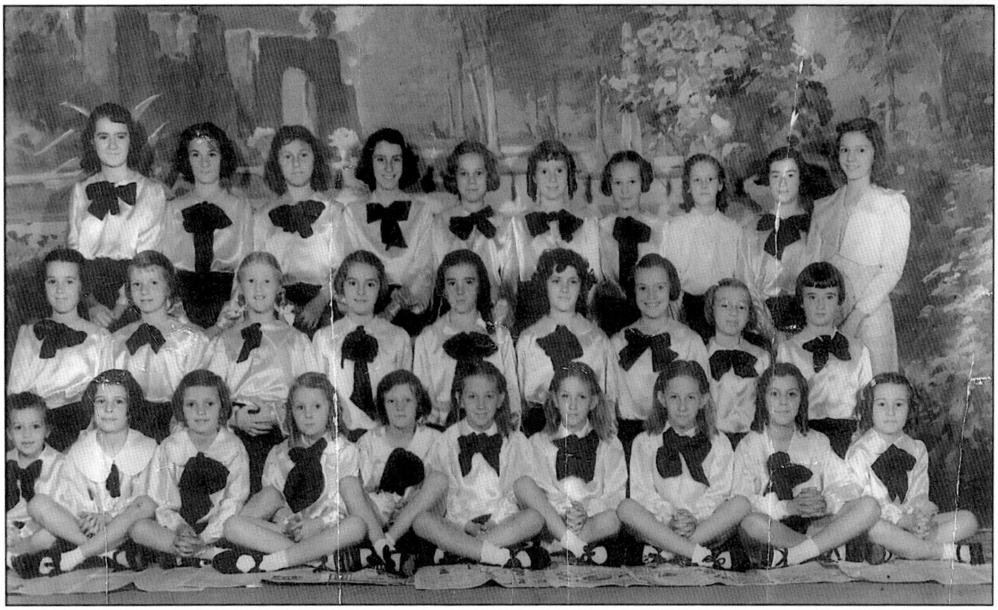

Many Roebling girls of the 1930s would spend their free time tap dancing. For 10¢ a lesson, Muriel Sweetman (back row, far right) would teach the girls how to tap dance in the basement of her Seventh Avenue home. Besides performing for Roebling residents in the Roebling Auditorium, the troupe shown in this 1936 picture went on the road and performed for many surrounding towns. (Courtesy Shirley and Tom Pierson.)

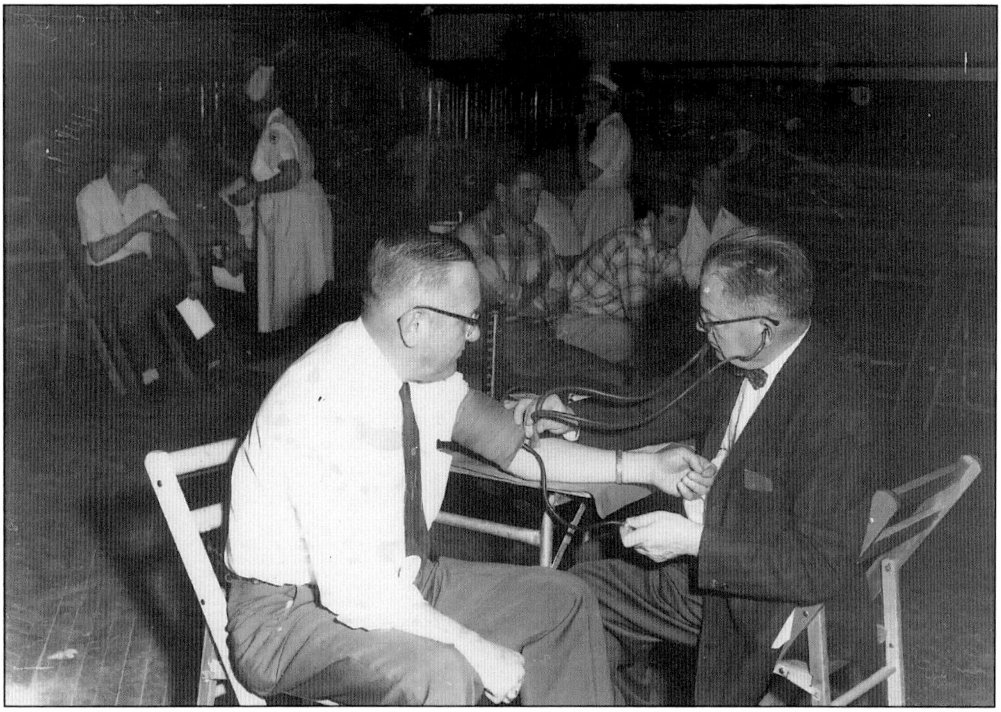

Dr. J. Howard Hornberger is checking Cap Blyne's blood pressure at a Roebling Blood Drive in the late 1940s. (Courtesy Louis Borbi.)

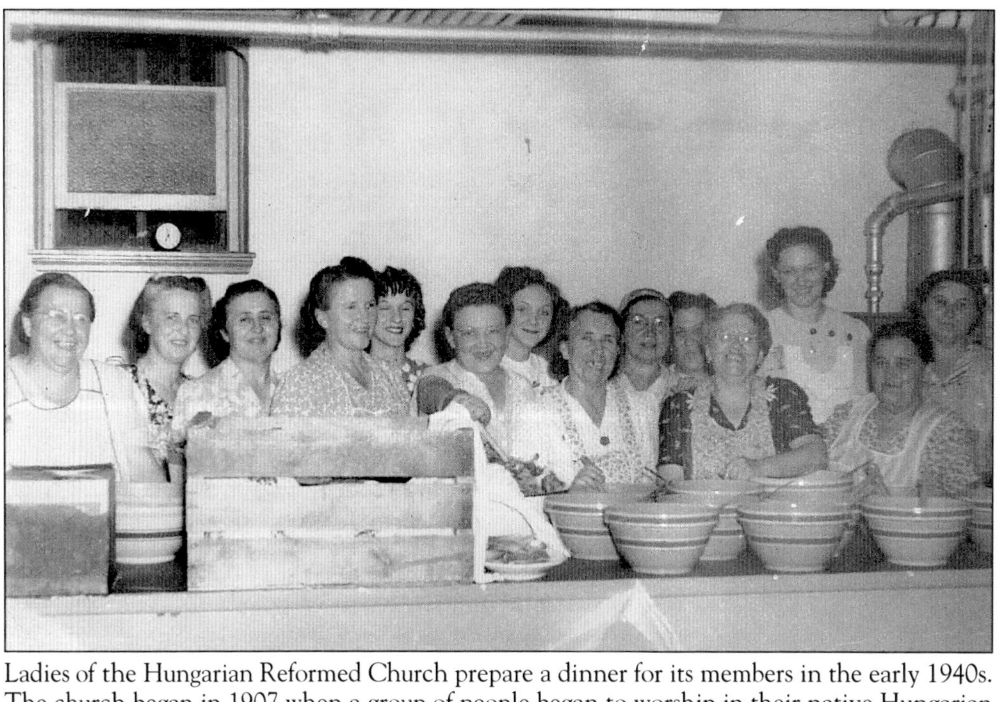

Ladies of the Hungarian Reformed Church prepare a dinner for its members in the early 1940s. The church began in 1907 when a group of people began to worship in their native Hungarian language. The official foundation was begun in 1913, and the church was completed in 1915. (Courtesy Louis Borbi.)

Morris and Mary Sheaffer pose in front of their home on 50 Main Street in 1950. Their home was located across from the Roebling General Store. Morris Sheaffer was one of Roebling's first inhabitants. (Courtesy Carol M. Sheaffer, M.D.)

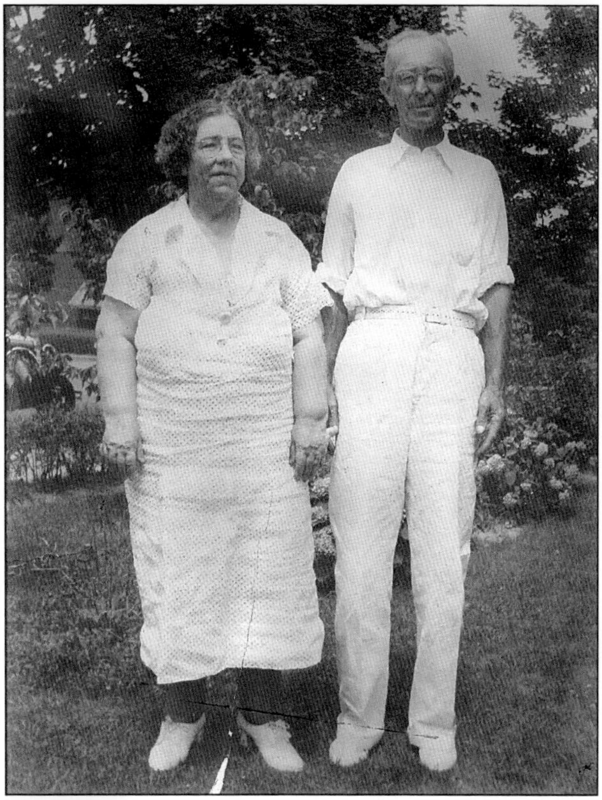

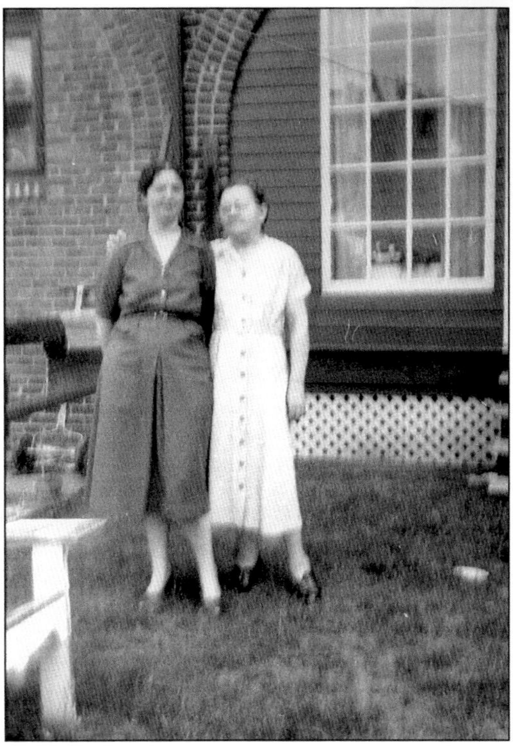

Margaret Earlin Sheaffer and Laura Elizabeth Earlin are standing in front of 106 Eighth Avenue *c.* 1950. (Courtesy Carol M. Sheaffer, M.D.)

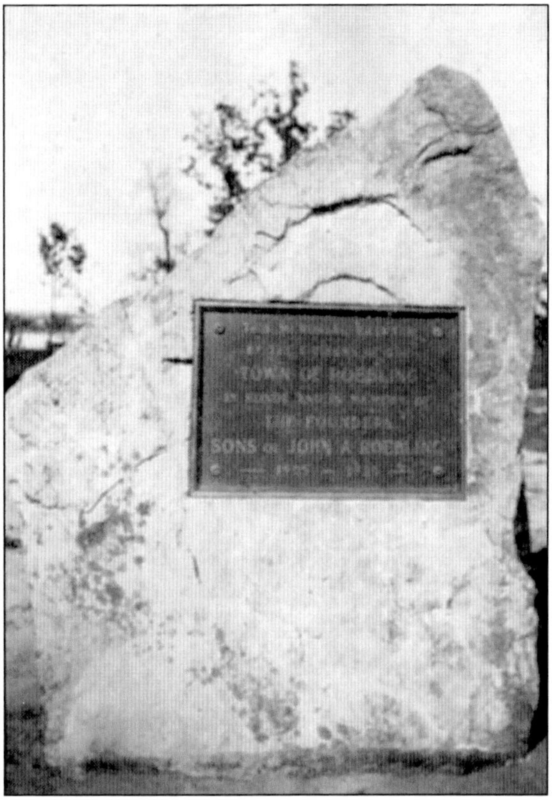

The dedication of this memorial took place on Saturday, November 9, 1930, at 1:30 P.M. It was donated by the citizens of Roebling in commemoration of the founding of the town. Helen Roebling Tyson, daughter of town founder Charles G. Roebling, unveiled the monument. (Courtesy Mary Arnold Montalto.)

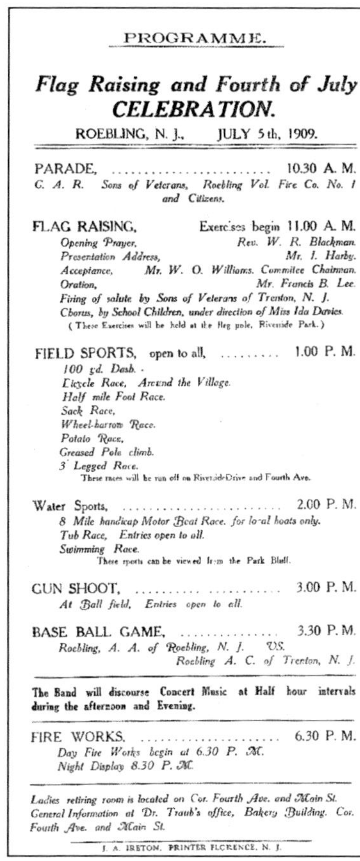

PROGRAMME.

Flag Raising and Fourth of July CELEBRATION.

ROEBLING, N. J., JULY 5th, 1909.

PARADE, ... 10.30 A. M.
G. A. R. Sons of Veterans, Roebling Vol. Fire Co. No. 1 and Citizens.

FLAG RAISING, Exercises begin 11.00 A. M.
Opening Prayer, Rev. W. R. Blackman.
Presentation Address, Mr. I. Harby.
Acceptance, Mr. W. O. Williams. Commitee Chairman.
Oration, Mr. Francis B. Lee.
Firing of salute by Sons of Veterans of Trenton, N. J.
Chorus, by School Children, under direction of Miss Ida Davies.
(These Exercises will be held at the flag pole, Riverside Park.)

FIELD SPORTS, open to all, ... 1.00 P. M.
100 yd. Dash.
Bicycle Race, Around the Village.
Half mile Foot Race.
Sack Race,
Wheel-barrow Race.
Potato Race,
Greased Pole climb.
3 Legged Race.
These races will be run off on RiversideDrive and Fourth Ave.

Water Sports, ... 2.00 P. M.
8 Mile handicap Motor Boat Race. for local boats only.
Tub Race, Entries open to all.
Swimming Race.
These sports can be viewed from the Park Bluff.

GUN SHOOT, ... 3.00 P. M.
At Ball field, Entries open to all.

BASE BALL GAME, ... 3.30 P. M.
Roebling, A. A. of Roebling, N. J. VS. Roebling A. C. of Trenton, N. J.

The Band will discourse Concert Music at Half hour intervals during the afternoon and Evening.

FIRE WORKS, ... 6.30 P. M.
Day Fire Works begin at 6.30 P. M.
Night Display 8.30 P. M.

Ladies retiring room is located on Cor. Fourth Ave. and Main St.
General Information at Dr. Traub's office, Bakery Building. Cor. Fouth Ave. and Main St.

J. A. IRETON. PRINTER FLORENCE, N. J.

Seen here is the program of the flag-raising and Fourth of July celebration held on July 5, 1909. Festivities included field sports, water sports, a gun shoot, and a baseball game. Fireworks were held, with a day fireworks display at 6:30 P.M. and a night display at 8:30 P.M. (Courtesy Ray Thompson.)

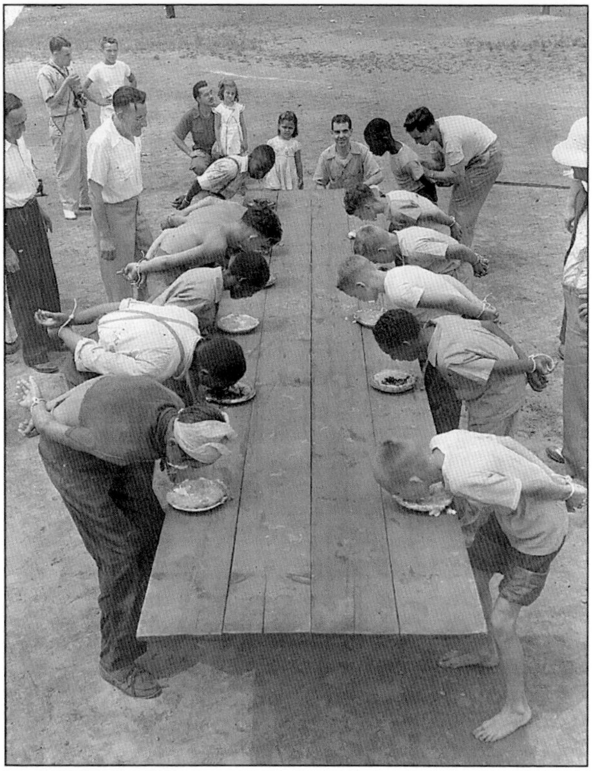

One of the events of the annual Fourth of July celebration was the pie-eating contest. These photographs show youngsters during and after competition. Note that no cheating was allowed because the youngsters' hands were tied behind their backs. Some of the adults shown are Raymond Bintliff, Walter Echgelmeier, William Lyons, Fred Linda, and Lou Wargo Sr. (Courtesy Joseph D. Zahorsky and Donna Orfe.)

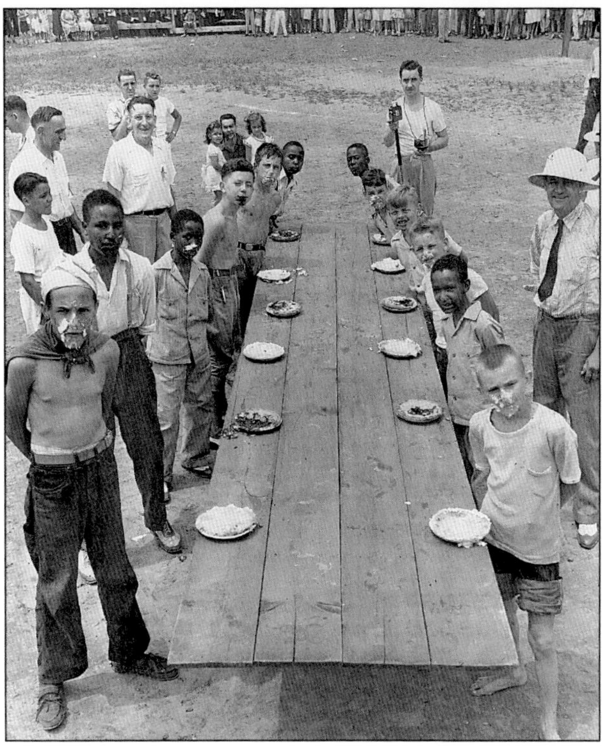

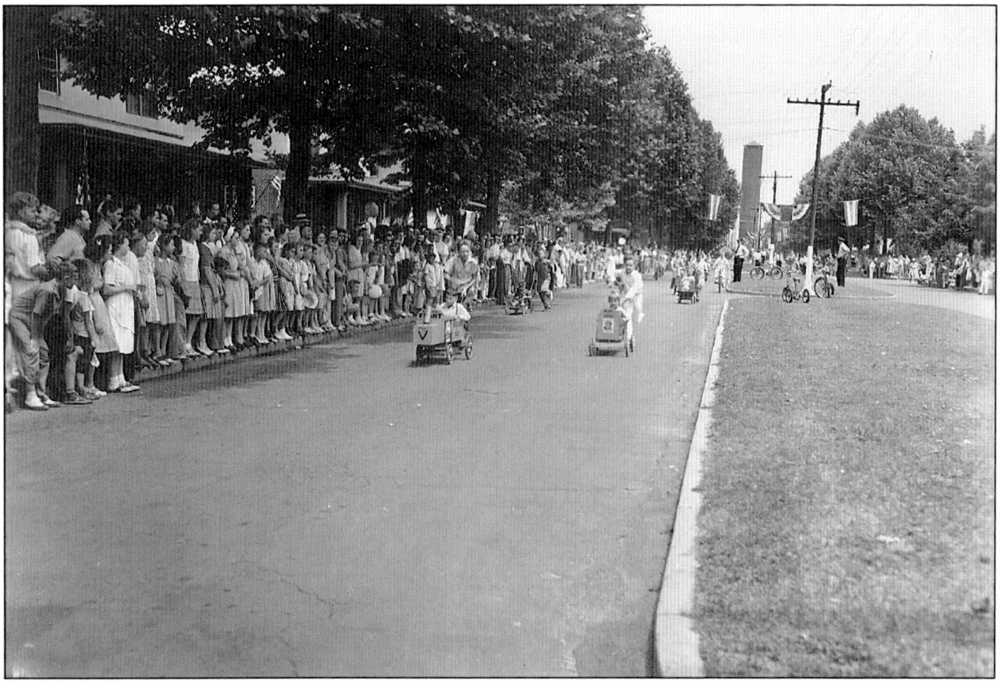

Roebling residents watch the soapbox races on Main Street in 1942. (Courtesy Joseph D. Zahorsky and Donna Orfe.)

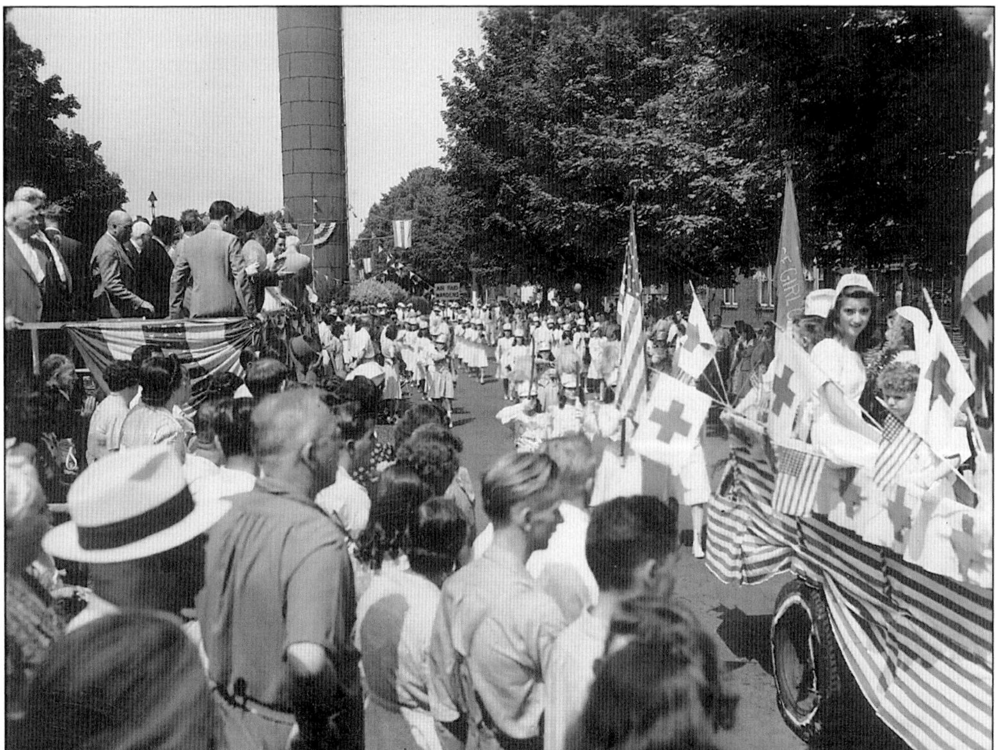

Roebling residents enjoy a Fourth of July parade. (Courtesy Joseph D. Zahorsky and Donna Orfe.)

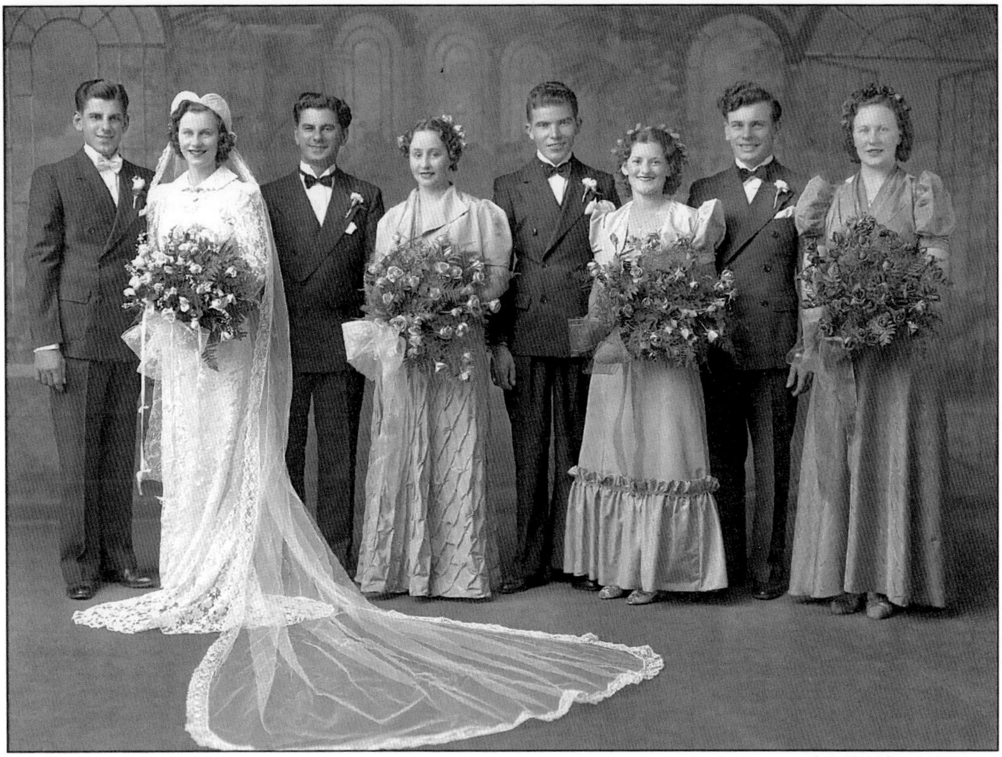

Residents Michael and Mary Bordas Zahorsky pose as newlyweds in this 1940s picture. Attending, to the right of the happy couple, are John Zahorsky, Mary Sabo, Joe "Pancho" Horvath, Helen Zahorsky, Joseph Bordas, and Betty Rusnak. (Courtesy Joseph D. Zahorsky and Donna Orfe.)

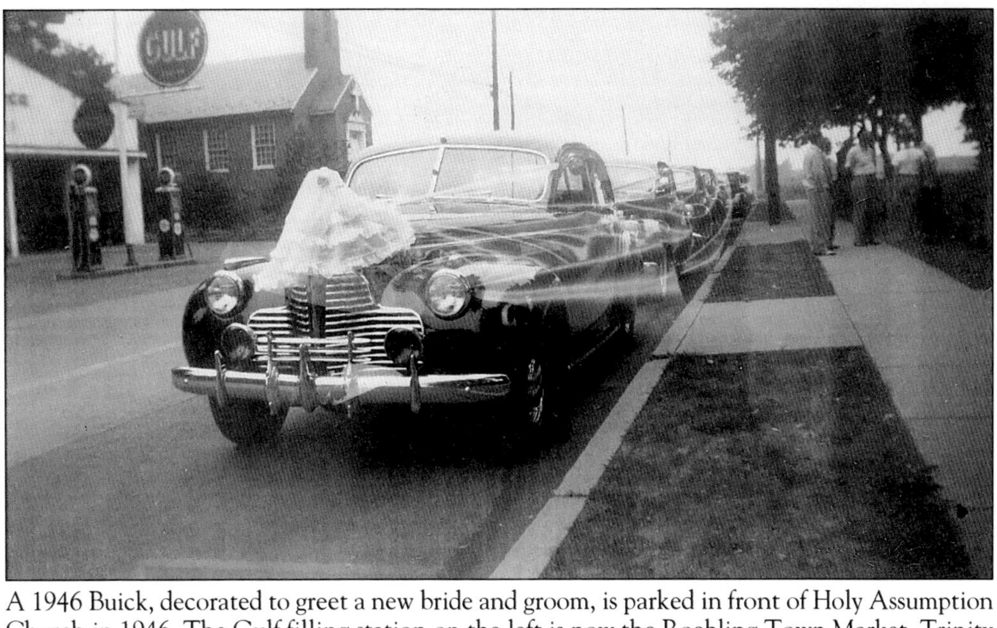

A 1946 Buick, decorated to greet a new bride and groom, is parked in front of Holy Assumption Church in 1946. The Gulf filling station on the left is now the Roebling Town Market. Trinity Methodist Church is also in the background. (Courtesy Louis Borbi.)

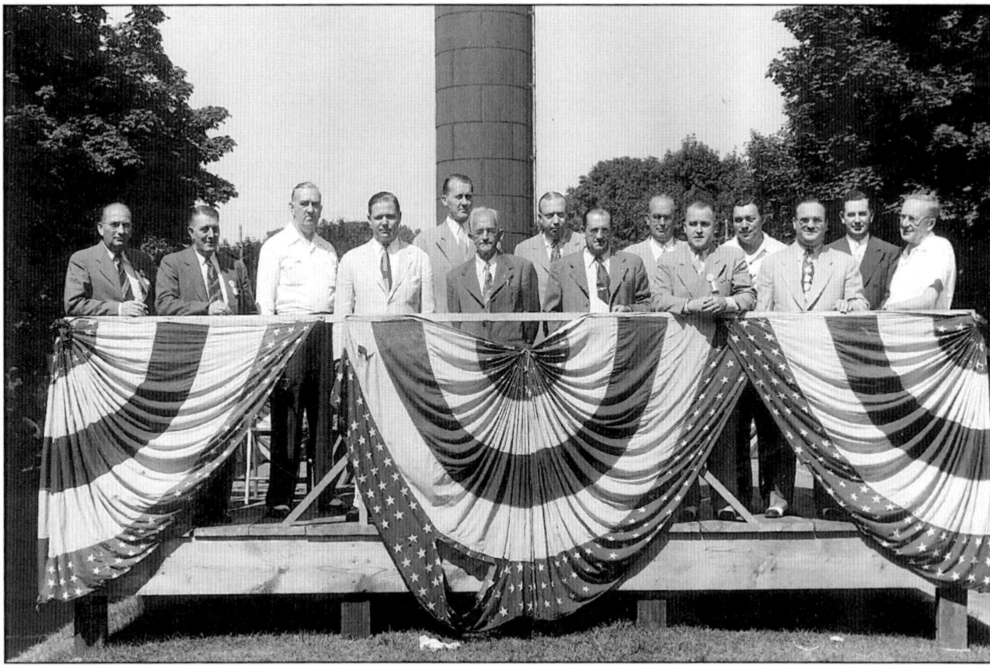

Celebrating Independence Day in 1946 is John A. Roebling's Sons Company president Charles Roebling Tyson (fourth from left). Among those standing with Tyson are Ray Bintliff, Paul Anderson, "Gip" Conrey, Paul Englund, and Nick Cantwell. (Courtesy Shirley and Tom Pierson.)

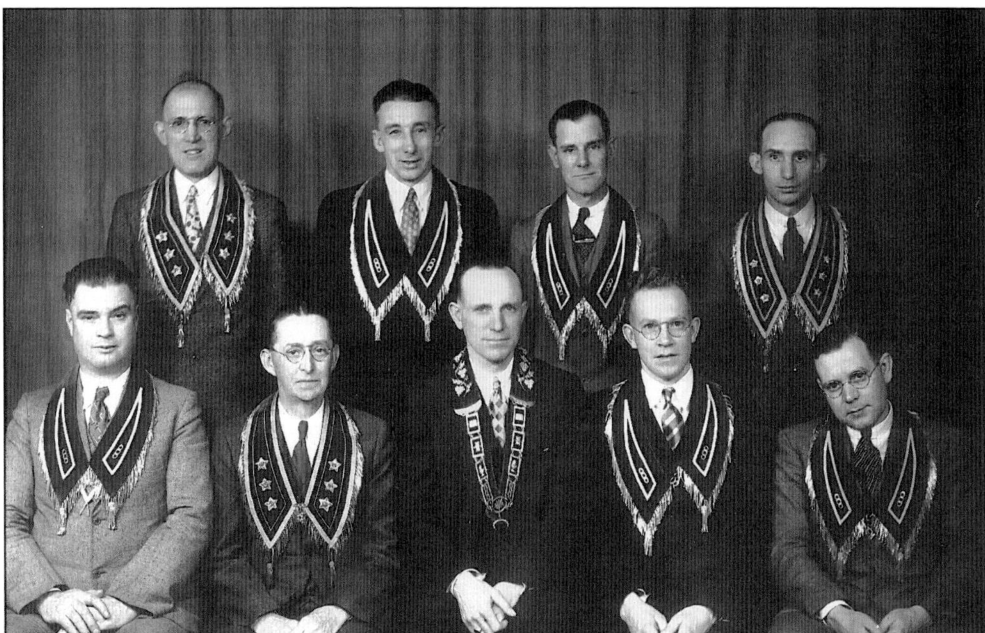

Members of the Roebling Odd Fellows pose in their Fourth Avenue lodge in the 1940s. They are, from left to right, as follows: (front row) Mr. Eckert, Mr. Kerr, Mr. Abrams, Mr. Segerstrom, and Mr. Larson; (back row) Mr. Vautier, Mr. Andrews, Mr. Lyons, and Mr. Katherine. (Courtesy of Shirley and Tom Pierson.)

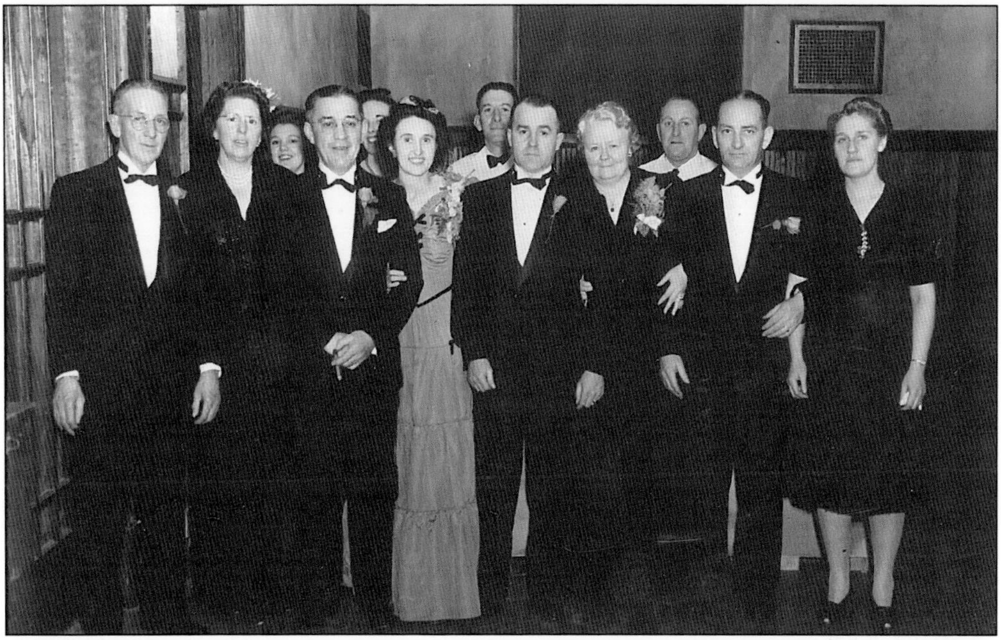

The Roebling Civic Association held a New Year's Eve party in the Roebling Auditorium in 1943. From left to right are the following: (front row) Ray Carter, Gladys Carter, Bruce Hubley, Agnes Kostrub, Nick Cantwell, Eleanor Earling, Ray Bintliff, and Mrs. Ginther; (back row) Muriel Sweetman, Irene Cantwell, Bill Lyons Sr., and Stump Malsbury. (Courtesy Shirley and Tom Pierson.)

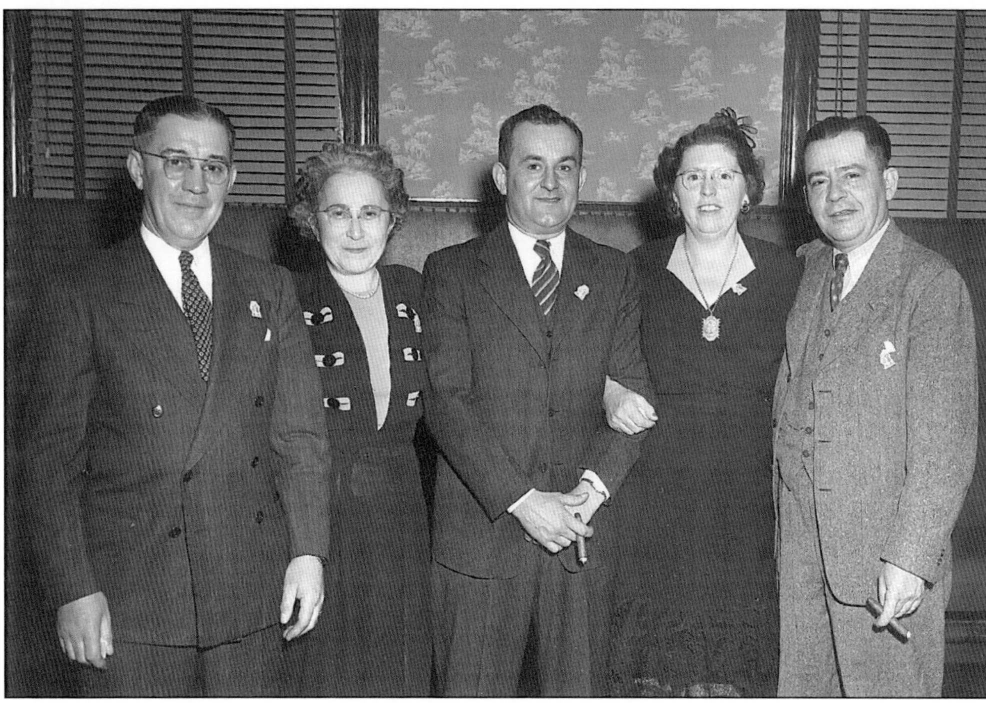

Members Bruce Hubley, Grace Bintliff, Steve Agoes, Gladys Carter, and Dr. J. Howard Hornberger are shown at a Civic Association meeting in the 1940s. (Courtesy Shirley and Tom Pierson.)

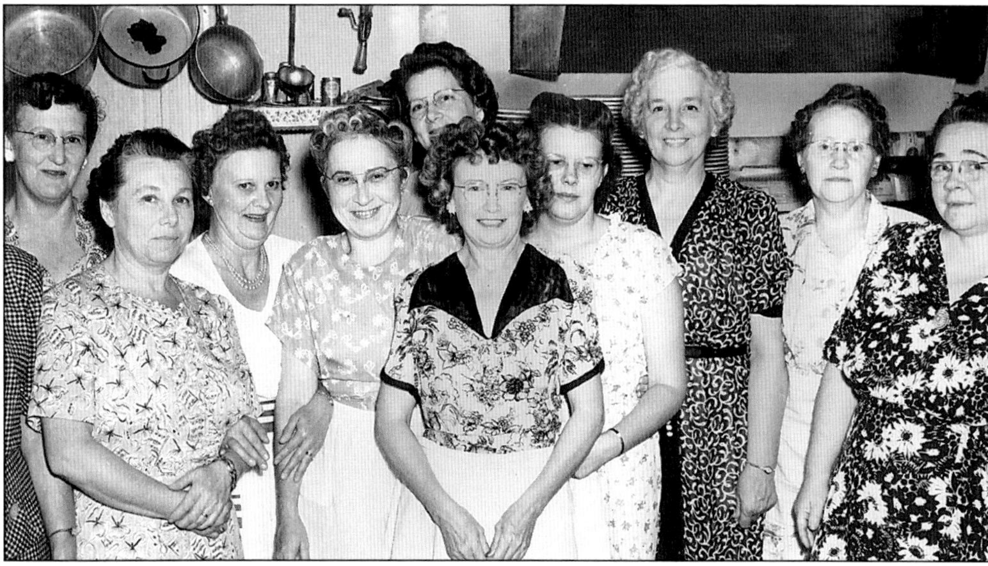

The ladies of American Legion Auxiliary Unit 39 always put in many long hours for veterans, their families, young people, and the Roebling community at large. Taking a short break from their work in the post kitchen to pose for this 1948 photograph are, from left to right, the following: Irene Ledger Rainier, Julia Shuler, Emma Sweetman, Grace Bintliff, Elsie Michalis Hoffman, Helen Elshove, Mrs. Sajeski, Mrs. Blakeslee, Carrie Tonne Elshove, and Carrie Mullins. (Courtesy Shirley and Tom Pierson.)

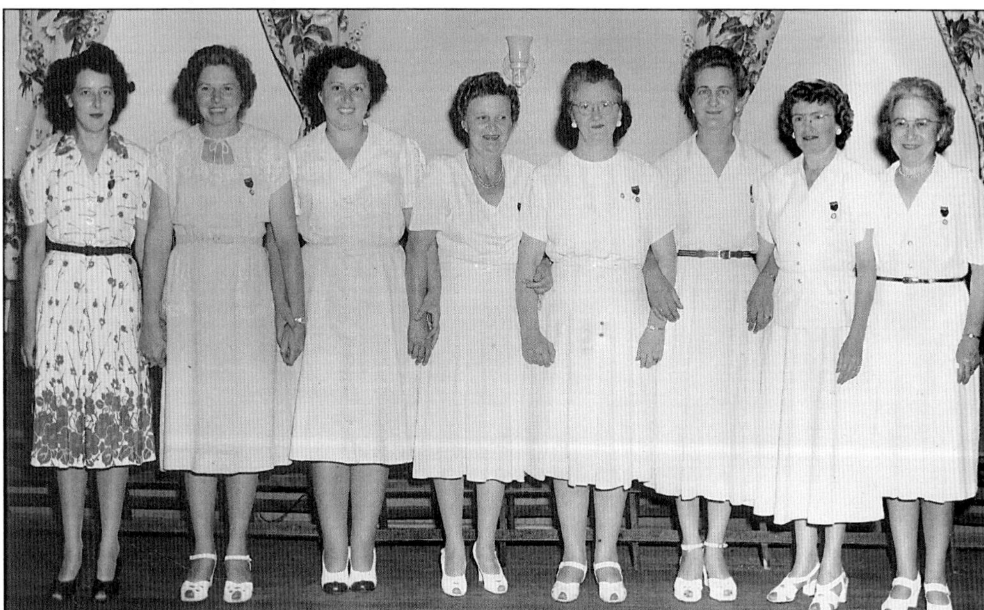

The women of Roebling's American Legion Auxiliary Unit 39 were very active in the community. Making bandages, knitting sweaters, and entertaining for the troops at nearby Fort Dix were just some of the activities they participated in. Shown in this 1948 photograph is the induction of officers at Post 39. From left to right are the following: Peg Sandusky, Betty Ibach, Mary Cronin Renzi, Emma Sweetman, Anne Cantwell, Kate Webber, Helen Elshove (vice president), and Grace Bintliff (president). (Courtesy Shirley and Tom Pierson.)

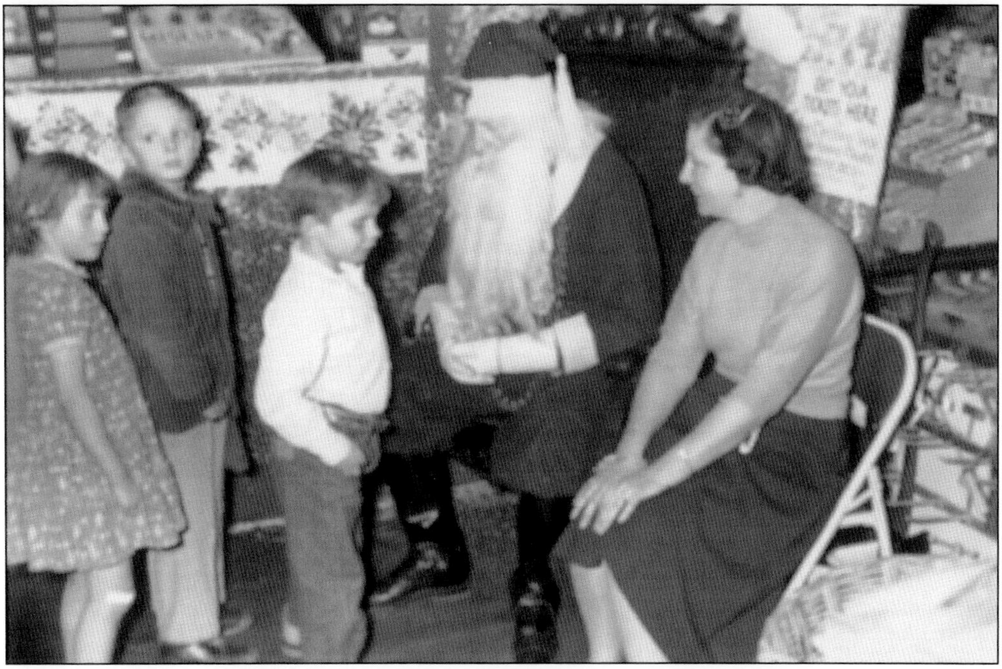

Santa Claus greets visitors at the Roebling General Store in this *c.* 1950 picture. (Courtesy Carol M. Sheaffer, M.D.)

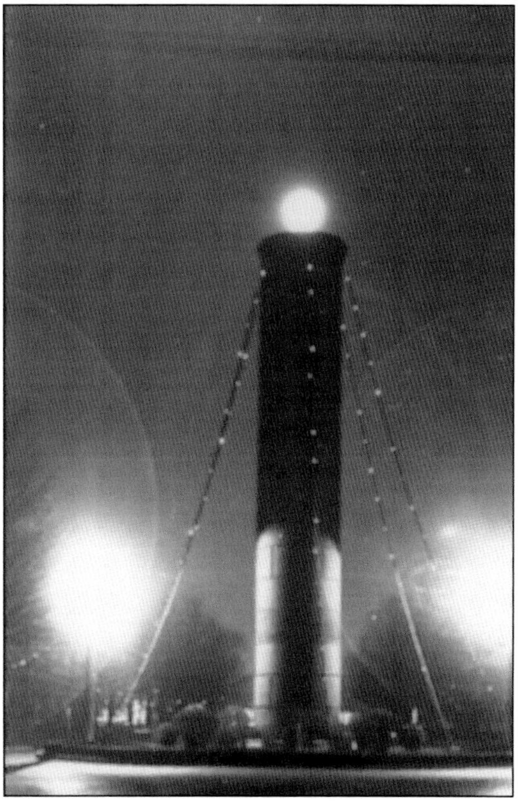

The Roebling Water Tower, located in the center of the village, is shown decorated for the Christmas holidays in the 1940s. (Courtesy Louis Borbi.)

In 1948, the water tower that had stood at the Fifth and Main circle from the town's inception was taken down. Being one of the initial structures built in the village, this standpipe was both a familiar friend and comforting beacon to the residents that grew up in the village. Resident Anne Dennis watched this landmark structure being dismantled and was moved to write the following poem.

Reverie of the Old Standpipe

I've slumbered silently these past few years
Life's dusk slowly creeping, 'till now appears
My death knell sounding—I hear the call—
Goodbye, folk of Roebling, I've loved you all.
They say a standpipe should have no soul,
That destruction alone should be my goal,
But I've lived and laughed and shared your tears,
Been a part of you throughout the years,
Yes, tear down the old, up with the new!
My job is finished, my work is through.
But before I go for old times' sake,
Down memory lane a glance with me take.
A unique little place, this Roebling town,
Its many products of world renown.
I've "landed" it high, keeping watch over you
A community strong, steadfast and true.
You've had your battles, stress and strife—
Love and marriages and new life!
But be trouble or joy, the issue at stake,
Roebling folk stand together for unity's sake
I've honored the years, I've been part of you,
I know many secrets—all standpipes do.
I've watched young lovers, thinking none could see,
Kiss goodnight on the steps—even thrilled me!
I loved the children when dusk was deep,
Playing "cops and robbers" around my feet.
And in their noisy, childish way
I've seen them "die" and run away.
On Christmas Eve when earth was stilled,
I've peeped down chimneys—saw stockings filled.
Though you heard not, I sang with you
The carols sweet, ever old, ever new.
Through the long years of war, I scanned the Sky,
Like some great black protecting eye
Silently praying this tranquil place
Might never glimpse war's ugly face.
I've watched your parades, celebrations grand,
And I've always been there right on hand
To stand at attention, saluting, head held so high,
As your colors gay marched proudly by,
Humbly I bowed as the Death Angel flew,
Through the skies to claim someone we knew.
But soon I'd smile with you happily,
For Mr. Stork loves Roebling chimneys.
So now as you stand and watch my "wake"
Grieve not, old friends, but in your hearts take
Pride in your village—the new lock is here—
We oldsters belong to yesteryear.
I want no plaque nor monument cold,
Just a small spot in your hearts to hold—
When in memory you go back again,
Let me be with you too, at "Fifth and Main"

—Anne Dennis
November 1948